D0205392

OCT 2 5 2004

D
648
.B77

194540

THE COST OF THE WAR
1914-1919

THE COST
OF THE WAR
1914-1919
British Economic War
Aims and the Origins
of Reparation

Robert E. Bunselmeyer

ARCHON BOOKS 1975

Library of Congress Cataloging in Publication Data

Bunselmeyer, Robert E.   1939-
    The cost of war, 1914-1919.

    Bibliography: p.
    Includes index.
    1. European War, 1914-1918—Reparations. 2. Euro-
pean War, 1914-1918—Great Britain. 3. Great Britain—
Politics and government—1910-1936. I. Title.
D648.B77   940.3'1422   75-14078
ISBN 0-208-01551-5

Printed in the United States of America

FOR JO AND ERIC

Contents

7

Preface

In 1932, near the end of the diplomatic tangle over reparations and other international payments, Sir Arthur Salter wrote, "To tell the tale of Reparation, and the questions with which it is intertwined, would be to write the history of post-war Europe."* Since 1932, historians have fairly heeded Salter's recommendation. Although there is today more work that might be done, we know a good deal about the economic peace of Versailles and the economic diplomacy of 1919 to 1932. However, the interest in these postwar subjects has not been matched by a similar concern for their wartime background. This work, I hope, will illuminate the British origins of reparation and related aspects of the economic peace.

I began my work thinking that all the origins that mattered were to be found in the politics and policies of late 1918, especially in the General Election campaign of November and December 1918. Research in Britain confirmed the importance of these developments, but it also showed that the 1918 agitation about the cost of the War had its own origins in earlier anxieties about what the War was doing to British trade and finance, and in protectionist preparations for a trade war with Germany that was expected to follow the military war. These wartime preoccupations were first efforts to alleviate the cost of the War at Germany's expense. Hence, the first part of this study, dealing with 1914 to 1918, is a necessary foundation for the second, which deals with 1918 and 1919.

Recovery: The Second Effort (London, 1932), p. 122.

9

During my researches, I also discovered the powerful and intimate relation between British economic aims and the anti-German temper of British opinion. Making Germany "pay" was not only an economic satisfaction; it was also a penalty for German misdeeds—some real, some imaginary—and especially for the presumed offense of having started the War. Economic policy and diplomacy, normally among the most dispassionate subjects, must here be dealt with in the context of the frustrations and animosities of war.

There were, of course, British politicians who opposed fear and hatred of Germany. In this respect, the dissent of the Independent Labour Party and of the Union of Democratic Control is well known. The present study shows that Germanophobia was also restrained by powerful Conservative* and Liberal spokesmen—among them Bonar Law, Lord Milner, Jan Smuts, and C. P. Scott. Bonar Law's decency and good sense were especially important. As Leader of the Conservative Party, he blunted many of the excesses of his more distracted followers. The voices of sensible men were not drowned completely by the shrill cry, "make Germany pay."

*   *   *

This study was first suggested to me by the late Professor Hajo Holborn; its completion was largely due to the advice and encouragement of Professor Gaddis Smith. Others who gave the most needed kinds of assistance were Raymond J. Cunningham, John Dunbabin, Wilton B. Fowler, Anne J. Granger, Margaret Jacobs, Colin Jones, Nicholas X. Rizopoulos, John and Alice Sell, and Robin W. Winks. The Council on International Relations of Yale University provided essential support for my travel and research. In Britain, I was helped by John Barnes, Geoffrey D. M. Block, Sheila Elton, Martin Gilbert, John M. McEwen, A. J. P. Taylor, D. C. Watt, and Trevor G. Wilson. I alone bear responsibility for the contents of this volume.

For the privilege of using and quoting from private papers and manuscripts, I am grateful to the Rt. Hon. Julian Amery; to the Beaverbrook Newspapers and Foundations; to the Birmingham

*"Conservative" is used in this study instead of "Unionist." The latter designation was still applied during the War, but "Conservative" is more descriptive of the politics and policies we will consider here.

University Library; to Mr. Henry Borden; to the British Museum,
Department of Manuscripts; to Viscount Buckmaster; to Mark
Bonham Carter; to Lord John C. C. Davidson and to Lady Davidson; to Lord Gretton of Stapleford; to Mr. Winston F. C. Guest;
to Lord Harmsworth of Egham; to Sir Geoffrey Harmsworth;
to Mr. Richard Hewins; to the Rt. Hon. Professor the Lord Kahn;
to Professor Ann K. S. Lambton; to the Marquis of Lothian; to
Lt.-Col. G. I. Malcolm of Poltalloch; to the Warden and Fel-
lows of New College, Oxford; to the Scottish Record Office;
to Mr. J. C. Smuts; to the Yale University Library, Department of Manuscripts; and to Viscount Younger of Leckie.
Crown-copyright materials in the Public Record Office appear
by permission of the Controller of Her Majesty's Stationery
Office.

My deepest thanks are to my wife and son for their kindness
and patience.

R. E. B.

New Haven, Connecticut
1975

Principal Abbreviations

ACC	Associated Chambers of Commerce
BED	British Empire Delegation
EDDC	Economic Defence and Development Committee
EOC	Economic Offensive Committee
FBI	Federation of British Industries
100 HC Deb 200	*Parliamentary Debates*. House of Commons. Volume 100, column 200.
ILP	Independent Labour Party
IWC	Imperial War Cabinet
NUM	National Union of Manufacturers
PRO	Public Record Office of Great Britain
	CAB class/volume. Records of the Cabinet Office
	FO class/volume. Records of the Foreign Office.
	BT class/volume. Records of the Board of Trade
	T class/volume. Records of the Treasury
TUC	Trades Union Congress
UBC	Unionist Business Committee
WC	War Cabinet

Chapter 1 INTRODUCTION

Paying for the War

OF ALL the sections of the Treaty of Versailles, none has provoked more debate than that dealing with reparation. Much of the controversy has focused on the first of the reparation articles, Article 231, which affirmed that German "aggression" had caused the War and that Germany was therefore responsible for the losses suffered by the governments and peoples who had opposed her. This affirmation, which Germany was obliged to accept, has generally been interpreted in two ways since 1919. One view has been that the Allies, conscious of the sacrifices of the War and prodded by the anti-German fervor of their publics, imposed a self-righteous verdict which was, in fact, an unnecessary and deliberate insult to Germany. Another interpretation has been that Article 231 was quite necessary as a logical premise for the economic compensation which the Allies naturally—and to some extent justifiably—expected of Germany. Thus, the Article was not really intended to brand Germany with "war guilt"; this connotation was only attached by the protests of the Germans themselves.

The present study suggests that this difference of opinion has been a misleading one. The British origins of reparation indicate that Article 231 expressed *both* moral outrage and economic anxiety, and that these two developments were mutually rein-

forcing. As we shall see later, most Britons had certainly come to
believe by early 1919 that Germany was guilty of aggression and
of a barbaric war effort, and that she ought to be made, somehow, to "pay."[1] That belief was one origin of reparation.
Closely related to it was another origin, the British Government's
wartime plans to ensure postwar economic security at German
expense.

These plans went through an interesting, two-stage evolution
from 1914 to 1919. First, during most of the War, the British
Government concentrated on making postwar British trade secure
and on planning for national self-sufficiency in raw materials
and militarily important products after the War. Since Germany
was expected to be the most aggressive postwar competitor, British
policy-makers hoped to minimize British dependence on German
products and to place restrictions on German trade that would
benefit British traders. These plans were embodied in the Paris
Economic Resolutions of 1916, in the policy of imperial
preference, and in the Government committees and memoranda
discussed in Part One of this work.

Of more direct importance for the peace settlement was a
second stage in British wartime planning: direct financial compensation from Germany. As long as the outcome of the War was
uncertain, this was a secondary idea and involved only reparation
for the physical damage done by warfare. However, toward the
end of 1918, the notion that Germany should pay an indemnity
which would defray a large part of all British war costs also
became part of British policy.[2] In fact, the political appeal of
reparation and indemnity became so great on the eve of the Peace
Conference that these policies displaced those dealing with
trade, raw materials, and "key" military industries. Yet insofar
as they were a means of achieving national economic security by
penalizing Germany, reparation and indemnity were an extension of the earlier policies.

Both stages of British planning were strongly influenced by
Britain's relations with her Dominions and with her allies. The
institution of an Imperial War Cabinet and Conference by
Lloyd George's Government in early 1917 meant that Dominion
statesmen were increasingly part of British politics and policy-
making. Prime Minister William Morris Hughes of Australia, in

particular, used the opportunity to project his anti-German, anti-American, and protectionist ideas into the British debate over economic policy. On the other hand, Canadian and South African representatives, especially Jan Smuts, exerted an influence that was usually counter to that of Hughes.

American policy, reflecting the views of President Wilson, opposed both penalties on German trade and a war costs indemnity. The third of the Fourteen Points envisaged freer international trade, and Wilson's adherence to that point was an important reason why the Paris Economic Resolutions and similar schemes did not survive the War. Also, Wilson's insistence on "reparation only" was the main obstacle to British hopes for indemnity. These disagreements over economic war aims, combined with the wartime growth of the American economy and the large sums which Britain was forced to borrow in the United States, produced considerable British resentment of America by the end of the War.

The British also disagreed with the French over economic policy. To be sure, the two Allies cooperated on economic matters during most of the War, and they were the principal sponsors of the Paris Economic Resolutions. However, their cooperation dissolved as victory became certain and reparation and indemnity replaced other wartime planning. Thereafter, they became the principal competitors for shares of compensation from Germany.

British economic planning was, of course, also affected by domestic politics. The political division which was most relevant to economic war aims resembled the prewar division over "the fiscal question." Just as most Conservatives, businessmen, and tariff reformers had favored some form of tariff protection before the War, so during the War they proposed an economic peace that would punish and restrict Germany. Meanwhile, most of the prewar opponents of protection—Liberals, Labourites, and "free food" Conservatives—opposed a harsh economic peace from 1914 to 1919.

However, unlike the prewar years, it was the former groups who enjoyed most success in the debate over economic policy. Conservatives, businessmen, and tariff reformers enjoyed the benefits of the patriotic atmosphere of the War. The Conservatives became the dominant political party, tolerating coalition only for the appearance of national unity and a Liberal Prime Minister only because he supported many Conservative policies. Businessmen used their share of the profits of wartime production to enter politics to an unprecedented degree. Tariff reformers, most of whom were Conservatives and businessmen, exploited the wartime desire for national economic security. They did not destroy the principle of free trade, but they did score important victories for tariff protection with the McKenna Duties, the Paris Economic Resolutions, imperial preference, and the Government election program of 1918. Moreover, they converted many Liberals to a measure of protection by appealing to the need for national unity and economic measures against Germany, and by designing new terms like "safeguarding of key industries" which had a cross-party appeal. However, this apparently new emphasis and new verbiage were really only a new mercantilism, a re-phrased philosophy of self-sufficiency which would subject many of the interests of private trade to the supposed requirements of the State. Underneath the rhetoric of wartime, tariff reform versus free trade remained, as before the War, an important economic dividing line in British politics.

Closely related to tariff protection, income taxation was another domestic issue which influenced British economic war aims. The War produced a startling increase in national debt and, consequently, in taxation. While the Labour Party sought to use the new situation for a progressive reform of taxation, many Conservatives and businessmen looked for ways to avoid such reforms. Just as they had found tariff revenue to be such an alternative before the War, so toward the end of the War they discovered the alternatives of reparation and, especially, indemnity. Germany had caused the War, the argument ran; it was only just that she should pay for it. Thus, the national debt and wartime taxation were important reasons why some Conservatives and businessmen proposed an economically punitive peace.

Surrounding the politics and diplomacy of economic war aims was an intensely anti-German public opinion, the other origin of reparation. The widespread belief that Germany had been the aggressor in 1914 and had fought with uncivilized methods thereafter affected even the most aloof policy-makers. Certainly

elected politicians who directly faced the electorate found it useful to "make Germany pay," partly through proposals which
would restrict German resources and trade, but mainly through
reparation and indemnity. The latter issues, along with war
crimes trials and the expulsion of enemy aliens, dominated the
General Election of 1918, during which public hostility toward
Germany reached its apex. The election in turn focused these
issues onto British peacemaking immediately before the Peace
Conference. It also produced a large group of anti-German
Members in the House of Commons who harried British statesmen throughout 1919. The most persistent fear of these MPs
was that the Government would moderate its demand for reparation and indemnity. This apprehension was partly accurate.
Lloyd George and the British Empire Delegation did attempt a
partial conciliation of Germany at Paris. On the other hand,
they could not completely free themselves from the wartime legacy
of anti-Germanism, as the last chapter of this study will show.

Thus, the Election of 1918 formed a link between the mentality of war, especially economic war, and the making of peace.
Likewise, British policy discussion on the eve of the Peace
Conference anticipated, to an impressive extent, what later
developed at Paris and Versailles on the subject of reparation.
That, however, is the last part of this story, the final transition
from war to peace in Britain. Before we can understand that
transition, we must first examine British wartime plans for the
postwar economic treatment of Germany.

Part One

THE SEARCH
FOR ECONOMIC SECURITY
1914-1918

Chapter 2 ANTI-GERMAN ECONOMICS

THE FIRST World War exacerbated, but did not create Anglo-German economic hostility; Britain and Germany had become industrial and trade rivals well before 1914. From 1870 to 1913, German industrial production had grown at a much faster rate than British production. German steel production, for example, which was less than half of Britain's in 1884, had surpassed British output by 1900. In rapid bursts of expansion in 1880-1885 and in the 1900s, Germany captured the major portion of Dutch and Belgian markets. In 1894 she surpassed Britain as the principal exporter to Russia; in 1907 she accomplished the same regarding Italy. In 1913, Britain herself received one-quarter of all her imports from Germany.[1]

Long before the Great War, this rapid growth of German industry and trade had been perceived as a threat in Britain, especially by protectionists. Britain's "unique position as unchallenged mistress of the industrial World is gone, and is not likely to be regained," wrote a widely read publicist in 1896.[2] Pessimism such as this was commonly expressed before the War, especially during the various business recessions. German trade was also a *bête noire* of the Tariff Reform League, founded in July 1903, at the outset of Joseph Chamberlain's unsuccessful campaign for imperial preference through tariffs. German economic expansion was considered by most tariff reformers to be an imminent threat to the economic solidarity of the Empire, as well as to Britain's home market.[3]

21

The coming of the War in 1914 naturally gave Germany's prewar economic competition a sinister appearance. W. A. S. Hewins, formerly Joseph Chamberlain's economic mentor and the most outspoken Conservative protectionist of the war years, wrote in 1915, "For many years before the war Germany . . . had in view an economic even more than a military or naval victory over the British Empire."[4] Hewins' interpretation of the prewar years was also held by Conservative leaders such as Sir Edward Carson and by prominent businessmen such as the President of the Associated Chambers of Commerce.[5] Likewise, a Cabinet Committee composed of Conservatives and Liberals reported in 1917 that Germany's past efforts to subject industry and trade to state needs was part of "an essentially militarist point of view" which had made Germany "the Japan of the European continent."[6]

Such views were naturally based on the hindsight of war with Germany. A similar foresight was commonly expressed. Hewins told the House of Commons many times that Germany would continue the economic war after the military war was over.[7] *The Times,* under the direction of its war-minded owner, Lord Northcliffe, shared this assumption. A leading article in that paper declared that a Reichstag bill for the postwar restoration of the German merchant marine was "fresh proof of Germany's determination to continue in the economic sphere after the peace the struggle for supremacy which will have ended on the field of battle."[8]

The German economic threat produced much self-criticism and a determination to mend old ways. In particular, the prewar free trade system of Great Britain was blamed by protectionists for facilitating Germany's economic growth and ambition. Leo Amery, a War Cabinet secretary and Conservative MP, felt that "with a different policy in England the expansion of Germany's industry and population would have been much less rapid, her ambitions would have been more restricted and more strictly confined to Europe, and she might have continued to regard the British Empire as a natural ally in her resistance to the pressure of Slavdom on her frontiers and not as a rival to be overthrown."[9] Another source of regret was that Britain had not contested the prewar monopolies of Germany in certain vital products, such as aniline dyes. The London *Globe* summarized the conclusion which most observers drew from this self-criticism: "We were unprepared for war; let us be prepared for peace."[10]

Preparing for peace in the *Globe*'s sense had a negative and a positive side. First, Britain and the British Empire must purge all German influence from their economies. A leading advocate of such purification, Prime Minister William Morris Hughes of Australia, advised the British to "go over Britain with the harrows of resolute purpose, tearing up every vestige of German influence and German trade."[11] Most British Conservatives agreed with Hughes. In the Commons on January 10, 1916, one Conservative MP said that it was necessary to "cut out from our social and political body the gangrene of German influence and German power."[12] This was one of the reasons for the widespread desire to intern or expel German aliens from Britain. Some believed that even naturalized Germans could be harmful to British economic security. One Liberal MP said, "I believe most of these Germans who are naturalized are Germans to the core. . . . It is that class of men who are doing injury to the trade of this country."[13]

The positive side of the British response to the German economic threat was the preparations that were made for a trade "war after the war." For the Government, the most important of these preparations were the Paris Economic Resolutions of the Allies and a new effort at imperial economic cooperation. Outside the Government, there were many schemes for postwar security, most of which involved tariff protection. For example, the arch-protectionist *Morning Post* advocated "a substantial but moderate tariff, with the easiest terms for our Dominions, the next for our Allies, and the highest rates for the enemy."[14] But whatever the scheme, it usually presumed the desirability of national and imperial self-sufficiency. As Leo Amery wrote, "In the economic sphere the great lesson brought home by the war to every combatant and neutral is the necessity of being self-contained."[15]

Not everyone agreed that this was the proper response to the German challenge; there were men in all parties who disliked the idea of carrying the economics of war into the postwar years. Most articulate were the prolific writers of the radical wings of

the Liberal and Labour Parties. For example, a brilliant attack
on the anti-German economics was made by the well known
author of *Imperialism*, J. A. Hobson. In 1916, Hobson published
The New Protectionism, in which he charged British protectionists with using the passions of war to enact their solution for the
fiscal problem. Hobson reminded his readers that "commerce has
always been the greatest civilizer of mankind," and that the
protectionists, under cover of war patriotism, were misrepre-
senting ". . . commercial competition as a struggle between two
nations for a limited amount of profitable foreign market, which
the one gains and the other loses. There is no such limit to the
quantity of the foreign market."[16] He further contended that the
essential interdependence of nations in trade made all plans for
postwar self-sufficiency illusory. These were among the traditional assumptions of free trade and it was on these foundations
that almost every critic of the anti-German economics stood.
Thus, the antebellum lines of fiscal politics remained quite
discernable during the wartime debate over economic policy.

However, during the War, the protectionist side of the traditional controversy gained the upper hand in the midst of an
increased awareness of economic organization. It is true, of
course, that in the first months of the conflict only a few people
saw the importance of the economic aspects of the War, and they
tended to be persons already preoccupied with economics. A
year later, however, the importance of the subject was widely
appreciated. The *Round Table*, a journal devoted mainly to
imperial federation, commented in September 1915, "The war is
becoming a war of exhaustion. As each month goes by the financial aspect of the war and its financial and economic results will
come more and more into prominence."[17] Tariff reformers had
always been more tolerant of state direction of the economy than
their free trade adversaries; hence, in the context of an organized,
national war effort, their ideas seemed more "modern."

The appeal of protectionism in wartime is shown most strikingly by the large number of free traders who converted to
protection during the War, one of the most important developments of that period. Harold Cox, free trade editor of the prominent *Edinburgh Review*, explained that he had changed his
principles because ". . . we have learnt by the war that it is

impossible to assume that other countries will look upon trade as Free Traders look upon it."[18] H. G. Wells wrote that he remained devoted to free trade, but that the prospect of continued German economic aggression had convinced him of the necessity for a postwar tariff against German goods and an anti-German customs alliance with Belgium, France, and Russia.[19] War with Germany also caused important Liberal organizations to alter their position on the fiscal question. Members of the National Liberal Club cheered Gordon Hewart, Liberal MP for Leicester, when he said, "it would be necessary, not only to defeat Germany, but to keep her crippled. To do this it might even be necessary to depart from those principles of Free Trade so dear to every member of the Club."[20] The Manchester Chamber of Commerce, formerly a bastion of *laissez faire*, voted in February 1916 to reject the resolution of its Executive to adhere to the principles of free trade.[21] Protectionists were elated. Prime Minister Hughes of Australia, then on an official visit to Britain, went to Manchester to congratulate the Chamber.[22]

In Parliament and Government there were more instances of self-searching and revised sentiments. Sir Arthur Markham, a Liberal MP, told the House of Commons that although all his interests were in free trade, he would never again have any sort of trade connection with Germany. He claimed this was also the determination of many other Liberal businessmen.[23] Halford J. Mackinder, the great political geographer, was a Conservative MP and tariff reformer who had himself converted from free trade in 1903. In early 1916, he related to the Commons what he thought was a symptomatic anecdote:

> I remember talking within the last two or three months to a gentleman, a very strong Free Trader, who was once a member of this House. We were talking quite peacefully, on this subject, and he said to me, "Eighteen months ago I would not have allowed you to talk in that manner under my roof. I freely admit we had no idea that any nation would be so wicked as the Germans have proved themselves to be." When things come to this, I think we have made very great progress towards that national unity which is necessary for action in the economic sphere.[24]

In the Government, the Liberal Secretary for India, Edwin S. Montagu, urged that free trade should be subordinated to national defense, especially in "key industries" necessary for a modern war effort.[25] Sir Alfred Mond, an important Liberal follower of Lloyd George, was formerly a staunch and vocal free trader. However, he came to believe during the War that "there is always an economic war in progress between competing industries in different countries" and that Britain should keep in mind that even Adam Smith qualified his philosophy of free trade by saying "that national security is [ultimately] of greater importance than national wealth."[26] The Conservative Foreign Secretary, Arthur Balfour, wrote on one of Mond's economic memoranda, "a remarkable paper within itself and from its authorship."[27]

Liberal acceptance of protection was reflected in policy as well as in memoranda. The Liberal Chancellor of the Exchequer, Reginald McKenna, in his September 1915 budget, introduced 33 percent duties on imports of certain luxuries, such as motor cars, watches, and films. The stated object of the McKenna duties was not protection, but revenue and the conservation of shipping space. However, free traders viewed the new duties with alarm, as a portent of things to come.[28] Their fears were heightened in the following year by the Paris Economic Resolutions, which the Liberal Prime Minister, H. H. Asquith, helped to negotiate. Furthermore, Asquith's defense of those Resolutions in Parliament resembled "the new protectionism": He said that Germany would continue her economic aggression after the War and that Britain must prepare to meet it, regardless of prewar fiscal dogmas.[29]

Not all Liberals agreed with their Leader. One Liberal MP, Gordon Harvey, replied, "It is quite significant to me to find that we are now asked to depart from Free Trade to barriers and tariffs amidst the spread of human animosity and hatred."[30] Like Harvey, many Liberals continued to believe in the material and ethical value of free trade. Moreover, a significant portion of those who had accepted protectionist measures during the War reverted to their old notions when the wartime emergency passed. Asquith himself began to do this after he lost the Premiership in December 1916; by the end of the War he insisted that the Paris

Resolutions were only meant to be war measures. The majority of Liberal MPs, who had followed him into opposition, argued likewise.

Nevertheless, the economic demands of the War and the widespread hatred and fear of Germany combined to make self-sufficiency and protection the dominant economic ideas of 1914 to 1918. J. A. Hobson and others might write well-reasoned refutations of protectionist arguments, but the atmosphere was not receptive. Hobson recognized this in a perceptive comparison of 1903 and 1916:

> In 1903 Mr. Chamberlain endeavored to float Protection upon the new tide of Imperialism and anti-Continentalism which the Boer War had evoked in this country. The political passions now available are far more concentrated and intense. Our nation is to be stampeded into Protection by hatred, fear, and suspicion of Germany.[31]

Indeed, a Conservative protectionist like Leo Amery might well feel that the War was the appropriate opportunity to do "what we had invariably done in the past, i.e. use a great national struggle as an occasion for reorganizing our economic system and developing new trades which more than met all the cost of the war."[32]

As in the years before 1914, the Conservative Party was the main bulwark of protection during the War. The position of the majority of the Party was reflected in its national publication, *Gleanings and Memoranda*, which consistently gave space and praise to protectionist ideas in its leading articles.[33] If the War brought some Liberals over to protection, at least temporarily, the majority of those who manned and led the protectionist campaign were Conservatives.

The most important center of protection and anti-German economics in the Conservative Party was a large committee of backbenchers, the Unionist Business Committee, founded on January 27, 1915, by twenty-five MPs.[34] From 1915 to 1918, almost one-third of Conservative Members attended the Committee's meetings at one time or another.[35] The Committee's importance is further shown by the fact that its first three chairmen were taken into the Government: Walter Long became

President of the Local Government Board and Colonial Secre-
tary, Ernest M. Pollock became Chairman of the Contraband
Committee of the Foreign Office, and W. A. S. Hewins became
Long's Under-Secretary at the Colonial Office.

The Business Committee was strengthened by the connections
it had with business and tariff reform organizations. Most
Committee members were businessmen themselves, several of
them quite prominent.[36] Many were also active in the Associated
Chambers of Commerce and the National Union of Manufacturers.[37] There was a close connection between the Business
Committee and the Federation of British Industries through the
friendship of Hewins and Sir Vincent Caillard, Chairman of
Vickers, Ltd.[38] Hewins was also the link between the Committee and the Tariff Commission, of which he had been Secretary since the founding of that protectionist study group in 1903.
During the War the staff and the great volume of economic
information which the Commission had compiled were largely at
the service of the Unionist Business Committee.[39] The Committee also had ties with the Tariff Reform League. Several men
were active in both groups: for example, Hewins, Alfred Bigland,
and H. J. Mackinder. In October 1917, Mackinder and Hewins
became Chairman and Vice-Chairman of the League.[40] These
connections with the business community and with the tariff
organizations made the Unionist Business Committee the main
Parliamentary spokesman for protectionist sentiment during the
War. Moreover, at the end of the War, these groups maintained
their informal ties in the campaign for an economically punitive
peace.

From 1915 to 1918, the main concern of the Business Committee was the economic side of the war effort, as shown by the
topics discussed at committee meetings: aniline dyes, aliens,
optical glass, food supply, national economy, contraband, trading with the enemy, excess profits tax, export licenses, foreign
exchanges, control of shipping, purchases by neutrals, sale of
enemy ships to neutrals, enemy debts, Empire minerals, and the
most-favored-nation clause. Of the twenty-three Commons
debates and deputations to ministers initiated by Business Committee members in 1916-1917, twenty-two dealt with economic
aspects of the War.[41]

Politically, the Unionist Business Committee was a "ginger" group; they were continually dissatisfied with the policies and policy execution of the wartime governments. They were especially distrustful of the Liberal-Conservative Coalition Government formed by Asquith in May 1915; they felt that Conservative vigor was being diluted by Liberal caution. Their typical attitude was, "Things look very bad—our Government is stone cold. . . . 'Wait and See' is fatal."[42] In particular, the Committee thought the Government too timid about economic war measures. They even attacked their own Party Leader, Bonar Law, on this score. Hewins recorded the following conversation with Walter Long on January 30, 1917:

> He talked violently against Bonar Law, whom he said he had spent the morning trying to understand. He said that B. L. was the chief difficulty in the way of Preference, that he was betraying his Party, was utterly without principle and thought of nothing but his own interests on which he had a false view.[43]

Hewins himself felt that Bonar Law "appeared to think that economic policy had nothing to do with the war."[44]

Protectionist disappointment with Bonar Law had a prewar source. Law had been one of the most active tariff reformers before his elevation to Party Leader in November 1911. However, in early 1913, he had publicly backed away from the controversial duties on grain that would have been necessary to implement imperial preference through tariffs. He did so in order to placate the moderate protectionists and "free fooders" in Conservative ranks, hoping thereby to strengthen the Party for the struggle over Home Rule. He remained a tariff reformer, to be sure, but he seemed to have deserted that aspect of tariff reform which ardent followers of Joseph Chamberlain had most cherished.

During the War, Bonar Law continued to de-emphasize tariffs, since protection was an issue that he could not press vigorously and openly, lest he alienate Liberal ministers, promote a split in the Coalition, and endanger wartime administration. Such considerations, however, did not impress the more extreme protectionists of the Business Committee. Despite Conservative prominence in the Government, they continued to demand a more protective, anti-German economic policy and, in 1918-1919, a punitive economic peace.

Nevertheless, Bonar Law withstood their discontent and maintained his Leadership. He was able to do so, in part, because of the free trade minority within the Conservative Party. Two of this minority were Lords Robert and Hugh Cecil, sons of the third Marquis of Salisbury. The Cecils were not enthusiastic about Bonar Law, but they preferred him to the imperialists and protectionists of their party.[45] Lord Henry Cavendish-Bentinck was another member of this minority. In his 1918 publication, *Tory Democracy*, he warned that wartime materialism threatened to transform the party of Disraeli into "A tariff-mongering faction."[46] Other Conservatives, like Colonel Aubrey Herbert, MP for Yeovil, Somerset, spoke in the Commons of the enormous sacrifice of British life in the War and said that this sacrifice required a more generous vision of peace than that put forward by protectionists.[47] Men like the Cecils, Bentinck, and Herbert found Bonar Law's leadership more attractive than the fulminations of his backbench critics.

Another source of Conservative support for moderate economic policies was the large number of MPs who were protectionist but who would not, for that reason, challenge their Party's leadership. This inhibition was even felt by some members of the Business Committee. At no time was the importance of such restraints more apparent than during the major wartime crisis within the Party, the debate of November 8, 1916 over the sale of enemy property in Nigeria.

The debate was initiated by the Unionst War Committee, a large backbench group concerned primarily within the military prosecution of the War. Under the leadership of Sir Edward Carson, this committee was even more anti-Coalition than the Business Committee.[48] They especially disliked the degree to which Bonar Law cooperated with Liberal ministers. In November 1916, they decided to attack the Government on an issue of colonial economic protection. Since Bonar Law was then Colonial Secretary, this was an affront to his Leadership from within his party. The War Committee resolution which he faced was designed to appeal to protectionists:

> That in the opinion of this House, where enemy properties and businesses in Crown Colonies and Protectorates are offered for sale, provision should be made for securing that such properties and businesses should be sold only to natural-born British subjects or companies wholly British.[49]

Hewins, Bigland, and Pennefather of the Business Committee spoke strongly in support of the resolution and many other members of the UBC voted for it.[50] Lord Robert Cecil denounced the resolution as inspired by selfish financial interests.[51]

Sir Edward Carson made the most strident speech of the debate. After a biting attack on the Colonial Office, he insisted that no other nation, including Britain's ally, France, would consent to a free auction. Then, despite Government assurances that no property would be sold to Germans, Carson made an anti-German appeal. Why not approve the resolution he asked, "What is the answer? Ah, we must hurry up and get money for the Germans!"[52] Sixty-five Conservatives managed to swallow those words and go into the division lobby with Carson.

Bonar Law defended himself by turning attention toward Carson's tactless vehemence:

> This is a motion of want of confidence in the Government, moved —and this I must say I do regret—with a violence which to my mind is hardly in keeping with the serious situation in which the country stands. . . . He [Carson] had behind him a very strong volume of sentiment, felt in the House and out of it, a sentiment based on the assumption that he is hostile to the Germans and that I, as represented by the policy which we are carrying out, am more or less friendly to them. I hope he is wrong.[53]

Furthermore, Bonar Law insisted that true tariff reform had never meant the total exclusion of foreign interests from the British Empire. He expressed concern about the effects this proposal would have on French and neutral opinion. H. J. Mackinder and Stanley Baldwin agreed with Law, saying also that an exclusionist policy would retard colonial investment and irritate British diplomatic relations with other countries.[54] Seventy-three Conservatives preferred these arguments and voted with the Government.

While 138 Conservatives took sides with either Carson or

Bonar Law, a similar number abstained or were absent. They may have agreed with Carson's resolution, but they probably also considered his challenge to Bonar Law harmful to the Party. Hewins wrote in his diary, "Carson's motion on Nigeria was badly worded and he made a bad speech. In fact he drove many of our men into the Government lobby."[55] And Winston Churchill, then a Liberal, explained to editor C. P. Scott that

> Bonar Law had been losing ground steadily to Carson . . . The charge against him now was that he was a mere echo of Asquith. Hence the vigour with which he asserted himself the other day against Carson on the Nigeria question. The effect had been to divide Carson's Party.[56]

With his "party" divided in this way, Carson's resolution lost by a vote of 117 to 231.

Thus, the debate of November 8, 1916, revealed three economic groups within the Conservative Party: a small free trade minority, a larger group of militant protectionists, and another large group of moderate protectionists who subjected their economic beliefs to party loyalty. This tripartite division, it is interesting to note, was basically the same as the prewar division between "free fooders," "whole hoggers," and Conservatives who took their cue from the Party Leader.[57]

The Nigeria debate also showed that the most intense protectionists were also those most adamant against Germany; the "new protectionism" and anti-German feeling were interdependent. Those who professed these two related lines of thought found several champions, but the most active and important was, in fact, the Labour Prime Minister of Australia, William Morris Hughes. Hughes came to Britain on official business in 1916 and again in 1917; he was also in Britain and France during the critical period from the summer of 1918 until June 1919. In this way he became for a time as much a British as an Australian political figure. During his 1916 visit, he made a speech which was typical of those which wartime protectionists found attractive:

> The German people, who for forty years were preparing for "the day," were able to recruit all the great commercial and financial

interests of their country by the prospect of much loot and no risk.
The hope that buoyed them up was not so much the downfall of
Britain but the industrial and commercial domination of the earth.
Early in the war Englishmen spoke of "business as usual." Patent-
ly, business as usual was impossible . . . we should be fools, and
worse, if we were not to learn something from the way in which we
have been betrayed. We have seen it in Australia, you have seen it
in Britain—you may yet see it before your eyes—men to whom
naturalization is nothing. We have declared for a policy which shall
pluck this cursed thing out root and branch and give us in truth
an Anglo-Saxon community. Germany has forfeited her right to
enter our shores on those terms of friendly intercourse and brother-
hood which we have extended to her for too long. The policy for the
Empire has many phases, trade and other. First of all, before you
build up, you must destroy; you must pluck out German influence
by the roots, wherever it is and at all costs, regarding everything
as subordinate to this one thing, and you must by settled determination, clearly expressed to the world, decide, whatever comes or
goes, to destroy German control of British trade. (Cheers) So you
will strike a blow at Germany equal to a decisive land battle.[58]

Here was the mentality of economic war and the spirit in which
Hughes and his British admirers eventually approached the
problems of peacemaking.

Chapter 3 TWO WARTIME POLICIES

THE VICTORY of the Western Allies in 1918 often obscures the deep sense of anxiety and pessimism felt in Britain and France during much of the War. Out of this foreboding arose the belief that men and governments should prepare for the possibility of a stalemated conflict, an undefeated Germany, and "a war after the war."

British protectionists reasoned that in such a war the most important weapons would be economic ones and that their effective use would depend on international cooperation. The most tangible results of this reasoning were the Paris Economic Resolutions, negotiated between Britain and the European Allies in June 1916, and imperial preference, agreed to by Britain and the Dominions in April 1917.

To some extent, these two policies were contradictory; one pulled toward Europe and the other overseas, in the traditional pattern of British foreign relations. However, they were also based on a common impulse, the search for postwar economic security at the expense of Germany. Few contemporaries saw them as incompatible until the end of the War, when the Allied victory opened new avenues for "making Germany pay." Therefore, the two policies are considered together in this chapter. More consideration is given to the Paris Resolutions partly because contemporaries paid much attention to them, partly because historians have paid very little.[1]

The Paris Economic Resolutions, 1916

In Britain, the idea of an Allied economic agreement to cooperate against Germany during and after the War appeared in
early 1915. The first advocate was H. G. Wells. In the *Daily
Express* of January 20, 1915, Wells called for a postwar economic
union of the Allies, within which there were to be no tariffs,
while a common external tariff would protect all members
against German "dumping." Wells' idea, however, did not
become current until later in the year. By that time it was clear
that the War would be a long one, and that economic organization and conservation of resources were vital necessities. On
October 18, 1915, the *Morning Post* advised that "the question
of the formation of a Commercial Union for the purpose of
threatening the trade of Germany and Austria is discussed in
various quarters as a weapon for future use, which should be
forged without delay." Business opinion was moving in the
same direction. On November 23, 1915, A. M. Samuel, an executive of the Associated Chambers of Commerce, proposed an Allied
conference at which "the general principle to be arrived at . . .
should be an offensive and defensive commercial alliance of the
Entente Powers against those Powers who are our enemies," to
take effect upon the signing of peace.[2] Even Dominion protectionists, despite their interest in imperial preference, were urging
Britain toward the same kind of agreement.[3]

The first diplomatic initiative for Allied commercial cooperation came from the French Director-General of Customs, Jean
Branet. In early September 1915, Branet proposed to Lord Granville, Counsellor of the British Embassy in Paris, a wartime
agreement between Britain and France to cooperate in repelling
imports from Germany after the War. The Frenchman admitted
that Britain might, as before the War, desire more German
products than would France and that Free Trade might stand in
the way, but he urged that at least an agreement to consult would
be possible and desirable. Although Branet said that he spoke
only for himself, Lord Bertie, the British Ambassador, reported
that other French officials had made similar suggestions.[4]

While these discussions transpired in Paris, Paul Cambon,
the French Ambassador in London, was reviewing the same sub-

jects with Sir Vincent Caillard and W. A. S. Hewins. On October
7, 1915, Hewins happily recorded in his diary that Cambon had
written to Paris for authority to open negotiations with the
British Government. By December 22, permission had been
granted. On that day, Cambon handed Sir Edward Grey an invi-
tation to arrange a conference that would study ways of liberating
the Allies "from any economic dependence on the German
states."[5] Gradually, in early 1916, the Asquith Government
agreed to such a meeting.

However, the Government's agreement was less a result of
French persuasion than of pressure from British protectionists.
Again, Hewins was the leading advocate. Throughout the fall of
1915 he sought a pledge from Asquith that the British Empire
would join some Allied economic combination.[6] In the House of
Commons, on January 10, 1916, he moved:

> That with a view to increasing the power of the Allies in the prose-
> cution of the War, His Majesty's Government should enter into
> immediate consultation with the Governments of the Dominions
> in order with their aid to bring the whole economic strength of the
> Empire into cooperation with our Allies in a policy directed
> against the enemy.[7]

In these carefully chosen words, Hewins united imperial and
Allied economic cooperation.

The resulting debate proved the skill of his wording. His
resolution was supported by eleven Conservatives and three
Liberals, a ratio which represented the relative support for
protectionist policies in the two major parties.[8] Significantly,
only one Liberal Member opposed the resolution. More important, Hewins' proposal was accepted by Walter Runciman on
behalf of the Government. Runciman said:

> When we are waging war we should wage it as war. An economic
> war should be well within the range of our powers. How long that
> economic war is to be waged is another matter. At any rate, we must
> see to it that, having ended this War victoriously, we do not give
> Germany a chance of reconstructing her commercial position.[9]

This acceptance was widely hailed in the Conservative and tariff
reform press,[10] despite its hesitation about a permanent eco-

nomic war, and despite the fact that the Government had already begun negotiations with France. And the elation was understandable: a Liberal Minister, speaking for a primarily Liberal Government, had accepted a protectionist suggestion. Hewins received dozens of letters of congratulation. William Cunningham, like Hewins an historical economist and tariff reformer, wrote to his colleague, "The victory of our cause is shown in the abandonment of Cobdenism by Mond and Runciman even more strikingly than in anything else."[11]

The Commons debate also alerted the business community to the possibility of an Allied economic league. On January 31, a large and varied assembly of businessmen at the Guildhall passed unanimously a motion quite similar to Hewins' and applauded the statement ". . . that above everything else they placed the smashing of Germany both as a maritime power and as a commercial competitor."[12] A special meeting of the Associated Chambers of Commerce on February 29, 1916, approved by a large majority a resolution calling for a British Empire-Allied commercial conference.[13] The President of the British Chamber of Commerce in Paris published a scheme that involved a post-war Allied tariff, a general British tariff, and a British Empire tariff.[14] It was in this atmosphere that the Manchester Chamber of Commerce rejected its traditional free trade position in late February 1916.

Despite the growing strength of protectionism and the Government's apparent concession to Hewins, Conservatives nevertheless worried about the reserved attitude of the Prime Minister and his Liberal followers. There were grounds for such concern. On March 9, Asquith warned the Commons that vindictiveness might be as harmful to the British economy as to the German, and that any Allied agreement must leave Parliament free to decide the fiscal system of the country.[15] His caution was probably reinforced by a memorandum from Sir Hubert Llewellyn Smith, Permanent Secretary of the Board of Trade, that expressed reservations about the effect of anti-German trade schemes on British relations with important neutrals, principally the United States.[16]

Asquith's lack of enthusiasm was also notable at the general Allied conference of March 27-29 in Paris. Aristide Briand, the

French Foreign Minister, played the leading part in the discussion of economic topics while Asquith and the other British
representatives were quiescent.[17] Finally, at the last meeting,
Asquith agreed that the next conference should concern itself
primarily with economic measures, but warned that these must
not limit Britain's freedom to make her own policies.[18]

Although Asquith did not intend to go in person to the
planned economic conference, Conservatives were wary of the
influence he would have on the negotiations. Consequently,
they mounted a campaign for the appointment of delegates who
could overcome the Prime Minister's inertia. Bonar Law and,
especially, William Morris Hughes of Australia were put for-
ard by the Unionist Business Committee and the tariff reform
press. Hughes, in Britain during the first half of 1916, was
regarded by Conservatives as an ideal choice since he was both a
Dominion statesman and an emphatic protectionist.

Asquith conceded. He selected both Law and Hughes to go to
the conference, and contented himself with Lord Crewe, then
Lord President, and Canadian Minister of Finance Sir George
Foster to represent free trade. Although nominally balanced,
this delegation pleased protectionists; Law and Hughes would
obviously dominate it.

Meanwhile, the Government, partly in conjunction with
France, prepared a program for the coming economic conference.
On May 1, Walter Runciman and French Minister of Finance
Etienne Clémentel agreed that the conference should produce
resolutions rather than a treaty and that the agenda should be
divided between wartime economic measures, reconstruction in
the immediate postwar years, and permanent economic cooperation.[19] In the Board of Trade, Runciman and Llewellyn Smith
prepared draft British resolutions along these lines. The two
most notable of these represented an attempt to balance protection and free trade. According to the fourth draft resolution, the
Allies were to deny Germany most-favored-nation treatment for
five years after the War. On the other hand, the seventh British
resolution proposed that "the means adopted by each of the
Allied countries [to achieve economic independence from Ger-
many] may vary, according to the different conditions applicable

to particular commodities, and the views held by the respective Governments on fiscal policy."[20]

The Paris Economic Conference of June 14-17, 1916, was attended by delegates from Britain, France, Russia, Italy, Japan, and Portugal. The brevity of the Conference was due to the careful planning of the French and, especially, of the British. The final statement of the Conference followed the format of the Runciman-Clémentel agenda and was definitely modeled on the British draft resolutions.[21]

The Resolutions of the Paris Economic Conference began with a condemnation of German plans for economic aggression after the War:

> They [the Allied delegates] declare that after forcing upon them the military contest in spite of all their efforts to avoid the conflict, the Empires of Central Europe are today preparing, in concert with their Allies, for a contest on the economic plane, which will not only survive the re-establishment of peace, but will at that moment attain its full scope and intensity.[22]

Proceeding on this premise, the first section of Resolutions declared that during the War the Allies would coordinate their laws to restrict trading with the enemy, would confiscate or control all enemy businesses in their territories, and would tighten their lists of contraband and export prohibitions so as to minimize German resources. Since most of these resolves had already been accomplished in Britain and France, their intent was to stiffen the policies of the other Allies.

The second section of Resolutions, on postwar reconstruction, proposed to give first choice of raw materials to those countries that had suffered most from German "spoilation." The Allies also resolved to deny Germany most-favored-nation treatment after the War. During the discussion of this Resolution, "Mr. Bonar Law said that it was one to which . . . the British Delegation attached great importance, and without it the work of the Conference would be unavailing."[23] However, the Russian and Italian delegates, mindful of their prewar dependence on trade with Germany, insisted that the period of this restriction be undefined and that the other Allies provide Russia and Italy compensatory trade opportunities.[24] The Russians and Italians also qualified the Resolution limiting German postwar shipping. Llewellyn Smith remarked, "We could not have carried a more definite and drastic proposal without raising a disagreeable debate on the rapacity of British shipowners."[25]

The "permanent measures of mutual assistance and collaboration among the Allies" included a pledge to coordinate commercial transport, communications, patents, trademarks, etc. Beyond this, the Allied resolve to secure "permanent" economic independence from Germany was hedged—as Runciman and Llewellyn Smith had hoped—by language that made clear the freedom of Allied Governments to determine their own fiscal policy. In the final paragraph, drafted significantly by Hughes of Australia, the delegates agreed that the effectiveness of the Resolutions depended on their speedy implementation, and resolved to recommend them to their Governments without delay.

In Britain, publication of the Resolutions brought forth a brief protectionist celebration, followed by a campaign for early and precise implementation. Already on June 26 Asquith was being hard-pressed in the Commons by Conservative questions along these lines.[26] From July 1 onwards, the *War Notes* of the Tariff Reform League regularly carried, as a banner slogan, a warning by Prime Minister Hughes: "The proposals of the Paris Conference are mere empty words unless Great Britain takes immediate steps to give effect to them."[27]

Protectionists were temporarily placated by Cabinet and Parliamentary approval of the Resolutions, and by the appointment of a Cabinet Committee to study implementation. The Cabinet approved the Resolutions on July 14, 1916.[28] On August 2, 1916, they were debated in the House of Commons.[29] Asquith opened the debate with a strong, anti-German statement (already noted in the previous Chapter) that emphasized the necessity and probable effectiveness of the Resolutions. At the same time, he held out to his free trade supporters the hope ". . . that we are left practically free in this country to pursue the policy which is best adapted and most suited to our own economic and industrial needs." Asquith's view was verbally supported by four members of his own party and by eight Conservatives, including Bonar Law, Sir Edward Carson, W. A. S.

Hewins, and H. J. Mackinder. Most of those who approved the Resolutions did so uncritically, but one supporter, Winston Churchill, thought the postwar Resolutions would be necessary only if there was an inconclusive peace. Events were to vindicate Churchill's view.

A strong attack was made on the Resolutions by four Liberals, one Conservative, and one Labour Member. The basis of the opposition was free trade. A Liberal, Sir John Simon, said the Resolutions would harm the great British industries which had been nourished on freedom of commerce, such as shipping and transport. Charles Carew, a Conservative free trader, could not see how "we are going to exclude Germany from trading in this country without receiving a very great setback to the commercial supremacy of this country." However, despite opposition, the Resolutions were approved by the House without a division.

The Government also tried to soothe protectionists through the establishment of a Cabinet Committee on Commercial and Industrial Policy. This was conceived at the Cabinet of February 23, 1916. Its original purpose was to have been quite general:

> The Prime Minister dwelt on the urgency of setting up without delay machinery to plan out the economic and industrial readjustments, both at home and in relation to foreign countries and to the Dominions, which will become necessary when the war is concluded. He suggested the formation of a mixed Committee comprising some of the most eminent Free Traders and Tariff Reformers to discuss freely the prospective situation.[30]

However, the Committee's specific terms of reference indicated that the Committee was "to consider the Commercial and Industrial policy to be adopted after the War, with special reference to the conclusions reached at the Economic Conference of the Allies. . . ."[31]

With this mandate, a committee of twenty-one members held its first meeting on July 29, 1916. The Committee continued to meet throughout 1916 but was unable to make even an interim report until the end of the year. Meanwhile, Conservatives grew impatient, and probably suspicious of the Committee's chairman, Lord Balfour of Burleigh, who had been a prominent free trader before the War. Hewins, a member of the Committee, was

asked by one Conservative, "What does the Morning Post mean
by saying that the Advisory Committee on the Paris Conference
has done nothing and will soon be abolished? If you have come
to a standstill we must take action in the House of Commons."[32]

The interim reports of the Committee, when they finally
appeared, did little to encourage the discontented. The first
report, of November 9, recommended that imports of enemy
origin be prohibited for one year after the War, but also observed
that Dominion and Allied cooperation would be necessary for
this and other postwar economic schemes. On December 14, a
second report proposed that Britain should restrict postwar
exports to Germany, except for articles which Germany could
get elsewhere, and excepting items not in demand at home.[33]
Such limited recommendations did not please many protectionists.

Therefore, they did not wait for the Balfour of Burleigh Committee to implement the Paris Resolutions. On October 12, 1916,
the Tariff Reform League decided to launch its own "vigorous
educational program" for executing the Resolutions.[34] In
November 1916, Conservative impatience with the Government's
failure to pursue the Economic Resolutions was one of the
motives for the Nigeria Debate of November 8. By the end of
1916, this failure had become one of the objects of a general
Conservative protest against Asquith's supposedly dilatory
prosecution of the War.[35] Moreover, Lloyd George's new
Government, formed December 7, was not immune from attacks
on account of economic delay. In early 1917, a Conservative MP
declared, "The question now is whether these [Paris Economic]
resolutions are to remain a dead letter. If not, when is the Government going to make a move? Time is running on."[36] W. A. S.
Hewins claimed that in April 1917, he convinced George
Younger, Conservative Party Chairman, to warn Lloyd George
that "a declaration on Preference and the Paris Resolutions must
be made at once or he would be out in three weeks."[37]

In July 1917, the Unionist Business Committee took strong
action. They wrote to Bonar Law in solemn tones, declaring
their belief in the Paris Resolutions and their doubt that the
Government intended to act.[38] When they failed to receive a
reply from the Conservative Leader, the Committee demanded an

interview, which Bonar Law granted. Hewins, present as Chairman of the Committee, recorded what Law thought most valuable about the Economic Resolutions:

> first, the withdrawal of most-favored-nation treatment from Germany, and secondly a period of continuance of war restrictions after the termination of the war during which we should have time to settle our policy. But he did not speak enthusiastically of the Paris Resolutions. He thought that in reality they concerned mainly Great Britain and France as Italy and Russia were not keen about them. The Government, he said, thought there should be another Economic Conference of the Allies.[39]

This cool explanation did little to deter Conservative backbenchers from further activity. On October 30, 1917, the Unionist War Committee resolved that the Government should immediately implement the Paris Resolutions.[40]

The Government did not capitulate to this agitation for various reasons. First, the Paris Resolutions placed both of the wartime Liberal Prime Ministers in a delicate position. Asquith, as we have seen, feared that a vigorous adherence to the Resolutions would alienate his free trade followers. His successor, David Lloyd George, had fewer scruples about free trade and fewer free trade supporters, but he was a superlative coalitionist who understood well the need to avoid divisive issues. He also disliked rigid diplomatic arrangements and once told W. A. S. Hewins that the Economic Resolutions ". . . tied our hands. He said there might be a revolution in Germany which would end the War, the Germans would in that case become our friends and we should want to make an arrangement with them."[41]

There were also inhibitions in Conservative ranks. One was a residual suspicion that the French were commercial competitors, not allies. For example, only five months after the Paris Conference, in the Nigeria Debate, Sir Edward Carson resolved that Frenchmen as well as Germans should be excluded from investment in Nigeria.[42] Many Conservatives also disliked the prospect of favorable treatment for French imports into the British home market, yet genuine implementation of the Paris Resolutions would have required such treatment. A related obstacle to implementation was the difficulty of coordinating the Resolu-

tions with imperial preference. In April 1917, Walter Long told
an Imperial War Cabinet Committee that French persistence in
urging Britain to denounce her present commercial treaties and
replace them with the Paris Resolutions was motivated by French
fear of postwar imperial preference.[43] Yet most Conservatives
preferred the latter to the former policy if forced to a choice.

The immediacy of the War also discouraged enactment of the
reconstruction and "permanent" Resolutions. The first section
of the Resolutions was relevant to wartime preoccupations, but
the necessity of the second and third was bound to seem con-
tingent upon the outcome of the War. H. J. Mackinder, initially
an enthusiast of the Resolutions, said in 1917:

> Just in proportion as we fail to defeat Germany at the present time
> will it be necessary to enforce economic control on her afterwards.
> The resolutions in Paris were war measures. They were a procla-
> mation to Germany of what we intended to do if she continued her
> policy of "peaceful penetration". . . .[44]

Along with Mackinder, many politicians came to believe that
enacting the Resolutions might be necessary only in the event
of an inconclusive peace; until then, their main value seemed to
be propaganda which might discourage the German war effort.

A similar attitude prevailed in the Board of Trade and Foreign
Office, where the Economic Resolutions were regarded in an
expedient, rather than wholehearted, manner. Officials in the
Board of Trade wanted to use the Resolutions as one method for
protecting newly-established "key" industries and ensuring adequate postwar supplies of specific raw materials, such as syn-
thetic dyes, spelter, tungsten, optical glass, etc. Authors of Board
of Trade memoranda did not consider the Paris Resolutions as a
firm pledge to conduct a general trade war.[45]

Foreign Secretary Arthur Balfour paid little attention of any
kind to the Resolutions. His principal subordinates were more
attentive, but had mixed feelings on the subject. Eustace Percy
and Arthur Zimmern of the Political Intelligence Department
remarked that ". . . the economic issue is by far the best leverage
at our disposal for influencing German opinion. . . ."[46] The
Chairman of the Contraband Committee, Sir Ernest Pollock,
also believed that the Resolutions were an effective psychological

weapon, but he doubted whether such measures ought actually to be taken because of the effect they might have on Britain's prosperity and because they might drive the commercial classes of Germany toward militarism.[47] A more decided critic of the Paris Resolutions was Lord Robert Cecil, Parliamentary Under-Secretary of the Foreign Office and Minister of Blockade. Although committed to economic war measures, Cecil deplored the diplomatic implications of the Paris program: He saw clearly that, aside from France, no Allied or Associated country was enthusiastic about the Resolutions.[48]

The most serious obstacle was the attitude of the United States Government, which was hostile to the Resolutions both before and after the United States entered the War. Only six days after the conclusion of the Paris Economic Conference, the British Ambassador in Washington, Sir Cecil Spring-Rice, sent home a pessimistic analysis of the reception the Resolutions had received in the United States, concluding with this warning:

> Whatever may be thought of the United States as a factor in war there can be no doubt as to its immense importance as a factor in the commerce and business of the world. The attitude of the United States towards a commercial combination, such as appears to be now contemplated, will, no doubt, be a matter of serious consideration. Should the United States take the side of Germany in the commercial war which as is planned is to succeed the present military war, the effect would no doubt be of serious importance to the Allies.[49]

In Britain, the Foreign Office concurred in this estimate and warned the Cabinet of the danger of encouraging a German-American commercial tie, and of the possibility that the Paris Resolutions would make American financiers less receptive to British requests for loans. To prevent these developments, the Foreign Office was anxious to assure American business interests that the Economic Resolutions would not be directed against the United States.[50]

The entry of the United States into the War in April 1917, relieved some of this anxiety. At the same time, it raised doubts about the practicality of an Allied economic arrangement negotiated without American agreement. An Imperial War Cabinet

Committee thought that the entry of the United States had introduced "doubtful and new elements into the situation" of the
Paris Resolutions.[51] The Board of Trade urged a reconsidera-
tion of the postwar Resolutions, since these were objectionable to
the United States.[52] An American official told Lord Robert Cecil
that the United States Government would probably agree to
economic "pressure on the Germans to put an end to the war, but
that they would be altogether against anything like a boycott of
Germany after the war. . . ."[53] British concern about American
opposition to the Paris Resolutions continued throughout the
War.

Protectionists, of course, disliked this solicitude for American
feelings. W. A. S. Hewins claimed it was merely subterfuge:
"Some silly people think they can preserve 'free trade' by running
America against the Paris Resolutions."[54] Likewise, Prime
Minister Hughes was not discouraged from his efforts for anti-
German protection. Even Lloyd George joined the protectionist
campaign, temporarily, in July 1918. Yet President Wilson made
clear in his 1918 speeches that the United States would accept
nothing resembling the Paris program.[55]

For that reason, and for the others already mentioned, the
Paris Resolutions were never implemented during the War. Nor
did they find any significant place in the peacemaking of 1919.
The economic clauses of the Treaty of Versailles, Articles 264
to 281, did not register an Allied agreement to restrict imports
from Germany or deny Germany most-favored-nation rights.
They made, instead, the negative requirement that Germany not
discriminate against Allied commerce. Moreover, on June 16,
1919, in the reparation section of the Allied reply to the German
counterproposals, the Allies recognized that German industry
and commerce would have to be restored on a sound basis if
reparation was to be paid. Trade war was thereby renounced in
favor of direct compensation from Germany, a shift that British
politics and policy at the end of the War did much to bring about.

In this way, the Allies eventually discarded the Paris Economic
Resolutions. During the War, however, they had been an important rallying point for protectionists, and as late as July 1918,
there was renewed (though mistaken) hope that the United States
might agree to the Resolutions. Thus, the British Government

never considered a definite, public renunciation of its resolves of June 1916. There were other reasons, too, why such a renunciation would have been impolitic: French sensitivity, the presumed propaganda value of the Resolutions, and, above all, the possibility of a negotiated peace with an undefeated Germany. This is why the Paris Resolutions remained a focus for British thinking about the economics of war and peace—until, during the Election of 1918, reparation and indemnity became more convenient instruments of economic security at German expense.

Imperial Preference, 1917

The wartime history of imperial preference followed a course similar to that of the Paris Resolutions: a protectionist campaign, official recognition, and practical difficulties. However, while the Resolutions faded from sight in 1919, imperial preference survived the War as an issue in British politics. The main reason for this different result was the greater loyalty of the Conservative Party to imperial preference.

Before the War, imperial preference was a source of contention between the British Government and the Dominions. Generally, it was the latter who urged reciprocal preference on imports within the Empire. They wished to provide the Empire with economic unity and security without losing their economic autonomy. However, their offers of preference were never sufficient to win the British Government or electorate away from free trade. Between 1897 and 1907, each of the Dominions granted some degree of preference to imports from Britain, but London failed to reciprocate.[56]

Naturally, this situation was disliked by most British Conservatives and tariff reformers, especially those led by Joseph Chamberlain. To Conservative imperialists, the policy of the British Government seemed ungrateful. To tariff reformers it seemed careless: They argued that the absence of any imperial economic policy was encouraging foreign inroads into Empire markets.[57] The reciprocity agreement of 1911 between the United States and Canada, though repudiated in the same year after a Canadian general election, seemed to support the tariff reform argument. A more constant source of concern was the growth of German trade with Australia and South Africa between 1906 and 1913.[58]

Then came the War of 1914, which appeared further proof of protectionist warnings. A Tariff Commission pamphlet of March 1915 urged that

> . . . a basis should be found for the economic partnership which overseas States of the Empire have long desired and which the facts of war have proved to be as much in our interests as theirs. The immediate object of Imperial cooperation is the permanent removal of that German menace which it is realized, as never before, is a menace against the whole British Empire. . . .[59]

The objective of imperial economic partnership was not forgotten by protectionists during the campaign for the Paris Resolutions. For example, Hewins' resolution for an Allied agreement on January 10, 1916, was carefully predicated upon Empire cooperation. Thus, two Dominion statesmen were British delegates at the Paris Economic Conference. After that Conference, protectionists searched for an opportunity to bring imperial policy up to the level of the Allied Resolutions.

The opportunity came in December 1916, when Lloyd George's new British War Cabinet decided to organize an Imperial War Cabinet and Conference to meet in March and April of the following year. As those meetings approached, three groups tried to persuade the Empire statesmen to consider imperial economic cooperation. On January 29, 1917, the Unionist Business Committee sent a resolution to Foreign Secretary Balfour urging the Imperial Conference to decide upon vigorous economic cooperation to combat "the recent developments of German economic policy" and to complement the Paris Resolutions.[60] Committee members then lobbied in favor of their resolution: In late March 1917, Hewins and four others of the UBC met with Walter Long, the Colonial Secretary, to ". . . consider what steps should be taken to make the Gvt. i.e. Ll.G. adopt preference at the Conference."[61] Similar pressure was applied by the Balfour of Burleigh Committee. On February 12, 1917, the Committee resolved that the Government should grant immediate preference to the Dominions and colonies on existing customs duties, or duties enacted in the future. The Committee also thought that "early consideration" should be given to the establishment of a wider range of British tariffs, enacted for the specific purpose of erecting a general system of imperial preference.[62] A third but more cautious recommendation was the report of the Dominions Royal Commission, presented to Parliament in March, 1917. The Commission, composed of six representatives of Great Britain and one from each of the Dominions, had been appointed in 1912 to study the possibility of greater imperial economic cooperation. Its report avoided the controversial question of customs preference, and argued that better communications and, especially, more shipping and lower freight rates were the surest avenues to economic unity.[63] These restrained suggestions, encased in a long, complicated state paper, probably had less influence than the well-publicized Balfour of Burleigh report and the political activities of the Business Committee.

Despite the enthusiasm of the latter two committees, economic cooperation did not receive much attention at the parallel meetings of the Imperial War Cabinet and Conference from March 20 to May 2. One reason for this may have been the absence of Prime Minister Hughes, who was detained by political difficulties at home. Hughes' absence left W. F. Massey, Prime Minister of New Zealand, the only determined advocate of tariff preference; and it was not until April 24, in the Imperial Cabinet, that Massey resolved for "a system by which each country of the Empire will give preference through its Customs to the goods produced or manufactured in any other British country. . . ."[64]

This explicit declaration was met by various objections. Lloyd George raised the well-established political fear that tariffs would increase the price of food; he preferred improved transport instead of customs preference. Sir Robert Borden, Prime Minister of Canada, and Arthur Henderson, Labour member of the British War Cabinet, agreed with Lloyd George. Jan Smuts, of South Africa, disliked the generality of Massey's resolution and reminded the Cabinet that he had no mandate to discuss "a definite Imperial Tariff system." Lord Robert Cecil pointed out that any resolution about preference would have to include an assurance that the policy was not directed against the Allies or America.[65] All of Massey's critics agreed that no British tariff should be enacted for the specific purpose of establishing a preferential system.

On the other hand, the same men agreed that greater economic cooperation was imperative. Therefore, they were willing to accept some British preference for imports from the Empire in present tariff schedules, and in any future tariffs legislated for reasons other than preference.[66] This consensus was strongly implied in the final resolution of April 26:

> The time has arrived when all possible encouragement should be given to the development of Imperial resources, and especially to making the Empire independent of other countries in respect of food supplies, raw materials and essential industries. With these objects in view this Conference expresses itself in favour of:—
>   1. The principle that each part of the Empire, having due regard to the interests of our Allies, shall give especially favourable treatment and facilities to the produce and manufacturers of other parts of the Empire.[67]

Thus, while customs were not explicitly mentioned in this declaration, Conservatives and protectionists could and did greet the statement as a victory for imperial preference.

It was not, of course, a conclusive victory. Differences over the best method of economic cohesion persisted. Officials in the Foreign Office remained anxious about the sensibilities of Britain's allies.[68] Nevertheless, the policy of customs preference survived the War. The Coalition election program of November 1918, pledged preference on existing and subsequent duties. The first postwar budget of April 30, 1919, redeemed this pledge. Two years later, the Safeguarding of Industries Act exempted Dominion products from the 33-1/3 to 50 percent duties levied on imports which might compete with Britain's "key" industries.

This success was mainly due to the continuous pressure Conservatives exerted in favor of imperial preference. That policy was more attractive to Conservatives than were other forms of protection, including the Paris Resolutions. A wartime comment by Leo Amery eventually became the Conservative view:

> . . . we should not let any pressure of our Allies, or of sentiment here, cause us to abandon or weaken the principle of preference in

any detail. Though Imperial preference is the foundation, it may be possible to put up a superstructure of inter-Ally preference on top of it. But that superstructure will never have the same internal strength or the same real meaning as Imperial preference, which is a recognition of our permanent unity.[69]

This attitude was reinforced by events in the immediate postwar years. Anglo-French tension at the Peace Conference, the disintegration of Allied organizations, and the general demand for de-control and retrenchment encouraged Conservatives to think more about the Empire than about economic cooperation with European allies.

However, until the end of the War the inconsistencies between the European and the imperial policies were usually disregarded in favor of the more important aims they seemed to have in common: the defeat of the German economic "menace" and the achievement of economic security. Because of these common objectives, the parallel campaigns for imperial preference and the Paris Resolutions both played an important part in forming the atmosphere for economic peacemaking.

Chapter 4 PREPARING TO NEGOTIATE

WHILE THE British Government made public commitments to the Paris Resolutions and to imperial preference, it was also making private economic plans for the postwar years. These confidential efforts were motivated by the same fear of an inconclusive peace that spurred the public policies. Government ministers braced themselves for the likelihood of negotiations with Germany by planning positions from which to bargain. Although few of these specific plans survived the War, their constituent ideas and attitudes did condition the general British approach to economic peacemaking in 1918-1919.

It was also during this planning that the Government first considered demanding German compensation for Allied material losses, a consideration which had already received some airing in the press and in the controversy which arose out of Norman Angell's *The Great Illusion*. Of course the possibility that the Allies might not win the War tended to discourage very detailed planning for reparation or an indemnity, just as it encouraged planning for relative superiority to Germany in trade and manufacture. Nevertheless, the wartime discussion, public and private, of reparation and indemnity did lay a foundation for the sudden and widespread popularity of these policies in late 1918. This process is examined in the second section of the present chapter.

Committees and Memoranda, 1915-1918

The first British plans for peace and postwar conditions were made during Asquith's Coalition. On December 15, 1915, Walter Runciman wrote a memorandum for the Cabinet in whch he noted the frequent Parliamentary questions about preparation for the end of the War. Runciman suggested that the different aspects of this preparation should be considered by the appropriate departments, whose efforts would then be coordinated by a Cabinet Committee. In March 1916, the Cabinet decided to adopt Runciman's suggestion by appointing a new Reconstruction Committee of Cabinet ministers.[1]

Throughout 1916 this Committee gathered information on the economic problems Britain would face after the War. One of its collections was a series of papers entitled "German Post-War Economic Policy." In January 1917, the Committee circulated a memorandum based on these papers. The memorandum stressed the importance placed on the economic side of the War in Germany, and gave a long analysis of *Mitteleuropa* and similar German schemes. The Committee said that such designs represented long-term German economic objectives, but they doubted that the outcome of the War would be sufficiently in Germany's favor to enable direct pursuit of these aims. Instead, the Committee predicted that Germany would try for indirect economic domination through "internationalist" proposals at the peace conference. German negotiators would probably seek freedom of the seas, most-favored-nation treatment, the "open door" in colonial markets, and other guarantees against discrimination. These demands would not be sincerely meant according to the Committee, but would be put forward as the most feasible way of promoting German economic expansion. Therefore, Britain should be wary of liberal German diplomacy at the peace conference.[2] This suspicion was akin to the current notion that liberal war aims, whatever the source, were "pro-German."

The Board of Trade was less apprehensive of German postwar commerce. In a memorandum of January 24, 1917, "Economic Desiderata in the Terms of Peace," the Board assumed that the Allies would win the War, but that the peace would be negotiated. The Board doubted the value of harsh economic peace terms:

. . . the Board of Trade have no desire to impose terms of peace on
the Central Powers inspired by motives of commercial revenge. The
permanent crushing of the commercial and industrial power of
Germany, even were it practicable, would not be to the eventual advantage of this country, while the attempt to effect it (though doomed
to failure) would alienate the good opinion and outrage the moral
sense of the civilised world.[3]

Naturally Britain would have to preserve means of defense against
German commercial aggression, especially if the War's outcome
was "inconclusive"; for this purpose the Board believed denial
of most-favored-nation privileges to be the most likely deterrent.
On the other hand, in the case of a conclusive Allied victory,
Britain would be wise to avoid a merely anti-German policy, for
that would disturb the European economic balance of power
in favor of France. Such a disturbance, the Board implied, could
be just as disadvantageous to Britain as a German commercial
hegemony. Thus, the return of Alsace and Lorraine would be
"a complete reversal of relative economic strength" between Germany and France which, according to the Board, would have to
be compensated by some French cession to Germany. In this
memorandum, as in subsequent ones, the Board of Trade related
the security of Britain, as a trading nation, to the sound development of European—including German—commerce.

Not long after the Board's report, the first Imperial War Cabinet received a similar report from one of its committees, also on
"Economic and Non-Territorial Desiderata in the Terms of
Peace." This study was conceived by Jan Smuts of South Africa,
with the support of Lord Milner, then one of the five powerful
men in the new British War Cabinet.[4] Both Smuts and Milner
were discouraged with the military situation and hopeful that a
reasonable negotiation with Germany could be arranged in 1917.
Later, Leo Amery vividly recalled these feelings:

. . . in the spring of 1917, with Russia on the verge of disintegration, with Germany in control of all southeastern Europe except
Greece, with the Ottoman Empire still substantially intact, with
the submarine menace threatening our very existence, with American help still remote, it was necessary to envisage the possibility
of a peace falling short of the enemy's unconditional surrender.
In that case, it was essential to make up our minds beforehand what
were the objectives most vital to our own security.[5]

With some reluctance, the Imperial Cabinet decided to prepare for a possible negotiation by appointing two committees, one on territorial and the other on non-territorial desiderata. The second committee was chaired by Lord Milner.[6]

Milner's committee deliberated from April 16 to 24, when they produced a final report.[7] The economic features of the report reflected the conciliatory attitude of Milner and Smuts. Although the Committee approved the Paris Resolution on most-favored-nation treatment, they emphasized the reservations expressed by several of the Allies and by the United States. Their report flatly stated that the Resolutions "do not, under present circumstances, provide any stable basis for the guidance of the British Government with regard to the objects to be aimed at in the negotiations for peace." The Committee was also cautious about reparation and indemnity, as we shall see later in this chapter. On the other hand, they warned that fundamental British interests must not be surrendered to German diplomacy: The Empire must not lose control over its natural resources, nor should it accept the freedom of the seas. Also, the Committee was dubious about ambitious schemes for a League of Nations. They preferred a less universal arrangement devoted to the needs of the "Powers."[8] Hence, the Milner report was between the conciliation of the Board of Trade and the suspicion of the Reconstruction Committee.

There was much criticism of the report in the full Imperial Cabinet. Bonar Law protested that the remarks on the Paris Resolutions would be interpreted as going back on those agreements. Lloyd George and Lord Robert Cecil disliked the cold water the Committee had thrown on the League of Nations idea. Consequently, there was no trace of the Milner report in the general and evasive "conclusion" about peace aims which the Imperial Cabinet reached on May 1.[9]

The efforts of the Milner Committee might, therefore, appear to have been fruitless; and the same could be said of the Reconstruction memorandum and the Board of Trade report. However, these three memoranda of January to April 1917, were the first clear articulation in government of ideas that would increasingly preoccupy British politics and diplomacy. Although the specific documents were almost forgotten by 1918, the thoughts they expressed were still evident when Britain made peace.

This, of course, is a retrospective view which could not be appreciated in 1917. Conservatives and protectionists quickly became exasperated with tentative reports, as mentioned in the previous chapter. Within the Government, the most powerful malcontent was Sir Edward Carson, champion of Ulster and of militant Conservatives. Having no ambitions to form a government of his own, Carson was watched carefully by those who did. In 1916, he had challenged Bonar Law and attacked Asquith, thereby undermining the first coalition and helping Lloyd George into power. In Lloyd George's government, he was First Lord of the Admiralty and, from July 1917 to January 1918, a member of the War Cabinet. His opinions were bound to be recognized.

In a "Memorandum on Economic Offensive" of September 20, 1917, Carson served notice to the War Cabinet that he considered the Government to be dragging its feet on the Paris Resolutions. He called for fresh British preparations for a postwar economic confrontation with Germany. France and the United States, Carson said, should be part of these preparations. Such a combination of the three Western powers was urgently needed:

(1) To convince Germany that the longer the war continues the worse will be her commercial prospects after the war, and
(2) To prepare for the Allies a sound economic foundation to serve as a basis for negotiation when serious peace proposals are being discussed.[10]

Carson was mainly interested in the psychological contribution that economic alliance would make to the war effort against Germany, less concerned with its merits as a permanent British policy.

Carson's initiative was greeted favorably. Albert Stanley, President of the Board of Trade, also urged "that steps be taken to clear up the position of the United States with regard to the conservation of the economic resources of the Allies during the reconstruction period."[11] The Liberal Secretary for India, Edwin Montagu, responded as if the Conservative Carson were stealing his program. Montagu reminded the War Cabinet of his own opinion that if Germany were threatened with commercial destruction after the War, she would agree to Allied terms.[12] More important, the War Cabinet did as Carson wished on October 9, 1917, by appointing a confidential Economic Offensive Committee, to be headed, of course, by Carson himself.[13]

At the first meeting of his new Committee, Carson assigned the members two general areas for investigation. First, they should study "methods of inflicting economic injury while the war is in progress. . . ." Second, they should devise a system of commercial treaties ". . . into which enemy powers will have to buy their entry by substantial concessions" at the peace conference and afterwards.[14] With this dual mandate, the Committee met from October 17, 1917 to June 4, 1918, producing eighty-one memoranda and eleven interim reports.[15] Most of these were technical and specialized, addressed to the first of Carson's purposes. A few dealt with postwar commerce; these were repetitive pleas for the necessity for collaboration between the British Empire, the Allies and, most of all, the United States.

The Committee's exhortations made little impression on the War Cabinet, which had to face American suspicions about trade war. In October 1917, the Government had learned of a French enquiry with Washington about postwar trade cooperation; there was no American response.[16] President Wilson, it is true, raised some protectionist hopes with a remark in his annual message to Congress of December 4: "It might be impossible to admit Germany to the free economic intercourse which must inevitably spring out of the other partnership of a real peace." On the other hand, in his more important Fourteen Points speech of January 8, 1918, Wilson made the lowering of economic barriers his third point. Near the end of his great address, the President said of Germany, "We do not wish to fight her either with arms or with hostile arrangements of trade if she is willing to associate herself with us . . . in covenants of justice. . . ." Hence, the British Government could be sure that proposals for economic offensive would mean a quarrel with the United States, a quarrel that would jeopardize American loans, and American cooperation on military strategy and on the Russian situation. The postwar recommendations of the Economic Offensive Committee went unheeded.

For that reason, Sir Edward Carson resigned his chairmanship of the Committee in January 1918, at the same time that he left the War Cabinet over Irish policy and military politics. While the latter were Carson's main grievances, he nevertheless found time, on January 21, for another long written complaint about economic policy. His committee, he said, had made little progress because the War Cabinet had ignored it. This indifference and consequent failure to take any official, public steps toward economic alliance were having ill effects. The Allies were confused about British policy. At home, Government silence encouraged misunderstanding and opposition:

> (a) *From the Trading Community*, owing to their fear that the Government policy aimed at putting them under the heel of bureaucratic interference.
> (b) *From the Liberal Party*, owing to their suspicion that anti-German sentiments were being exploited for partisan purposes, and as a means of making a covert attack upon the principles of Free Trade.
> (c) *From the Humanitarians*, owing to their belief that the Government policy was inspired merely by vindictive feelings against Germany. . . .[17]

Carson recommended that the secret Economic Offensive Committee be disbanded in favor of an "Economic Defence and Development Committee" which would enjoy real authority and be publicly acknowledged.[18] Carson's idea was endorsed by the full Economic Offensive Committee.[19]

However, it was not until June 10, 1918, that the War Cabinet established the suggested Committee.[20] The authority granted was not so definite as Carson had proposed; the Economic Defense and Development Committee could not infringe on economic policy being made in departments and ministries. And despite the appearance of being a fresh start, the new Committee was little more than an extension of its predecessor. The only changes in membership were the assumption of the chairmanship by Austen Chamberlain and the addition to the new Committee of G. H. Roberts, Minister of Labour, and H. A. L. Fisher, President of the Board of Education. The minutes of the last Offensive Committee meeting were read at the first Defence and Development meeting on June 18, 1918. The eighty-two memoranda which the latter Committee produced from June until its last meeting, on December 17, 1918, were similar in their specialization to those of the Offensive Committee.[21] Likewise, the Defence and Development Committee had no important effect on the policy of the War Cabinet.

The expiration of the Economic Defence and Development Committee only one month after the Armistice symbolizes the fate of almost all the British "economic offensive" planning. As the War drew to a conclusion, three developments retarded that planning. One was a rising confidence in the Allied military position, increasingly buoyed by American aid. Despite the German spring offensive in the spring and summer of 1918, British policy makers were more and more certain that a decisive blow was within their grasp. This feeling removed the imperative from plans for postwar economic alliance against Germany. Instead, as victory became more likely, the Allies began to differ among themselves over the terms, economic and other, to be imposed on Germany. A second restraint on "economic offensive" was the opposition of the United States. With American men and material pouring across the ocean, Allied statesmen tried to evade issues that might offend President Wilson. Third, in the last half of 1918, the appearance of reparation and indemnity as widely popular ideas offered a method for economic security more direct than the complicated "economic offensive."

Nevertheless, the British committees and memoranda of 1915 to 1918 did establish an atmosphere in Government deliberations similar to that which developed in public during the protectionist campaigns for the Paris Resolutions and imperial preference. They also originated important perspectives on the economic peace. For example, the difference of opinion between the Reconstruction Committee and the Board of Trade—suspicion of German liberalism versus reintegration of Germany into European commerce—became an especially crucial dialectic in 1919.

Reparation and Indemnity, 1911-1918

First thoughts about reparation and indemnity during the war years in Britain were affected by the prewar controversy over Norman Angell's *The Great Illusion*. Originally published in 1909 as *Europe's Optical Illusion*, by 1911 this book was being widely discussed in most Western countries, especially in Britain.

The author, a young British journalist who then directed Lord
Northcliffe's new *Paris Daily Mail*, intended his work as a coun-
terpoise to the notion that war was an inevitable, periodically
recurring phenomenon among the great powers, a belief he feared
might soon become a self-fulfilling prophesy in Europe. He also
hoped to refute the popular idea that territorial conquest and
commercial aggrandizement could make war "pay."

What denied both the current fatalism and the wishful notion
that war could be profitable, according to Angell, was the in-
creasing commercial and financial interdependence of the Western nations. War might once have been a periodic and expectable
scourge which elevated one nation's fortunes at the expense of
another, but in the new conditions of interdependence the expectation of gain was illusory. A "victorious" power, by damaging
the prosperity of its opponents and disrupting the delicate mech-
anisms of international trade and finance, would only penalize
its own trade and thus its own citizens. Unless this truth were
recognized, the old ideas about war might lead Europe into tragedy.

As one part of his general argument, Angell tried to show that
the concept of direct compensation for war damages and costs was
futile: ". . . in our day the exaction of tribute from a conquered
people has become an economic impossibility; the exaction of a
large indemnity of doubtful benefit to the nation receiving it, even
when it can be exacted."[22] Whatever gain might be had through
indemnity would almost surely be cancelled by other considerations: trade lost through disruption on the exchanges caused by
large, unilateral transfers of gold or goods; a rise in prices and
consequent check to the exports of the nation receiving the indemnity; and the loss of the earnings the recipient's citizens would
otherwise have enjoyed from producing the transferred wealth.
Angell found evidence for these contentions in the indemnity
of £212,700,000 which France was compelled to pay to the German
Empire after the War of 1870-71, the only really instructive example of an indemnity imposed on one great power by another in
the recent past. The indemnity consisted partly of gold and silver,
but mainly of German currency paid in installments from 1871 to
1873 and financed by London banking houses. These sums,
Angell believed, had been the main cause of the speculative burst
which had produced the German financial panic and depression
beginning in 1873.[23]

Angell's theory of the economic senselessness of war attracted a good deal of attention before July 1914, probably because it seemed to offer some relief from the oppressive realities of alliance and arms race. Hence, the popular impression that *The Great Illusion* attempted to prove war impossible under modern conditions, a misrepresentation contrary to Angell's essential purpose and against which he had to work for many years to come.[24] Yet he had considerable assistance in explaining this and other nuances of his theory: *The Great Illusion* aroused the interest of Viscount Esher, influential chairman of the Committee on Imperial Defence, and of his industrialist friend, Sir Richard Garton. In 1912, Esher and Garton established and financed a foundation and a monthly, *War and Peace*, to promote the study of Angell's ideas.[25] From this base the young author was able to expound his notions and to attract a considerable following to his "new pacifism" just before the War. Among those who Angell later recalled as having sympathized with his movement were Arnold Bennett, H. N. Brailsford, Viscount Bryce, G. Lowes Dickinson, Francis W. Hirst, J. A. Hobson, John Maynard Keynes, Ramsay MacDonald, E. D. Morel, Arthur Ponsonby, Bertrand Russell, Philip Snowden, and G. M. Trevelyan.[26] Many of these men carried their affinity for Angell's ideas into the war years through their opposition to punitive trade schemes and war costs indemnities.

Nevertheless, the influence of Angell's movement dissipated after the outbreak of the War. The cataclysm of 1914 seemed to lessen the usefulness of *The Great Illusion*, which was written, after all, in the hope of averting just such a catastrophe. Angell himself spent most of the War in the United States and his main concern in Britain was the radical Union of Democratic Control, of which he was one of the original members. In 1915 he resigned from the foundation which had been set up on his behalf.

At about the same time, certain of Angell's economic ideas came under close and critical scrutiny. Already in the last year of peace a fellow of the Royal Economic Society, H. H. O'Farrell, had written a careful, statistical study showing that *The Great Illusion* had misrepresented the indemnity of 1871: It was neither so harmful to Germany nor so important a cause of the depression of 1873 as Angell had supposed.[27] In early 1915, J. H. Jones, a young lecturer in social economics at the University of Glasgow, published a more thorough critique, *The Economics of War and Conquest: An Examination of Mr. Norman Angell's Economic Doctrines*. Jones, like O'Farrell, maintained that Angell had oversimplified the indemnity of 1871. This was only one of several factors causing the panic of 1873, and much of the indemnity had been converted into tangible assets—for example, factories and railways—which remained valuable regardless of the depression of the 1870's. Moreover, Angell had unduly minimized the economic benefits Germany derived from the annexation of Alsace-Lorraine: the more plentiful supply of raw materials, the larger home market, the wider tax base. Thus, conquest and confiscation had not been so futile as Angell claimed. Neither could Jones accept Angell's confidence that gain from war would be impossible in the future. While war would certainly damage international trade and finance, this did not disprove the possibility of profit by an individual belligerent. That possibility was enlarged by the more sophisticated forms of modern exploitation, such as the manipulation of most-favored-nation clauses and tariff policy generally. Also, there was certainly no reason why a triumphant power or powers might not reasonably expect that direct compensation could defray at least part of their damages and costs. "If Britain and her allies prove to be victorious in the present struggle, an indemnity to Belgium, if not also to France, will undoubtedly be provided for in the final settlement."[28] Furthermore, "it is conceivable that Germany will be compelled to compensate Britain for the material loss involved in the present war . . . ," which Jones predicted might approximate £ 100,000,000.[29] If such "indemnities"—or, technically, reparations—were paid gradually and in goods which were scarce in the recipient countries, Jones saw no reason why harm should result.

These were important and precocious observations. Indeed, Jones' critique of Angell was one of the most perceptive comments on the general question of reparation and indemnity to appear during all of the war years. Yet there was almost no mention of it in subsequent discussions of economic war aims! Perhaps this was because Jones himself was not well known; he was only 34 years old in 1915 and *The Economics of War and Conquest* was his first book.[30]

However overlooked Jones may have been, Angell's theory and the criticisms it aroused must nevertheless be considered the first origin of British thinking about reparation and indemnity. The controversy over *The Great Illusion* established foci around which later commentators debated. The precedent of 1871, the problem of how to transfer wealth without harming the recipient, whether indemnities were compatible with sound international economy, the wisdom of gradual payment in scarce goods—these remained important concerns for journalists, economists, and policy-makers who foresaw the possibility of compensation from Germany.

Yet to trace these considerations alone would not be to tell the story of the course of reparation and indemnity in politics and public opinion during the war years. *The Great Illusion* and the other writings it provoked were too specialized to have very much effect on popular and party political opinion about direct compensation from Germany.

This more general opinion proceeded from several simple assumptions. One was that, in the event of an Allied victory, Germany would be compelled to repair the physical damage done in the invaded territories of the Allies. Compensation to Belgium, whose violated neutrality was Britain's main public reason for going to war, was considered especially vital. In Asquith's early declaration of British war aims on November 9, 1914, reparation for Belgium held first place: "We shall never sheath the sword which we have not lightly drawn until Belgium recovers in full measure all and more than all she has sacrificed. . . ."[31] Here even the Labour Party, generally sceptical of forcing German compensation, agreed:

> The [Labour] Conference once more declares that the foremost condition of peace must be reparation by the German Government of the wrong admittedly done to Belgium; payment for all the damage that has resulted from this wrong; and the restoration of Belgium to complete and untrammelled independent sovereignty. . . .[32]

Also popular, though to a lesser extent, was the demand for reparation of damage done in France and in the territories of the other Allies.

Britain, though free of invasion, was nevertheless considered by most of her citizens entitled to compensation for certain non-territorial damages. One of these catagories was reparation for ill-treatment of British prisoners-of-war. Already on April 27, 1915, speakers of all parties in the House of Commons agreed that the Government should hold Germany liable for such maltreatment.[33] This issue, as we shall see in a later chapter, reached an emotional climax in late 1918. A similar category was compensation for the spectacular "outrages" of the War, such as the sinking of the *Lusitania* and the execution of Nurse Edith Cavell. In his first speech as Prime Minister, Lloyd George asked:

> Are all these outrages against humanity on land and on sea to be liquidated by a few pious phrases? Is there to be no reckoning for them? Are we to grasp the hand that perpetrated these atrocities in friendship without any reparation being tendered or given?[34]

And the great majority of Britons naturally expected compensation for British merchant shipping sunk during the War, especially that destroyed by German U-boats. Few people would have questioned *The Times'* demand that "we should compel Germany to understand that the day is coming when for all the devastation wrought by her submarines payment will be exacted and punishment will be awarded to the uttermost."[35]

However, only a few wartime commentators envisaged either a very large British share of reparation, or an indemnity for the cost of the War to the Allies. One who did was Sir Leo Chiozza Money. A Liberal MP who later joined the Labour Party, Money was a fervent believer in economic planning and a prolific writer on economics. In November 1914, he wrote the first article on indemnity to appear in Britain after the outbreak of the War. He proposed:

> . . . Germany and Austria must be made to pay for this war. I have reminded the reader that Germany made France pay £ 200,000,000 forty years ago. . . . In this, the second decade of the twentieth century, productive powers are so very much greater than they were in 1870, that the cost of the war to the Allies, although so great, can in practice be levied upon the defeated powers. Even if the total cost of the war to the Allies be as much as £ 3,000,000,000 that is far less than one year's income of Germany and Austria-Hungary on the basis of 1913. . . . Presumably the indemnity would be payable over a period of ten, fifteen, or even twenty years.[36]

Thus, unlike Angell, Money used the precedent of 1871 to support, rather than deny, the feasibility of an indemnity; and this interpretation eventually became more popular than that of *The Great Illusion*.[37] Money continued to favor indemnity in his wartime writings, though by 1918, when the Allied cost of the War had risen from £ 3,000,000,000 to £ 24,000,000,000, he was much less optimistic than in the third month of the War.

Meanwhile, a scattering of other articles and schemes appeared which placed great faith in the capacity of an indemnity to erase Britain's financial problems and to penalize Germany for her "crimes." A writer in the *Nineteenth Century and After* of May 1916, thought that the total indemnity which Germany should pay to the Allies should be between thirty and forty billions sterling, of which Britain was to receive slightly less than 25 percent. The proposed method of finance was a mortgage held by citizens of the Allies on all German industry or a "Germany exploited by the capitalists of the Allied countries."[38] In this way, Germany was to be carved into spheres of influence. A similar proposal was made in August 1916, by the President of the Liverpool Exchange, Edgar Crammond. Crammond forecast a total German payment of fourteen billion pounds, to be exacted by a great variety of methods, including ". . . a first charge on the State Railways and the Customs and Excise."[39] Four months later, a Germanophobe group of Britons and Frenchmen in Paris, the "Look Ahead" Committee, circulated a scheme based on the premise that "it is only right and proper that for the next two generations all the effort and all the productions of the enemy countries should be devoted to repairing the damage they have wilfully caused." The Committee defined "damage" so broadly as to be, in fact, war costs. They held the Central Powers liable for "any material damage of any description caused by the War." Significantly, this was to include pensions for relatives of deceased Allied servicemen and for disabled servicemen and their relatives, categories of "damage" later included in the Treaty of Versailles.[40]

Until the last half of 1918, these expectations of a war costs indemnity were not widely shared. All elements of the Labour Party were opposed to indemnity, as distinct from reparation. The Labour Executive would claim no more than reparation for Belgium; the Conference took the same view. The Trades Union

Congress of September 1916 urged the Treasury to finance British war costs, not by indemnity, but through

1. The heavier graduated taxation of all large incomes.
2. A special tax on land values . . .
3. An increase in the estate duties on large estates.
4. The taxation of capital on a justly graduated scale.
5. The taxation of personal wealth.[41]

Philip Snowden, of the more radical Independent Labour Party, proposed that *all* belligerents contribute to a common fund for reparation and reconstruction in Europe.[42]

Many Liberals were also sceptical of indemnity. Walter Runciman, out of power after 1916, told the Commons on February 13, 1918:

> What is to be done with regard to indemnities must depend on the end of the War, and no sensible man, looking at the situation as we find it to-day, is likely to regard penal indemnities as an item of our war aims. We could get rid of indemnities provided we adhered to reparation as an essential element of our policy. When one deals with reparation there are more ways of acting than by merely humiliating your opponent.[43]

Several Liberal writers thought it a fallacy to count on indemnity to alleviate postwar financial problems, which could only be solved, in their view, by the traditional methods of taxation and frugality. So reasoned Francis W. Hirst, the Liberal editor of the *Economist*. In 1915, Hirst published *The Political Economy of War*, which concluded that the war debt could be defrayed only by repudiating or reducing the value of war bonds, or by taxation, or by disarmament. Hirst preferred the latter. He had little confidence that an indemnity could dissolve war debts as it had done in 1871:

> Even if this war lasted only one year the exhaustion of credit would probably be twenty times, and the destruction of property fifty times, greater than in the Franco-German conflict. In 1871, though Paris had lost much of its financial power to London, France was solvent. But who can guarantee the solvency of Europe when the post-bellum liquidation takes place? In 1871, the credit of London was unimpaired, and it was able to finance the indemnity. In this war all the

great financial centres of Europe are being exhausted . . . even the resources of New York have been heavily drawn upon by the belligerent governments.[44]

This was an acute foresight. Other Liberals predicted a further difficulty that would be raised by indemnity: One could not expect a significant indemnity if Germany were subjected to commercial restrictions such as those projected in the Paris Economic Resolutions.[45]

Prominent Conservatives also cast doubt upon indemnity. Lord Milner, in a prescient speech of March 24, 1915, warned against high expectations:

> Needless to say in these [eventual peace] negotiations we shall not be able to have things our own way: In the first place a great deal depends on the extent of our victory. But even assuming it to be complete, assuming the enemy to be utterly beaten—a very large assumption—it is not Great Britain or even the British Empire which will be the only conqueror. Our Allies, who have borne the brunt of the struggle, will have to be considered, and the compensation which will have to be given to them may go very near to exhausting the damages, in money or kind, which the enemy can be made to pay.[46]

Foreign Secretary Balfour, in response to a radical war aims resolution of July 30, 1917 in the House of Commons, denied that indemnity was a British objective. "We did not go into this war for an Imperialist policy, and certainly not to get indemnities."[47]

The cautious attitude toward indemnity and the near consensus about physical reparation help to explain the infrequent attention given these subjects by the Government during the War. Indemnity seemed too indefinite, reparation too obvious to merit extensive study. Of course some policy-makers were probably aware of Norman Angell's thesis about indemnity, though they may have discounted it, given its *ante bellum* origin and Angell's association with the Union of Democratic Control. Some may also have read J. H. Jones' trenchant reply to Angell. It is especially likely that John Maynard Keynes and the other economists who came into the Treasury early in the War were acquainted with the Angell controversy. Keynes himself was one of Angell's

prewar sympathizers, though he was not a close associate and
there is no reason to think that Keynes' Marshallian, free-trade
economics or wartime thoughts about reparation and indemnity
were much affected by his contact with Angell.[48]

Whatever information policy-makers may have gathered on
their own, the only written analysis of reparation and indemnity
which the Government had before 1916 was an outdated essay of
1874 by Adolph Wagner, a professor at the University of Berlin,
"The Indemnity of 1871 and Its Effects." Wagner admitted that
the French indemnity payments may have had inflationary effects
in Germany and may have encouraged the financial crisis of 1873.
He suggested that it would have been wise to have required smaller
payments over a longer period and more payments in kind than
in cash. On the whole, however, he thought the indemnity beneficial for reducing public debt and taxation.[49]

In December 1915, Walter Runciman of the Board of Trade
noted the absence of any current study of reparation and indemnity, and suggested that the Treasury prepare such a report. The
task fell to Keynes and to another Treasury recruit, Professor
W. J. Ashley, a leading historical economist and protectionist
who was well acquainted with the German academic world and
with German economic thought.[50] Despite their different economic views, Keynes and Ashley quickly produced a memorandum
"On the Effect of an Indemnity" on January 2, 1916.[51]

The Board of Trade had asked the two Treasury officials to
consider the economic effects of a German "indemnity" that
would "make good the damage in the territories overrun"—that
would, in other words, be reparation for the physical damage
suffered by the Continental Allies. Thus, in their final report,
Keynes and Ashley assumed that if Britain were to receive payments, it would be only as "a trustee, receiving wealth to be
passed on." Britain might, however, enjoy an indirect but important benefit from such an "indemnity": the avoidance of
expenditure that would otherwise be necessary if she were to assist her Allies toward recovery.

Regarding the effects of German payments on the recipients
themselves, Keynes and Ashley accepted the "presumption of
unsophisticated common sense" that such payments would be
helpful rather than harmful. They also agreed with the main

contentions of Wagner and O'Farrell—to whom they referred in their text and footnotes, repectively—about the precedent of 1871-73: First, while that indemnity had worked some ill-effects, its net result had been beneficial to Germany. Second, harmful side-effects might have been avoided through more payment in kind and less in currency. Payment in kind was also to be preferred for positive reasons, according to Keynes and Ashley. If, for example, the reparation payments were to consist of raw materials and machinery in kind, Allied rather than German industry would enjoy the stimulating effects of manufacturing for reconstruction. Other payments in kind favored by the two authors were state railways and public property in ceded colonies, and especially the surrender of German naval and merchant ships. They recognized that these kinds of payment would have to be changed into wealth more suitable for repairing territorial damage, but they made no specific suggestion as to how this might be done. They did imply, however, that Britain might receive German ships and pay the Continental Allies equivalent value for territorial repairs.[52] Whatever the methods of payment, the period allotted for payment would probably have to be prolonged in order to allow Germany to recover from the War, and this would entail some continuous Allied means of enforcement. Keynes and Ashley also warned that discriminatory Allied tariffs would lessen Germany's capacity to pay, though they admitted that tariffs might be beneficial to the Allies for other reasons.

The care with which Keynes and Ashley set about their task was impressive, yet in early 1916 they did not feel able to estimate a total figure for either territorial damage or Germany's capacity to pay. Hence, their report did not remain for long the most significant or conclusive British analysis of reparation and indemnity. Nevertheless, Lloyd George later tried to give another impression in his *Memoirs of the Paris Peace Conference.* He blamed Keynes and Ashley for encouraging the indemnity agitation in British politics at the end of the War and charged them with responsibility for the reparation clauses of the Treaty of Versailles. The two economists were ". . . the joint authors of the long-term indemnity which was incorporated in the Treaty."[53] These accusations were historical nonsense. The Keynes-Ashley report could not have had any effect on British opinion since it was neither released nor "leaked" to the public. Also, its language was restrained, that of advisors who had been assigned to report on a future contingency, not—as Lloyd George claimed —that of "extortionate zeal." While the report foreshadowed several aspects of the Treaty of Versailles, it did not anticipate more than reparation for physical damage or a direct British share in compensation.[54] Moreover, the report was superseded by other studies, as will be shown, and practically forgotten by 1919. Lloyd George, writing in the 1930's, may have been justly angry with the political effects of Keynes' *Economic Consequences of the Peace*, but here he made a poor sort of counterattack.

Surely as important as the Keynes-Ashley conclusions was the long discussion of compensation in the Board of Trade's January 1917 memorandum on economic desiderata. Unlike the two Treasury servants, the Board did not exclude Britain as a possible recipient. The Board also went beyond Keynes and Ashley to consider whether a war costs indemnity was feasible and how much could be expected. On both points they were cautious:

> The possibility of exacting an indemnity from the Central Powers, and the magnitude of any such indemnity, must obviously depend on the circumstances in which the war comes to an end. . . . Assuming a complete victory, the Board of Trade see no reason to doubt the expediency of exacting an indemnity, though the proceeds of any indemnity which the Central Powers could pay will necessarily go but a short way toward meeting the cost of the war.[55]

The Board agreed with the Keynes-Ashley recommendation of payments in kind, especially in merchant ships. The Germans should replace destroyed Allied shipping on a ton-for-ton basis, which implied that Britain's greater maritime losses would be taken into account. The Board also believed the enemy should restore devastated territory with machinery and raw materials, especially raw materials in which Germany had a monopoly before the War, such as potash. Altogether, the Board's memorandum gave the impression that Germany could not be expected to do much more than repair the extensive physical damage done on land and at sea.

A similar position was taken by Lord Milner's Imperial

Cabinet Committee in April 1917. They also favored payments in kind, in merchant shipping, and in scarce raw materials. In addition, they stressed a consideration that previous reports had not emphasized: the British Empire share of compensation. That share, the Milner report said, would be limited by the claims of Belgium and France based on the enormous damage done in their occupied territories. "The only claim of equal strength with those . . . is that of Great Britain and other Allied countries for shipping destroyed in a manner contrary to the hitherto recognized laws of maritime war."[56] Clearly, however, that "claim of equal strength" would not result in equal payments, unless territorial cessions were taken into account:

> In the case of France, for instance, the re-acquisition of the provinces ceded in 1871, especially of the rich iron ore field of German Lorraine, might be regarded as in itself representing some measure of indemnity for the destruction wrought in her territory by the invading armies.[57]

Here was a bargaining point *vis à vis* the French that would appear again and would cause friction between the western Allies, since all Frenchmen naturally felt that the retrocession of Alsace-Lorraine was a matter of historical right, beyond the mundane trading of diplomacy.

After the Milner report, there was no further British study of compensation until the end of the War, when the subject quickly became more feasible and popular. Nevertheless, before that happened, public discussion and government studies had established a rough British consensus: that reparation was more just and more likely to be realized than indemnity; that payments in kind were preferable to payments in cash; that Britain's principal claim to reparation would be through her shipping losses; that payment would have to be spread over time, perhaps over a considerable number of years; and that the indemnity of 1871 formed the only plausible precedent, however limited, for the current problem. Thus, the British Government was modestly prepared for the emergence of reparation and indemnity as political issues when victory became certain in the latter part of 1918.

They were not, however, prepared for the intensity of those

issues. They did not anticipate the depth of popular feeling that would marshall behind reparation and indemnity; their wartime search for economic security had focused in other directions. Consequently, the last months of 1918 were a time of considerable turmoil about economic and other issues of peacemaking. The result was an important transformation of British attitudes toward the economic peace on the eve of the Paris Peace Conference.

Part Two

FROM WAR TO PEACE
1918-1919

Chapter 5 BRITAIN, WILSON, AND REPARATION

PRESIDENT WILSON's attitude toward the postwar economic treatment of Germany played an important part in the transformation of British economic aims in 1918. Until July of that year, the British Government remained deferential to Wilson's objections to a postwar economic alliance; and the British position on compensation from Germany was modest, tentative, and compatible with the desires of the President. However, serious disagreements arose between the end of July and early November. Britain made a final plea for the Paris Economic Resolutions and was decisively rebuffed by Wilson. Leaders of Britain and the United States also quarreled over basing the Armistice on the Fourteen Points. These differences were resolved by diplomacy in September and October; and in November, the Board of Trade and Treasury recommended economic terms of peace that would have been acceptable to the United States. Nevertheless, the appearance of indemnity in British politics in November and in British policy in December again disturbed Anglo-American relations, on the eve of the Peace Conference.

The outward unity of the Allies and Associates in 1917-18 concealed important tensions. In Britain, for example, there was considerable suspicion of the limits which the Wilsonian program seemed to place on British as well as German ambitions. Protectionists and British officials also resented the wartime shift of economic power to the United States.[1] Before the middle of 1918, discretion required that these jealousies be withheld from view; but with the exhaustion of the German offensive in mid-July, the British Government regained confidence for a more independent and public expression of policy.

One of these expressions was a temporary revival of hopes about the Paris Economic Resolutions. The revival was instigated in July by British businessmen. On July 22, the British Empire Producers Organization sent a resolution to the Government urging a reaffirmation of the Paris Resolutions and of imperial preference, and calling for definite preparations for "the economic struggle which must follow the war."[2] On the next day, Sir Edward Carson, out of office but convinced as ever of his economic ideas, persuaded the National Union of Manufacturers to press the Government for a statement of postwar economic policy.[3] These and similar appeals were fully reported in the press.

Lloyd George decided to placate his critics. He received a deputation from the NUM on July 31, and told his guests:

> Up to the present time America has expressed no opinion on them [the Paris Resolutions], and it is vitally important that the policy of America and that of this country should be in complete agreement on economic as well as other problems. An agreement among the Allies means that the economic fate of the world will be in the hands of the great Allied powers federated together at present. . . . The longer the war lasts the sterner must be the economic terms we impose on the foe. I think the sooner he realizes that the better. He is fighting in order to impose his own economic terms on the Allies. He will never succeed in doing so.[4]

These sentiments were widely reported in the United States. In Britain, the press remarked on the belligerence of the statement. The Germanophobe *Daily Mail* declared, "Mr. Lloyd George has gone far towards giving what Mr. Hughes and the *Daily Mail* have been asking him for two years to give."[5]

Despite Lloyd George's earlier scepticism of the Paris Resolutions, there is no reason to doubt the sincerity of his comment of July 31. The Prime Minister apparently decided that the brightening military situation permitted the Allies to consider imposing their most desired peace terms. At Imperial War Cabi-

net meetings in August he made this very clear. He told the
meeting of August 15 that continued Allied military pressure
would ". . . inflict upon them [the Germans] such a defeat as
will enable you to dictate terms, and the terms that should be
dictated ought, in my judgment, to be such as will mark the view
which humanity takes of the heinousness of the offence committed by Germany. That is the only basis of a League of Nations."[6] As the German army retreated, Lloyd George seemed
to find greater dangers in the diplomacy of President Wilson. He
remarked to his Imperial colleagues on August 18 that the gist
of Wilson's attitude toward peacemaking was "Gentlemen of
the Conference, we come here asking for nothing ourselves, and
we are here to see you get nothing."[7]

If these private expressions did not augur well for British-
American relations, neither did Wilson's failure to make any
public response to Lloyd George's suggestion of July 31. The
President did, however, make a confidential reply to Sir William
Wiseman. On August 20, Wiseman cabled to the British Ambassador to the United States, Lord Reading, then in London on a
visit:

> The President . . . had understood that the Allied Governments
> decided that they would not officially resort to the punitive trade
> policy advocated by the Paris Conference. He was disturbed there-
> fore on reading the reports of the Prime Minister's speech of July
> 31st . . . which seemed to recommend the crushing of Germany's
> trade after the war. . . . He fully appreciates the value of the
> economic weapon which the Allies, particularly England and the
> U.S., possess and he is in favour of using that weapon to the full in
> order to bring Germany to her senses and to ensure that a just
> peace, when signed, will be scrupulously observed. He is convinced,
> however, that it is a great mistake to threaten Germany now with
> any kind of punitive post-war measures against her trade. In his
> view this threat is one of the strongest levers with which the German
> militarists suppress the growth of any liberal movement in Ger-
> many. . . . Col. House says he fears that, if the Allies persist in
> making similar statements regarding their economic policy, the
> President will feel obliged, as he did one before, to make some
> statement dissociating this country with [sic] that policy.[8]

On August 28, Reading replied to Wiseman. He agreed with
President Wilson and was attempting to persuade British minis-

ters to accept Wilson's views. In a few days he would have an interview with the Prime Minister on the subject.[9]

Reading's presentation must have influenced Lloyd George. In his next major address, at Manchester on September 12, the Prime Minister expounded a philosophy of peacemaking quite different from his views of a month earlier. Germany was to be punished for her "crimes against civilization," to be sure, but she was also to be admitted to the League as soon as she had rid herself of Prussian influence. More important, Lloyd George called for a moderate peace settlement:

> It must be a peace that will lend itself to the commonsense and conscience of the nation as a whole. It must not be dictated by extreme men of either side. . . . We must not arm Germany with a real wrong. We shall neither accept ourselves nor impose on our enemies a Brest Litovsk Treaty.[10]

The Prime Minister appeared to be back in the Wilsonian fold.

Nevertheless, this did not dissuade Wilson from making public, once again, his objections to projects such as the Paris Resolutions. On September 27, in the fourth of his "Five Particulars," the President said:

> . . . there can be no special, selfish economic combinations within the League and no employment of any form of economic boycott or exclusion except as the power of economic penalty by exclusion from the markets of the world may be vested in the League of Nations itself as a means of discipline and control. . . . Special alliances and economic rivalries and hostilities have been the prolific source in the modern world of the plans and passions that produce war.[11]

This proclamation largely sealed the fate of the Paris Resolutions. Their demise was confirmed by the near-collapse of Germany in late 1918, which removed the original motive for the Resolutions, and by the consequent possibility of imposing a large indemnity. A few protectionists clung to the Resolutions, and the British Government remained concerned about scarce raw materials and German "dumping"; but the program of June 1916 disappeared from British displomacy.

Meanwhile, Lloyd George's Manchester speech had averted a clash between his Government and the United States. Yet this apparent convergence of views was only temporary. A month later, British-American tension over economic aims reemerged during President Wilson's negotiations with the German Government regarding an armistice based on the Fourteen Points. As Wilson and the Germans exchanged notes, the British Government had to debate two questions: Was this the proper time to suspend warfare? Were the Fourteen Points a desirable basis for an armistice and future peace terms? These questions strained Anglo-American relations.

Initially, Lloyd George doubted the value of an early armistice. At an informal meeting of British Cabinet ministers on October 13, he predicted that Germany would make war again in twenty years if her armies were not driven onto German soil and defeated there. Balfour and Milner replied that a continued war might completely disintegrate German institutions and encourage European revolution.[12] Nevertheless, the Prime Minister remained dubious. As late as the War Cabinet meeting of October 26, he declared:

> . . . there was an important school of thought which at times made considerable appeal to him, who said that we ought to go on until Germany was smashed . . . that we should actually dictate terms on German soil . . . that the enemy should be shown that war cannot be made with impunity . . . industrial France had been devastated and Germany had escaped. At the first moment when we were in a position to put the lash on Germany's back she said, "I give up." The question arose whether we ought not to continue lashing her as she lashed France.
> Mr. Chamberlain said that vengeance was too expensive in these days.
> The Prime Minister said it was not vengeance but justice.[13]

Despite Lloyd George's fervor, the rest of the War Cabinet supported Austen Chamberlain.[14] Reluctantly, the Prime Minister agreed to an armistice, provided that Germany consent to disarmament and reparation. Jan Smuts then tried to bolster Lloyd George's decision with some profound considerations:

> . . . peace made at the present time would be a British peace. We had now got into our hands everything of material importance that we required. . . . Were we, he asked, to continue the War for the advantage of Central Europe? . . . The longer we continued the

greater he believed would be Germany's chance of once more getting
on top. . . . In the anarchy and revolution that would follow the
War, the strong hand of Germany would prevail. . . . If we were
to beat Germany to nothingness, then we must beat Europe to
nothingness, too. As Europe went down, so America would rise.
In time the United States of America would dictate to the world in
naval, military, diplomatic and financial matters. In that he saw
no good.[15]

Smuts was, on many questions, a friend of the United States;
that he was also suspicious of American power indicates the
latent Anglo-American tension at the end of the War.

This tension was also present in British discussions of the
Fourteen Points. On October 25, Lloyd George warned the War
Cabinet that if the British Government agreed to the Points as a
basis for negotiations, they must make certain reservations. "Otherwise the Germans would have a perfect right to assume that the
Fourteen Points were the worst conditions that could be imposed
on them."[16] Here Lloyd George enjoyed the support of his colleagues. Thus, in the pre-Armistice negotiations of October
29 to November 4 at Versailles, the British expressed several
reservations about the Fourteen Points. One was a formal dissent
from the "freedom of the seas." Two others related to economic
questions.

One of the latter concerned the third of the Fourteen Points:
"The removal, so far as possible, of all economic barriers and the
establishment of an equality of trade conditions among all nations
consenting to the peace and associating themselves for its main-
tenance." At Versailles on October 29, Clemenceau pointed out
the vagueness of this declaration. Lloyd George deprecated the
Point, remarking that the most important words were "so far as
possible."[17] Meanwhile, the British War Cabinet took a more
serious view. On November 1, they cabled to Lloyd George their
fear that the third Point would interfere with physical reconstruction in Belgium and France ". . . and prejudice our own economic policy in the future. . . ."[18] Later on the same day, the Prime
Minister explained these fears to the American representative,
Colonel Edward M. House:

We should all be short of various kinds of raw material. . . . What
was the meaning of the point in question? After the signature of

peace, were we to share all stocks equally among all peoples? If so, Germany would benefit, as her machinery was intact, whereas that of the Allies, especially Belgium, was to a great extent damaged or destroyed . . . did President Wilson mean that when peace was signed no country should have preferential tariffs?[19]

House promised an early clarification.

No clarification having been made by November 3, Lloyd George grew impatient and raised the matter again. House replied with what was to become an American theme: The Allies must not wage commercial discrimination against Germany while expecting large reparation payments. Prime Minister Hymans of Belgium denied any desire for an economic war, but stressed the special needs of Belgium and France. Lloyd George intervened to suggest that all fears would be removed if they could agree that "so far as possible" applied to "equality of trade conditions" as well as to "the removal of all economic barriers." House accepted this suggestion and promised to bring it to the attention of President Wilson.[20] Wilson did not object. Hence, there was no formal Allied reservation about Point Three. Instead, the United States agreed to tolerate discrimination for the purpose of conserving reconstruction materials, while the Allies foreswore a general trade war against Germany.

Another clarification, eventually of greater importance for peacemaking, was required by the absence of any reference to reparation in the Fourteen Points. On October 29, Colonel House tried to cover this deficiency by assuring the Allies that the word "restored" in Points Seven, Eight, and Eleven included German compensation for damage to civilians and civilian property in invaded territories. Referring to British concerns he said, "The same principle applies to illegal sinkings at sea, and to the sinkings of neutrals."[21] The Allies, however, wanted more than an oral assurance. On November 1, they drafted a written reservation. The crucial sentence read, "By it [restoration] they understand that compensation will be made by Germany for all the damage done to the civilian population of the Allies and their property by the invasion by Germany of Allied territory by land, by sea and from the air."[22] The British then had second thoughts about "invasion." On November 4, they successfully insisted on broader phraseology: "by the *aggression* of Germany by land, by sea, and from the air."[23] Thus altered, the reservation was cabled to President Wilson. On November 5, it was communicated to the German Government by Secretary of State Robert Lansing, as part of the Allied and Associated pre-Armistice Agreement.

In this manner, British diplomacy first introduced the fateful word "aggression" into the history of reparation. At the time, Sir Maurice Hankey, Secretary of the War Cabinet, explained, "The object of the alteration was to include compensation for damage inflicted at sea."[24] This was only one motive. Another was recalled in 1931 by Lloyd George's former private secretary, Philip Kerr, Lord Lothian:

> I remember very distinctly discussing with L. G. the interpretation to be put upon the question of "restoration" or "reparation." His view was—"We must make it clear that we cannot charge Germany with the costs of the war. . . . She could not possibly pay it. But she must pay ample compensation for damage and that compensation must be equitably distributed among the Allies and not given entirely to France and Belgium. Devastated areas is only one item in war loss. Great Britain has probably spent more money on the war and incurred greater indirect losses in, for instance, shipping and trade, than France. She must have her fair share of compensation." He then instructed me to prepare a form of words. . . . I therefore revised it to read "damage to the civilian population of the allies by the aggression of Germany by land, air, and sea."[25]

This desire for a "fair share of compensation," especially relative to France, continued to preoccupy British policy and diplomacy. "Aggression," however, soon became more than a diplomatic concept since, as we shall see, it coincided with a widespread desire to censure Germany.

Nevertheless, it is important to note that in early November 1918, Lloyd George did not yet envisage what would soon be such a popular demand, an indemnity for war costs. When the Belgian Prime Minister urged that Germany be responsible for "all damage caused by the war," rather than civilian damage only, Lloyd George objected. He said, ". . . that to insert M. Hymans' words would be to tell Germany that she had to pay so huge an indemnity that it would probably be better for her to go on fighting."[26] He also opposed Article 19 of the Armistice terms: "With the reservation that any future claims and demands by the Allies and the United States remain unaffected, the following conditions are imposed:—Reparation for damage done."[27] It was later argued that this provision reserved an Allied claim for indemnity, as distinct from reparation. At the Allied meeting of November 2, 1918, Lloyd George thought the Article superfluous.[28] Furthermore, when he returned to London on November 6, the Prime Minister told the Imperial War Cabinet that at Versailles "a war indemnity had been ruled out because, beyond full reparation, Germany would have no means of paying further."[29]

This scepticism was surely influenced by a short memorandum, "Notes on an Indemnity," written by John Maynard Keynes and rushed to the Armistice discussions on October 31. After reviewing the various kinds of payment Germany might be able to make, Keynes had estimated that the Allies could expect no more than one billion sterling "without crushing Germany."[30] This total was not likely to go beyond the physical damage done on land and at sea.

The moderate assessment by Lloyd George and Keynes was similar to that of the American Government. Indeed, by November 1918, British and American economic aims seemed in close alignment: The British had backed away from the Paris Resolutions, a mutual understanding had been reached about Wilson's third point, and Britain was aiming for "reparation only." As long as the United States respected the British concern for a "fair share" of compensation, there seemed no obstacle to cooperation in economic peacemaking.

This cooperative trend was reinforced by three confidential British studies done in November and December 1918, by the Foreign Office, the Board of Trade, and the Treasury. The first of these was a handbook prepared in the Historical Section of the Foreign Office, entitled "Indemnities of War."[31] This was one of a series of pamphlets designed to inform British diplomats of the historical background of the problems they would face at the peace conference. "Indemnities of War" asserted that previous international practice sanctioned indemnity for damages and costs. However, after reviewing the eighteen treaties of the previous century that had included an indemnity, the handbook concluded that the only relevant instance was that of 1871. Following the lead of wartime writings on that indemnity, the Foreign Office handbook said the lesson of 1871 was that an indemnity *per se* was not harmful to the recipient, especially if payment were exacted in "things" over a number of years. The handbook's estimate of what Germany might be able to pay after the current war was in the comparatively modest range of £ 900 to £ 1,000 millions.

Many of the Foreign Office handbooks prepared for the peace conference had a definite influence at Paris in 1919, but "Indemnities of War" seems not to have been one of them, probably because it showed only scant historical precedent for direct financial compensation from the enemy. The British position on reparation and indemnity was much more affected by the analyses done by the Board of Trade and the Treasury in late 1918. The Board's contribution was a one hundred page report on "Economic Considerations Affecting the Terms of Peace," a study ordered by the War Cabinet on October 17, 1918, ". . . following a preliminary discussion on the preparations required for an eventual peace conference. . . ."[32] The Board's memorandum was presented to the War Cabinet on November 28.

The Board of Trade report was an elaboration of their January 1917 memorandum. In 1918, however, the Board was directly confronted with the difficulties of postwar trade and reconstruction during conditions of scarcity. Consequently, they recommended terms of peace which would prevent Germany from adding to those difficulties. The Board urged that for twelve months after the War, German exports to Allied countries be prohibited except under license; that for five years after the War, or until Germany was admitted to the League, whichever came sooner, no Allied country conclude a most-favored-nation agreement with Germany without the consent of the other Allies; and that after five years every Allied nation have the right to insert special protective measures into their commercial treaties with Germany. These policies would discourage German "dumping" and German purchases of scarce raw materials.

While the Board's commercial suggestions were more stringent than their position of 1917, their analysis of reparation and indemnity had not changed. The Board's only insistence was that Britain receive a share of shipping reparation proportionate to her losses.[33] The general problem of compensation, however, they continued to view with caution. The Board calculated that the Allied claims for reparation would amount to at least £ 2,000,000,000. They questioned whether it was within Germany's capacity to pay so large a sum. Even if she could pay, collecting the total sum would probably require an Allied army of occupation over a considerable period. Since this would be unpopular in the war-weary Allied nations, the Board recommended a moderate, clearly fixed sum of reparation. Indemnity for war costs seemed to them almost out of the question:

> . . . the total claims under the head of reparation will certainly be very great, and as the satisfaction of these claims must take precedence over an indemnity proper, it is suggested that no useful purpose would be served by putting forward a claim for an indemnity proper unless it be thought expedient to do so for bargaining purposes.[34]

Most of the Board's recommendations were similar to those of the Treasury memorandum "On the Indemnity Payable by the Enemy Powers for Reparation and Other Claims." This study had been requested by the War Cabinet on October 26. Bonar Law summarized its findings for the Imperial War Cabinet of November 26, but the report was not printed until December; it was not fully discussed until the Imperial War Cabinet of December 24.[35] Nevertheless, Lloyd George referred to it, obliquely, in public on December 11 at Bristol. The memorandum was prepared by the "A" Division of the Treasury, a group of economists under John Maynard Keynes who had been assigned most questions of external finance beginning in January 1917. Keynes was the principal author of the memorandum, which was based on his recent "Notes on an Indemnity."[36]

Like the Board of Trade, Keynes and the "A" Division limited their expectations to "reparation only." They were moderate for three reasons. First, they believed that "civilian damage" in the Allied reservation of November 5 excluded any claim for a war costs indemnity. The argument that Article 19 of the Armistice permitted such a claim was strained, in their view, and would be resisted by the United States. Second, Keynes and his associates doubted that Germany could pay more than £ 3,000,000,000. "An actual payment of £ 2,000 million, if effected without evil indirect consequences, would be a very satisfactory achievement in all the circumstances." Certainly German capacity was insufficient to pay the Allied cost of the War, estimated at £ 24,350,000,000 or even the British Empire war costs of £ 6,600,000,000 plus pensions and war loans. Third, the "A" Division feared the effect of large German payments on British trade:

> An indemnity so high that it can only be paid by means of a great expansion of Germany's export trade must necessarily interfere with the export trade of other nations. . . . It will be very disadvantageous to this country artificially to stimulate German exports in order that the proceeds of these exports may be paid over (e.g.) to France. [37]

The Treasury authors shared Board of Trade fears about Britain's position in the possibly fierce competition that would follow the War; their fears on that score outweighed any hopes they may have had for a large indemnity.

The "A" Division also restrained their expectation of the share of total reparation that might be enjoyed by the British Empire. They forecast 15 percent, considerably less than British negotiators tried to achieve at Paris in 1919. Furthermore, they believed this share would depend on illegal damage being accepted as a principal criterion of reparation by the peace conference, since 93 percent of all British "civilian damage" had been "illegal" sinkings of ships and cargoes by German submarines.

Only in one respect did the Treasury memorandum have a belligerent ring. Feeling that a lengthy series of large, annual payments would be an excessive stimulant to German exports, the Treasury authors believed a better method of reparation would be

> To obtain all the property which can be transferred immediately or over a period of three years, levying this contribution ruthlessly and completely, so as to ruin entirely for many years to come Germany's overseas development and her international credit; but, having done this (which would yield more than £ 1,000 million, but less than £ 2,000 million), to ask only a small tribute over a term of years, and to leave Germany to do the best she can for the future with the internal resources remaining to her.[38]

While this was harsh, the "A" Division considered it more beneficial for Germany than the alternative. Numerous and large annual payments would probably entail an oppressive army of occupation and tempt Germany into unwholesome methods of discharging or avoiding her obligation. German states might, for example, secede in order to avoid the financial commitments of the central government. Also, the central government itself might try to alleviate its external burden by repudiating the internal German debt. Keynes and the "A" Division solemnly warned that "repudiation is a contagious disease, and each breach in the opposite convention brings it nearer everywhere."

The reports of the Board of Trade and the Treasury were, in fact, a studied articulation of two policies the War Cabinet had already adopted in early November 1918. One of these policies was preparing for postwar scarcity and trade competition with Germany and other foreign nations. Here, however, only the Board of Trade remained loyal to the essentials of the Paris Economic Resolutions, which their minister had been mainly responsible for drafting in 1916. Otherwise, the emphasis on Allied cooperation had faded, in favor of a more unilateral policy which envisaged competition with "friendly" nations, including France. The second policy was "reparation only," of which the British Empire should have a just, if minor, share. This was consistent with the desire to minimize German competition in export and raw materials markets.

While the first of these policies was a conceivable irritant in Anglo-American relations, the second was a definite and immediate basis for cooperation with Woodrow Wilson in making the economic peace. In fact, there was little in the priority of trade over reparation and indemnity that might interfere with British-American harmony at Paris. Yet even as the memoranda which expressed this priority were printed, their recommendations were challenged by demands for more punitive and less consistent terms of peace that would include a large war costs indemnity. These demands arose out of two developments in British politics. One was the General Election of 1918, to be discussed presently. The other was a conflict between Prime Minister Hughes of Australia and the British Government. Both events moved British peace aims away from those of President Wilson.

Chapter 6 BRITAIN, HUGHES, AND INDEMNITY

FEW MEN chose to quarrel with William Morris Hughes; none enjoyed doing so. Hughes was partly deaf, easily irritated, and seldom afflicted by doubt. Many of his British Empire colleagues regarded him as *l'enfant terrible,* to be avoided when possible and accommodated when necessary.

In November 1918, Hughes became embroiled in a dispute with the British Government that affected imperial unity, British peace aims, and Anglo-American relations. The controversy was over the Armistice. Hughes was enraged because he had not been consulted about the Versailles discussions and because the Armistice had been based on the Fourteen Points. He especially objected to the fact that the Armistice did not provide for a war costs indemnity.

In the summer of 1918, Hughes had returned to Britain to represent Australia in imperial discussions. He continued a vigorous exposition of his economic philosophy. Privately, he reminded the Imperial War Conference that "the struggle between the two races [British and German] is for economic domination or supremacy."[1] Publicly, he adhered to the Paris Resolutions and the eradication of all German influence from the British Empire.[2] His speeches were widely reported in Britain and in the United States, where they so incensed President Wilson that he considered denying Hughes an American visa.[3] Hughes hoped to influence the armistice and peace terms. On

October 11, he told the War Cabinet that "an armistice must approximate to the basis of the conditions of peace" and that one of these conditions must be complete Allied freedom to take economic measures against Germany after the War.[4] Two British politicians who knew Hughes warned that he expected to be consulted in the making of the armistice. "After a long talk with Hughes," Leo Amery wrote to Bonar Law on October 15, saying that imperial unity depended on close consultation with Dominion statesmen about the peace terms.[5] Walter Long told the Cabinet of October 18, "The Australians had, in fact, done a good deal more than the Americans towards winning the War, and had, therefore, just as good a right to a voice as President Wilson."[6]

Hughes made consultation difficult by going on a speaking tour of the North of England at the end of October and beginning of November. His private secretary gave Hughes' itinerary to the War Cabinet secretariat on October 24, and said that Hughes could return to London on four hours notice,[7] but the Australian Prime Minister was not recalled for the important War Cabinet meetings which were held simultaneously with the Versailles discussions. In part, this was because meetings were called on less than four hours notice; in part, because other Dominion prime ministers had not yet arrived in London; and perhaps in part, because of Hughes himself.[8]

When Hughes did return to London, he initiated a rancorous controversy at an Imperial War Conference on November 6. He implied that he had been deliberately excluded from the Armistice discussions, and warned that the Imperial system was failing in its consultative function. He then attacked the Fourteen Points, protesting the limits they placed on Allied aims. He was especially distressed with the third point. That provision, he said, denied Allied tariff autonomy and would thereby impede reconstruction. Hughes also claimed that the Germans might not adequately compensate the British Empire for shipping lost, and that the third point would prevent alternative economic penalties.[9]

Lloyd George and Bonar Law hit back sharply about consultation. Lloyd George noted that Australia had been reluctant to attend Imperial meetings during the War. He reminded the

meeting that Hughes had been sent the minutes of recent War
Cabinets, but that the Australian Prime Minister had made no
protest. Bonar Law recalled two occasions when Hughes was to
have been chairman of Imperial War Cabinets, but did not appear and could not be reached by telephone. Lloyd George added
that Hughes, like other ministers, must hold himself ready for
official business and not treat personal engagements as more
important.[10]

The British ministers also rejected Hughes' interpretation of
the Fourteen Points and the Armistice agreements. Lloyd George
said that President Wilson fully understood that tariffs and
imperial preference were domestic questions of the British Empire. Anyway, Bonar Law interjected, at Versailles "they had all
agreed that the terms of Clause 3 were so vague that we could
really place any interpretation upon them that we liked."[11]
Lloyd George then explained the view taken of reparation and
raw materials at the Allied meetings. Full reparation would be
demanded of Germany, in the range of one to two billion pounds
sterling. However, the Germans could pay no more than two
billion and, therefore, indemnity for war costs had been "ruled
out." Furthermore, the payment of reparation alone would require German access to raw materials. Nevertheless, the Allies
would take measures to prevent that access from interfering with
their own reconstruction. Hughes, perhaps sullen from earlier
remarks about his official duties, tamely replied that Lloyd
George's exposition "cleared up the point."[12]

In fact, he was not satisfied, and on the following day, November 7, he made his case public. In a widely reported speech to
the Australia Club, Hughes repeated almost literally his arguments of the day before. He then advanced a new grievance about
the Armistice agreements:

> I object to these terms of peace because they do not provide for
> indemnities. (Hear, hear) . . . Why? Do my friends realise the
> position for which [these terms] stand? . . . that for generations
> we shall be staggering under a . . . burden of taxation which it
> was not imagined before the war could be borne? And is Germany
> to escape bearing at least some share of these frightful burdens?[13]

This was the first public plea for indemnity by a major politician
in Britain.

Then, on November 9, Hughes delivered a formal protest to the British Government on behalf of the Australian Government. He wrote that his Government regarded the failure to consult as "a painful and serious breach of faith," that they would not accept any interpretation of Wilson's third point which would limit their tariff automony, and that they would insist on retaining the ex-German colonies in the Pacific.[14] On the same day, there appeared in the press an assurance by the British Government that all the Dominions would be continuously consulted in peacemaking, and that the Allied Governments were confident "that the language of President Wilson's Fourteen Points was wide enough to cover all that they [the Allies] intended to raise when the issues of peace came to be dealt with."[15]

If this assurance had any soothing effects on Hughes, they were nullified by certain remarks which Lloyd George made to a pre-election meeting of Liberal MPs on November 12. The Prime Minister told his fellow-Liberals that he was "as much a Free Trader as ever" and that he believed that the third of the Fourteen Points "imposed considerable limitations" on the Paris Economic Resolutions, "inasmuch as it makes economic war after the war impossible."[16] The next day, the energetic Leo Amery warned his chief, Sir Maurice Hankey, that Lloyd George's remark "has made matters much worse and will give Hughes a fresh handle for saying that the whole economic settlement has been jumped by the Prime Minister with an eye to the Liberal vote in England. . . . We must get L. G. to see the seriousness of the thing and set the matter right."[17]

Amery's assessment was correct. On November 14, the Australian Prime Minister, addressing the Agents-General of the Australian States, criticized the British Government even more strongly than he had on November 7. He rejected almost all of the British assurance of November 9. He claimed that the third of Wilson's points either threatened tariff autonomy or was meaningless rhetoric and a grave reflection on the President. Hughes also revealed his basic motive in calling for indemnity. Australia would get very little from reparation for civilian damages, even though she had "poured out blood and treasure." Reparation without indemnity would reward France and Belgium and modestly compensate Britain, but deny the *entire* British Empire of its just share.[18] Here, roughly articulated by Hughes, was logic that quickly impressed imperialists and protectionists in Britain.

The reaction of the British press to Hughes' protest was mixed. *The Times*, the *Scotsman*, and the *Glasgow Herald* thought that the Australian had overstated his complaints.[19] On the other hand, that warlike monthly, the *National Review* charged that the Fourteen Points—which editor Leo Maxse despised—had been accepted "behind the back of Hughes" and that they did, indeed, "infringe the fiscal freedom of the Dominions."[20] More important, the *Morning Post* adopted Hughes' case, especially on indemnity, and clung to it for the rest of November.[21] Meanwhile, other newspapers, including *The Times*, gradually moved toward the view of peacemaking taken by Hughes.

Various Conservative politicians also tried, unsuccessfully, to convince Bonar Law to support Hughes and the Hughes view of peacemaking. On November 12, in the House of Commons, three Conservative Members closely questioned their Leader for assurances that the Armistice agreements did not limit Allied demands and that Hughes would be consulted in the peace negotiations.[22] Bonar Law heard from a Conservative candidate that there was popular support for Hughes' position on indemnity.[23] Nevertheless, on November 11, Law replied:

> Wilson's terms are so vague that the terms of peace can be fully discussed under them except perhaps an indemnity in one sense. As a matter of fact however, under the term reparation for all acts of damage caused by her aggression a far larger sum can be claimed than Germany can ever pay.[24]

Thus, Bonar Law adhered to reparation only, and to the advice of his civil servants at the Treasury.

The most persuasive Conservative to support Hughes was Cabinet secretary Leo Amery. Amery feared the British-Australian quarrel would impair the Imperial War Cabinet system, which he had helped to initiate.[25] He urged the British War Cabinet to prevent this by accepting "the direct representation of the Dominions and India in the British delegation at the Peace Conference."[26] He also became convinced that Hughes was right about the Fourteen Points and the economic peace. On November 19, in long letters to Foreign Secretary Balfour and Jan Smuts, Amery elucidated Hughes' attitude about reparation and indemnity. France, he wrote, should not receive the industrial value of Alsace-Lorraine and large reparation payments without agreeing to corresponding economic rewards for the British Empire. Furthermore, within the British Empire, those rewards should be divided fairly. On that score, Amery said several things should be borne in mind: Britain would get direct reparation for shipping lost, in any case. Canada and South Africa had made industrial gains during the War and had not had their shipping seriously disrupted. However, "the Australasian Colonies have suffered enormous indirect loss in diversion of all their shipping in addition to the actual cost of the war, and as things stand they are getting nothing . . . except the probability of their retaining certain German islands."[27] The clear implication was that a fair division of the "spoils" between the Allies and within the British Empire required some larger basis of claim than reparation for physical damage done.

The issues raised by Hughes and Amery could not be dealt with until the Prime Ministers of Canada and South Africa arrived in London later in the month of November. Sir Robert Borden of Canada grasped the problem of indemnity almost immediately after his arrival. On November 23, he wrote to Lloyd George:

> One nation or Dominion may have suffered greatly in loss of manpower with a resulting pension roll which will impose heavy burdens for half a century; another nation or Dominion may have sustained . . . a greater loss in the destruction of shipping or other property. Accessions of territory with large supplies of raw material may wholly or partially compensate one nation or Dominion and not another; a powerful and wealthy nation like the United States may be opposed to any indemnity; the enemy nations may not possess material resources sufficient to pay an indemnity comparable with the appalling losses they have inflicted upon the world.[28]

There was no better short comment on the difficulties of the general question.

Those difficulties were considered by the important Imperial War Cabinet of November 26. Not surprisingly, Hughes initiated the discussion with a long recapitulation of the views he had publicly advanced in previous weeks. On the subject of compensation by Germany, he made explicit what he had previously implied: reparation should not be considered more valid than indemnity. If it was, "an invidious distinction is at once made between a country like Belgium and, say, a country like Australia, or even like England."[29]

Lloyd George immediately replied that expectations of German payments must be tempered by certain practical difficulties. Germany did not have enough gold to pay, the Prime Minister said, and if the Allies carried out plans to restrict Germany's trade and her supply of raw materials, she would be even less able to pay. How, he asked, was Germany to compensate Australia for £ 300,000,000 war costs when Australia refused to import German goods? He could promise the British electorate that Germany would pay all of Britain's £ 8,000,000,000 war costs, but if he asked them how she could do it there would be no answer. Germany was responsible for the War, to be sure, and ought to pay all the costs, but if the Allies demanded that, they would encourage German exports to the detriment of their own trade. "All these policies were hopelessly inconsistent," the Prime Minister said. Therefore, he proposed the appointment of an Imperial Cabinet Committee to study further how Germany might pay to the limit of her capacity without harmful side effects for the Allies. No one objected.

However, the chairmanship of the intended committee was difficult to assign. Lloyd George first suggested Bonar Law and when the Chancellor of the Exchequer said he was too busy, both he and Lloyd George asked Sir George Foster, Canadian Minister of Finance. Foster also declined. As the meeting progressed attention turned to Hughes, who Lloyd George thought should be on the committee "because he is raising the question." Hughes' response was a *faux pas*: "I much prefer to remain free so I can criticise." Lloyd George instantly replied, "Well, that is not quite playing the game here." The entire Cabinet agreed and pressed Hughes to accept the chairmanship, which he did only with reluctance.

A long, revealing discussion was required to appoint the other members of the committee. At the Cabinet's urging, Walter Long and Sir George Foster agreed to serve. Hughes suggested W. A. S. Hewins, who was subsequently appointed. Then Bonar Law proposed that civil servants who had already worked on the problem should be included. He described the report of the "A" Division of the Treasury as "hurried" and probably too pessimistic, but he felt that Hughes' committee should "make the fullest use of our Government officials, who . . . have the economic side thoroughly at their fingers' ends." Eventually, Maynard Keynes and Llewellyn Smith did sit in a few committee meetings, but only as advisers. The Imperial Cabinet preferred businessmen to civil servants, following the argument of Sir Joseph Cook of New Zealand: "You have to satisfy the outside public view . . . that Germany is capable of paying far more than we have demanded, and you can satisfy that view best by having a couple of business men to represent it." Consequently, two businessmen were selected as members: Herbert Gibbs, a prominent City of London banker and Conservative, and Lord Cunliffe, an ex-Governor of the Bank of England and eventually a British reparation delegate at the Peace Conference.

Of the six men chosen, all but Sir George Foster were protectionists who favored a large indemnity. This suited the purpose of some members of the Imperial Cabinet. Austen Chamberlain, for example, said the committee should start with the Treasury's report ". . . and set to work to prove it to be wrong, and to prove how much more Germany can pay." With Hughes as chairman, backed by a sympathetic majority, it is not surprising that the committee took just this approach.

Yet this preconceived, dialectical attitude was not in keeping with Lloyd George's original concern about the practical difficulties of reparation and, especially, indemnity. Why then did the British Prime Minister raise no objection to the appointment of men who were purposely included because they favored large payments, nor insist on precise terms of reference for the committee?

Lloyd George later explained in his *Memoirs of The Peace Conference*, first published in 1938, that he had simply miscalculated in November 1918. He had considered the committee to be "men of real practical ability" who, once they studied the situation, would moderate their expectations and those heard in the current election campaign. He especially counted on Gibbs and Cunliffe to be cautionary because of their long financial experience. Thus, Lloyd George recollected, when he read the committee's final report of December 10, he was shocked at its optimistic conclusions. He and Bonar Law regarded the report as "a wild and fantastic chimera." For that reason and "in view of the election then proceeding I decided not to publish it."[30]

This retrospective explanation is only partly credible. Certainly Lloyd George hoped that committee work would convince Hughes to modify his position. Surely, also, the British Prime Minister would have been pleased with a moderate report. On the other hand, it is hard to imagine so acute a politician as Lloyd George being misinformed about the views of prominent financiers or over-confident that committee work would change their views.[31] Nor can Lloyd George have been very surprised at the committee report, which was not exactly unpublished, since the Prime Minister himself described its conclusions at the most important of his election meetings, at Bristol on December 11.

The election, in fact, must have been a more critical element in Lloyd George's thoughts about the Hughes committee in 1918 than he later remembered in 1938. Hughes' public criticisms of the British Government had been made at the beginning of the election campaign of November-December. Conservative and protectionist confidence in the Government might have eroded had Hughes not been placated. A new study of the "indemnities" problem would help to pacify Hughes and his followers. And there was a further advantage in having Hughes himself on such a committee: Even if this didn't reduce his expectations of Germany, it would at least obligate the Australian not to make further speeches critical of British economic aims, in which the electors were showing a surprising interest. Furthermore, even if the Hughes committee reached excessive conclusions, Hughes would at least have to share responsibility for introducing indemnity into British politics and diplomacy. The Hughes committee was very likely a political convenience as well as an economic study group. This is substantiated by the record of the committee's deliberations and reports.[32]

On November 26, Sir Robert Borden warned that the committee

". . . will have to work pretty fast if their report is to be of any value to us."[33] Accordingly, the newly designated Imperial War Cabinet Committee on Indemnity began their deliberations a day later. The Committee met four times between November 27 and December 2, when they produced a report for the Inter-Allied Conference of December 1-3. On December 3, the Committee was reconvened to consider additional subjects, and held seven further meetings, submitting a final report on the evening of December 10.

During the first phase of their meetings, the Committee discussed four aspects of the general problem: Whether the Allies should claim indemnity as well as reparation, how much Germany could pay, the total claim that the Allies should put forward, and the effects of payment on the British economy. On the first matter, Hughes repeated his view that "indemnity and reparation are both necessary in order that all nations may be treated alike." (meeting of November 29) Here the Chairman was supported, as he would be throughout, by Long, Hewins, Cunliffe, and Gibbs. There was no serious opposition, though Keynes and Llewellyn Smith remarked that their departments had assumed that the Fourteen Points limited claims to reparation only.

How much Germany could pay aroused more controversy. Hughes and his supporters asserted that Germany could, over time, pay more than £ 20,000,000,000. Keynes, Llewellyn Smith, and Foster rejected this as an unthinkable burden; Llewellyn Smith said it would simply force many Germans to emigrate. The replies of the Committee majority were not very cogent. Cunliffe admitted that in regard to capacity to pay "my knowledge of Germany and German trade is not sufficient." (meeting of November 29) The other City businessman, Herbert Gibbs, remarked, "I have merely thought of [German capacity] just as any other individual has thought of it. . . . I should have thought she could have afforded to pay a very considerable indemnity" (meeting of November 29). Hughes, faced with resistance, belittled the question of German capacity: "What we have to consider is whether we ought to claim an indemnity. Then the onus is on Germany to prove she cannot pay it" (meeting of November 28).

Agreeing with Hughes, the Committee majority was willing

to recommend an Allied claim for the entire cost of the War, approximately £ 24,000,000,000. Specifically, Cunliffe proposed a scheme of five percent gold bonds issued by the German Government, through which the Allies would receive an annual payment on principal and interest of £ 1,200,000,000.[34] The Committee majority would claim from Germany in one year what the "A" Division expected in total.

The effects of large German payments on the British economy were stressed by Keynes and Llewellyn Smith. Like the British Prime Minister, the two civil servants believed that a large indemnity would encourage German exports to a degree harmful to British traders. Hughes replied with a circuitous argument: In that case, Britain and the Allies should raise tariffs against Germany as Australia had done. Yet he made no effort to discover how Germany could pay the entire cost of the War except through an export surplus.

On December 2, the Committee submitted to the Imperial Cabinet what was to have been its final report.[35] This was drafted by Hughes and Hewins on December 1.[36] The report denied that there was any real or just distinction between reparation and indemnity and urged the Allies to claim compensation for the cost of the War as well as for physical damages, though it did admit that reparation should be the first claim on German resources. It presented the various Committee opinions on German capacity to pay but came to no definite conclusions, only warning the Cabinet not to rely on the advice or evidence of those who had an interest in resuming trade with Germany. Despite this uncertainty, the report approved Cunliffe's bond scheme and said that "it seems likely that the Enemy Powers could provide 1,200,000,000 pounds sterling per annum for the service of the debt." The report inaccurately described the Committee as "unanimously" of the opinion that fears of economic ill-effects were "groundless." To all the previous arguments for indemnity, the report added that of indemnity as penalty and deterrent: Germany would be deprived of the capacity to finance an army or navy capable of aggression, and the example of the indemnity would discourage Germany and any other aggressor from provoking wars.

The report was hurried together as a guide for British policy at the Allied Conference of December 1-3, in London. These discussions were convened by the Western Allies in order to prepare for the peace conference, although the United States was not represented since Colonel House was ill in Paris. At the beginning of the meetings, Lloyd George was still sceptical about the practical problems of reparation and indemnity. On December 1, he told his Allied colleagues "that one of the difficulties of demanding an indemnity [in the sense of general compensation] was that the enemy had no means of paying except in goods; and none of the Allies, at any rate, wanted to take their goods in payment."[37] On the following day, the Prime Minister mentioned the high expectations of payment held by the Allied publics. "The general public were commonly under some illusion in this matter," he said. Therefore, the Conference ought to establish an Allied commission of experts to determine how much Germany could pay. "If Germany, for example, could pay fifty thousand millions, the claims would be put forward on a different basis from what it would be if she could pay only two or three thousand millions."[38] The Allies agreed and decided that the peace conference should include two reparation commissions: One to study Germany's capacity to pay and the best forms of payment, and another to decide on the priority of the various Allied claims. Nothing other than reparation was mentioned as being within the purview of the two commissions.

However, an important change in the commissions' terms of reference resulted from a brief Imperial War Cabinet on the morning of December 3. Hughes insisted that the commissions should consider Germany's capacity to pay indemnity, as well as reparation. Lloyd George, having theoretically admitted that Germany might be able to pay "fifty thousand millions," agreed.[39] At an Allied conversation immediately following the Imperial Cabinet, "Mr. Lloyd George said that . . . it was proposed to ask for *indemnity* as well as reparation."[40] Hence, the instructions of the commission on capacity were changed to ". . . examine and report on the question of the amount of the sum for reparation and indemnity, which the enemy countries are capable of paying. . . ."[41] Indemnity for war costs was no longer "ruled out."

Why, on December 3, did Lloyd George depart from his cau-

tion of early November? First, because the British Prime Minister was under heavy electoral pressure to seek large payments,
as we shall see in a later chapter. Second, because the optimistic
Hughes committee report of December 2 meant that Lloyd George
would not have to bear sole responsibility for claiming indemnity.
Third, because there was no American representative at the Allied
conference to resist the change of policy. The importance of
the third reason was made clear on December 5, when Colonel
House told the Allies that the United States would agree to the
proposed commissions, "eliminating the word 'indemnity.' "[42]
This certainly coincided with the views of President Wilson,
who became more and more suspicious of British economic aims
just before the peace conference, as Britain refused to forego a
claim for war costs. The Allied decisions of December 2 and 3,
instigated by Hughes and Lloyd George, opened a divide between the British Empire and the United States.

Those Allied decisions also extended the life of the Hughes
Committee. On December 2, Hughes thought his endeavor complete, but on the following day the Imperial Cabinet directed his
committee to prepare for British Empire participation on the
Allied commissions. The Committee was to delve further into
the mysteries of German capacity and to submit to the Imperial
Cabinet the names of three candidates for British Empire reparation delegates to the Peace Conference.[43]

These assignments prompted Jan Smuts to warn Lloyd George,
on December 4, that the Hughes Committee was gaining too
much influence. They were making "impossible recommendations on Indemnities" which would require an army of occupation and thereby "play into the hands of the French." Lloyd
George should at least withdraw the privilege of nominating
reparation delegates from the Committee. Smuts said his concern was shared by Lords Reading and Curzon.[44] There is no
record of how Lloyd George received these criticisms, but he
did not find them persuasive enough to interfere with the further
activity of Hughes' committee or to ignore their final recommendations. To have done either would have offended Hughes
and destroyed the political purpose of his committee.

Thus, the Committee on Indemnity reassembled on December
3 and continued meeting until December 11.[45] None of these

meetings included Keynes, Llewellyn Smith, or any other civil servant. Instead, the Committee called three witnesses who, presumably, would be more sympathetic to their purposes: Sir Charles Addis, a director of the Hong Kong Bank, Sir Eric Geddes, First Lord of the Admiralty, and Hugo Hirst, a British subject of German origin who had founded the General Electric Company in Britain. None of these three men altered the views of the Committee. Geddes reinforced the majority's opinions by telling them that the blockade would enable the Allies to "squeeze . . . everything of value" out of Germany, a metaphor the First Lord also used in his election campaign. Addis and Hirst gave informed testimony, but their evaluations were ignored when they conflicted with those of the committee majority.

Indeed, from December 3 to 11, the Committee developed few new ideas about the size or method of payment. They did, however, expose some of their basic motives, as shown by these remarks of December 6:

> Hugo Hirst: If we have to pay [war debts without any assistance], we may be in a very difficult position in five years' time. We may not reap the fruits of victory . . .
> The Chairman: . . . Now, we have to carry on our backs the interest on 8,000,000 sterling of debt plus pensions for 1 million dead, pensions for those who are living . . . and we are asked to compete with America . . .
> Lord Cunliffe: It is rather a choice of who is to be ruined, we or them [the Germans]. Are we to be ruined?
> Hugo Hirst: Certainly not.
> Mr. Hewins: On the whole I think we had better ruin them.
> Lord Cunliffe: I think so.
> Mr. Herbert Gibbs: Is it too strong, referring to what you were saying about America, to say that, if there are to be no indemnities, it is impossible to say that in the course of time British trade may not be completely ruined by American competition?
> Hugo Hirst: If there are no indemnities, yes; I am willing to agree to it. . . . I feel that if we have to carry this sacrifice, and America has to carry no sacrifice, we may have fought for the greatness of America.

Here, as in other discussions, the Committee worried as much about American competition as about German.

This was especially true of Herbert Gibbs, who embodied his ideas about the United States in a confidential letter, which the Committee approved and sent to Lloyd George covering the final report. As the letter explained:

> The Committee for obvious reasons has not referred to American competition in their Report, but they think it is important that the Cabinet should be informed that in their opinion the great menace to the trade of the British Empire comes from the U.S.A. America made large profits during the first two and a half years of the war. . . . The British Empire on the other hand has been pouring out great streams of blood and treasure during the whole period of the war. From a great creditor nation she has become a debtor nation. The crushing burden of debt which she now carries must inevitably most seriously handicap her in any competition with a nation such as America whose financial and economic position is now much stronger than before the war.[46]

Therefore, the letter continued, Britain must have a war costs indemnity from Germany. In this way, America's wartime prosperity strengthened the desire of many British protectionists for a punitive economic peace.

Another consideration which weighed on Committee minds was the General Election. The campaign was then in full swing, the balloting scheduled for December 14. Chairman Hughes told the Committee many times that the Government, especially the Prime Minister, was in urgent need of their conclusions. On December 9, Hughes warned, "Mr. Lloyd George must have some resting ground for his feet, and, if we are uncertain, then he is launched into a sea of uncertainty." The only ground the Committee could discover was a large indemnity. On December 5, for example, when Sir Charles Addis estimated that Germany could pay the Allies no more than £ 60,000,000 annually, the Committee majority replied that such a modest figure would cost the Government the election. On the other hand, they were unable to gather convincing evidence that Germany could pay —or be compelled to pay—Allied war costs. Sir George Foster pointed this out again and again, until he finally surrendered his lonely opposition on December 10. At that meeting, Hughes said that Lloyd George had asked for a report immediately. The Chairman had promised that one would be ready after the current meeting. Pressed by the majority, Foster surrendered his argument, though not his scepticism. Consequently, a unanimous report went to Lloyd George on the evening of December 10.

The Committee's final report was an expansion of their recommendations of December 2. Their first conclusion of December 10 was the central principle: "The total cost of the war to the Allies is the measure of the Indemnity which the enemy Powers should in justice pay."[47] The Committee admitted, again, that German payments should be first applied to reparation. On the other hand, and somewhat inconsistently, they asserted the equal validity of indemnity: "To make good the expenditure on troops and munitions of war is precisely the same kind of thing as to make good the destruction of property." To bolster their position, they reminded their readers that Germany and Austria had caused the War and waged it by illegal means.

The most important conclusion came second, giving the Committee's estimate of what Germany could pay. Here the reasoning was tortured. The Committee confessed that they lacked evidence for an accurate forecast of German capacity. They also granted that the cession of territory might reduce that capacity. Nevertheless, the Committee were optimistic. They believed that estimates by persons interested in trade with Germany could be discounted. They also rejected prewar statistics. Instead, they emphasized the rapid expansion of German production during the War as an indication of what Germany could pay in the future. Therefore, the Allies should claim all damages and costs, totalling £ 24,000,000,000. "The Committee have certainly no reason to suppose that the enemy Powers could not provide 1,200,000,000 l. per annum as interest on the above amount when normal conditions are restored." This could be accomplished without an army of occupation, a crucial point which the Committee did not substantiate.

The remaining conclusions closely resembled those of December 2. Cunliffe's five percent bond scheme appeared again, as did the value of large payments for discouraging German rearmament. Harmful side effects on Allied trade were once more rejected, but with more conviction: Far from being harmful, a large indemnity was indispensable; without it the Allies ". . . would be unable to compete successfully in the markets of the world."

Here the Committee hinted at the apprehensions of their private covering letter.

This was the report which Lloyd George was anxious to receive and which Chairman Hughes was anxious to give him on the evening of December 10. The election campaign was drawing to a close, but the British Prime Minister had not yet taken a clear stand on the important issue of "making Germany pay." Public expectations were running high, far beyond the analyses by the Board of Trade and Treasury. If Lloyd George was to say pleasing things to the electorate, some more optimistic report was necessary. The Hughes Committee report was placed in his hands just before he left London on the eve of an important address at Bristol.[48] There, on December 11, the Prime Minister cited the conclusions of the Hughes Committee as the basis for his dramatic assertion that Germany should pay all damages and costs, and for his hope that she could, in fact, do so.

On the same day, the Committee on Indemnity was performing its final task: the nomination of three British Empire reparation delegates. Eschewing modesty, the Committee selected three men from their own ranks: Hughes, Cunliffe, and Gibbs.[49] On December 13, these nominations were sent to Lloyd George, who eventually appointed Hughes and Cunliffe but passed over Gibbs.[50] Hughes would, of course, create trouble if left out. Cunliffe, as the most prominent businessman on the Indemnity Committee, could hardly be excluded. Herbert Gibbs, however, was rejected in favor of Lord Sumner, a distinguished Lord of Appeal.[51] Sumner had no experience in international economics and at the Peace Conference followed the views of his two fellow-delegates.

The nomination of delegates who favored indemnity was the last step in the shift of British policy away from "reparation only" and the economic aims of the United States. The shift had begun with Hughes' discontents of early November, and continued with the appointment of the Committee on Indemnity, the Allied decision of December 3, the Hughes Committee report of December 10, and the Bristol speech of December 11. By mid-December, the British Government seemed committed to an indemnity for war costs that would, hopefully, afford all members of the British Empire just compensation and also bolster Britain's economic position relative to Germany and the United States.

The emergence of indemnity was closely related to the General Election campaign of November and December. Hughes and his committee, after all, could not and did not influence British policy by the mere force of their arguments. They were influential largely because their image of Germany coincided with a deep antipathy that pervaded Britain at the end of the War.

Chapter 7 THE ANTI-GERMAN TEMPER

ALTHOUGH anti-German feeling dominated the General Election of mid-November to December 14, 1918, that feeling had gathered force in the months just before the campaign began. In fact, hatred of Germany became more intense in the early autumn of 1918 than at any time during the War. A remarkable instance of the general mood may be seen in the lines by Rudyard Kipling which appeared in the *Daily Telegraph* on October 24:

> A people and their King
>   Through ancient sin grown strong,
> Because they feared no reckoning
>   Would set no bound to wrong;
> But now their hour is past
>   And we who bore it find
> Evil Incarnate held at last
>   To answer to mankind.[1]

Some people doubtless thought expressions of this sort excessive and harmful; yet the accumulated and terrible loss of life the War had brought about made public moderation difficult, just as any-one who knew that Kipling himself had lost a son would scarcely have contradicted his severe verse.

Popular hatred of Germany, and the obstacles to speaking against it, originated at the very beginning of the War. The Germans and Austrians had, so it seemed, willed a general conflict in their diplomacy during the July crisis. Their apparent guilt was quickly made more plausible by the arrogance the Germans

106

displayed toward Belgians and Belgian neutrality.[2] This and more was "documented" in 1915 by a semi-official committee, chaired by the respected Liberal, Lord Bryce.[3] Also in 1915, the British nation was faced more directly with German methods as the U-boats struck British commerce with surprise sinkings in violation of established maritime rules. Riots against "German" shops in the East End of London followed the *Lusitania* sinking of May 1915. A merchant captain, Captain Fryatt, who was executed by the Germans for ramming a German submarine became, understandably, a national martyr. The same mantle fell upon Nurse Edith Cavell, whose execution for harboring Allied prisoners-of-war became widely regarded as typical of German treatment of women and innocents. These events, and others like them, received detailed coverage in a newspaper press that was starved by censorship of more substantial war information. Thus, the normal penchant of the newspapers, especially of the London papers, for sensational crimes found an outlet in the marginal pathos of the War.

That there were criminal acts by German combatants easily led many British observers—including many in the Government—to believe that Germans were also secretly at work in Britain. As early as August 1914, aliens of enemy origin were interned in camps and later deported.[4] Throughout the War there was a popular campaign to make this safeguard more inclusive.[5] Likewise, German influence was suspected in businesses supported (even partly supported) by German investors. In politics, efforts for a negotiated peace, such as that by Lord Lansdowne, were stigmatized as pro-German. Some observers even saw German influence in the Government. Sir Eyre Crowe of the Foreign Office, whose wife and mother were German, was publicly harassed throughout the War.[6] More important, Lord Milner was suspected because of his German-English parentage. Lord Northcliffe thought that Milner, because of his ancestry, was lenient toward Germany and enemy aliens.[7]

In its most shrill form, Germanophobia was to be found on the fringe of serious politics. Fear and hatred of Germany were especially sensationalized by Pemberton Billing and Horatio Bottomley, independent MPs for East Hertfordshire and South Hackney. In the House of Commons and in his publication,

Vigilante, Billing campaigned against "pro-Germanism." He achieved his greatest notoriety in 1918 with the allegation that the Germans possessed a list of 47,000 prominent British subjects whose sexual weaknesses made them prey for German agents.[8] Bottomley, in his weekly *John Bull*, was only slightly less virulent than Billing. These two were joined by Leo Maxse, a long-time Germanophobe who continued to agitate against Germany in his *National Review* from 1914 to 1919. During the same years, the militant suffragettes transformed some of their passionate hostility into hatred of Germany. A National Party, formed in September 1917 by a small group of Conservative MPs, based part of their appeal on the "eradication of German influence."[9]

Antipathy for Germany was also expressed and stimulated by the daily newspaper press. Here genuine feeling against Germany was reinforced by the natural desire of each paper to have its own proper share of the enlarged reading public of the War years. At the center of this patriotic competition stood Lord Northcliffe, owner of *The Times* and *Daily Mail*, who had developed an almost psychopathic fear of German aliens and of German influence.[10] His *Daily Mail* drummed out a steady anti-German line, and other papers tried to keep its pace. *The Times*, though a finer instrument, gave the same lead.

Official propaganda against Germany began in January 1917, when the Lloyd George Government created the Department of Information. In March of the following year, the Department was transformed into a ministry, led by the contemporary Lords of the press, Beaverbrook, Northcliffe, and Rothermere. Talented writers such as H. G. Wells and John Buchan were on the staff and all available media, including films, were used by the Ministry. The character of its publications is suggested by two titles: a pamphlet, *A Corpse-Conversion Factory*, and a film, "Once a Hun Always a Hun."[11]

For several reasons, the anti-German temper did not recede at the end of the War, but instead reached a high pitch. The Ministry of Information, only recently established, was just reaching its full momentum in the summer and fall of 1918. Furthermore, on October 10, a needless U-boat attack in the Irish Sea revived British convictions of German barbarism. The sinking was of the mail packet, *Leinster*, which went down with the loss of 451 lives, all civilians. Coming seven days after the German request for an armistice, the attack appeared especially prefidious. Foreign Secretary Balfour, in a rare display of emotion, expressed the reaction of his countrymen: "Brutes they were when they began the war, and as far as we can judge, brutes they remain."[12] Another graphic reminder of German warfare was provided by the advance of the Allied armies into French and Belgian towns formerly occupied by the Germans. During the German retreat of summer and fall 1918, the British press carried daily pictures of destruction, allegedly the result of German policy.[13] *The Times* headline covering the entry of British troops into Lille was a typical response: "The Agony of Lille. Four Years of German Rule. Brutality and Plunder."[14]

The most important stimulus of anti-German sentiment in Britain at the end of the War was German mistreatment of prisoners-of-war. Germany held about 60,000 British prisoners in 1918. Most of these men had performed hard labor in Germany or behind the German lines, often in dangerous situations and without adequate food. As the German armies retreated in the fall of 1918, German authorities began to release their prisoners, and after the Armistice all were released, usually without transportation or provisions. Some of the British prisoners did not reach home until early 1919.

The British public and press showed the greatest interest in the returning prisoners-of-war. Local newspapers gave prominence to interviews with the men returning to their locality. The national press made the question a constant news item well into 1919. As the conditions under which the prisoners were released became widely known, newspapers and journals of all persuasions joined in outrage. *John Bull* spoke of "prisoner torturers" and cried for vengeance.[15] The *Daily Mail* described "Prisoners' Agony. Skeletons Drag Their Way Into France. Many dying on the Road. Demand for Hun Retribution."[16] The Radical weekly *Nation* added its voice to those of the jingo press, calling the conditions in which the prisoners-of-war were released the result of "stupid brutality."[17] A similar assessment appeared in *The Times*:

> Military and civil prisoners from Germany are flocking into France by all roads. Ten thousand are reported to be on their way to Paris.

Many of them, owing to their treatment, are in a state of deep physical and moral depression. Everyone of them is unanimous that no prisoners have been more shamefully and brutally treated than the English.[18]

On October 23, *The Times* called the prisoners-of-war "the subject nearest the heart of the House of Commons." On that day both the Unionist and the Liberal War Committees resolved a Commons debate on the question. During the subsequent debate on October 29, Captain C. C. Craig, Conservative MP for South Antrim, described his own captivity under the German "brutes." Other MPs, mostly Conservatives, demanded Government reprisals and the trial as war criminals of the Germans involved. The Home Secretary, Sir George Cave, agreed: "We have to take these people by the throat if we can and let the punishment given to them be an example for generations to come."[19]

The War Cabinet had already decided, on October 11, to warn Germany that if the abuses did not stop within 28 days, the British Government would take reprisals against German prisoners-of-war in Britain.[20] When the 28 days had elapsed, the War was nearly over and the reprisals were not taken. However, the British Government sent a further warning on November 20: If British prisoners-of-war were not released under better conditions, the British Government might refuse to send food relief to Germany.[21]

The prisoners-of-war question also promoted the idea of war crimes trials. The War Cabinet of October 11 decided to inform Germany " . . .that we would take all steps in our power to insist that the persons responsible for these outrages [against prisoners] should be punished for their misdeeds."[22] This demand was also taken up in the House of Commons and the press, and expanded to cover every kind of German misbehavior. Gradually attention focused on the Kaiser himself, who came to be regarded as the single instigator of the War. In October and November, a trial for the Kaiser and other German "war criminals" was demanded by periodicals as diverse as *John Bull*, on the right, and the *New Statesman*, on the left.[23] On November 15, the Leader of the Labour Party, Arthur Henderson, declared that the Allies should "begin at the top" in trying German war criminals.[24]

Meanwhile, the Government was considering definite steps in this direction. The prime movers were F. E. Smith, the Attorney General, who first suggested war crimes trials to the War Cabinet on October 17, and Lord Curzon, who emphasized the idea throughout October and November.[25] At the Imperial War Cabinet of November 20, Curzon called the Kaiser "the archcriminal of the world." Practical doubts about trying the German Emperor and his cohorts were dismissed by Lloyd George, who agreed with Curzon that William "ought to be tried for high treason against humanity." Consequently, the Imperial Cabinet agreed to ask the Law Officers of the Crown to study the possibility of such a trial.[26] Shortly thereafter, at the Allied London conference of December 2, the British and the French agreed that the peace conference should establish a tribunal for war crimes.[27]

In this way, concern about prisoners-of-war helped to introduce war crimes trials into British and Allied diplomacy. The same concern, along with the other grievances of the anti-German temper, encouraged the economic punishment of Germany. For example, a member of the Associated Chambers of Commerce who visited the Western Front in early October 1918, returned to tell his organization of "the atrocities which the Germans had committed" and to urge severe restrictions on German trade after the War. Consequently, the ACC resolved that imports of German goods into Britain should be prohibited for several years after the War and that "the conditions should be extremely drastic."[28] Likewise, in the October *Edinburgh Review*, editor Harold Cox surveyed the "crimes" Germany had committed and reaffirmed his wartime belief that free trade principles and the lure of profit were less important than the safety of the British market against German penetration and the need to penalize Germany economically. "It were better to remain poor for many decades rather than permit Germany to go unpunished."[29]

The parallel desires for economic protection and punishment played an important part in party politics and Government policy

at the end of the War. On October 5, Bonar Law wrote to Arthur
Balfour:

> The pressures to have a statement on our economic policy was
> almost irresistible before the House rose. Our Party were kept
> quiet by a promise of a statement immediately on the re-opening
> of Parliament and I am sure that there will be serious trouble if
> we are not prepared, as a Government, to say more than has yet
> been said as to the security of home markets after the war.[30]

Bonar Law judged correctly. When Parliament resumed on
October 16, a determined band of Conservatives began pressing
the Government for a statement of economic policy.[31] Privately,
Lloyd George and Bonar Law were encouraged to make such
a statement by Sir Edward Carson and by his friend and former
secretary of the Economic Offensive Committee, F. S. Oliver.[32]
On October 30, 69 members of the Unionist War Committee
adopted a set of resolutions for a "National Economic Policy"
which would alleviate the current uncertainty in business circles,
eliminate "undue foreign influence and dumping" after the war,
implement imperial preference, and provide for the rational
allocation of raw materials among the Allied countries.[33] A
deputation headed by the Marquis of Salisbury and Sir Edward
Carson was appointed to present these resolutions to the Chancellor of the Exchequer, Bonar Law.

Bonar Law and Lloyd George placated the Conservatives in
the formal election program the two leaders composed on November 2, 1918. This was later issued on November 18, in the form
of a public letter from the Prime Minister to the Leader of the
Conservative Party. The paragraph on economic policy was
the first substantive declaration in the program. In that paragraph, Lloyd George repeated his acceptance of imperial preference on existing and future duties, with the proviso that no
tariffs be levied on imported food stuffs. The Prime Minister
also agreed that "key industries" must be protected against
cheap imports, regardless of "theoretical opinions about Free
Trade or Tariff Reform."[34]

At a meeting of Conservative MPs and candidates on November 12, the economic paragraph was loudly cheered. Bonar Law
told the gathering that even if they were campaigning as an

independent party, they could not improve on the Coalition's economic statement. Sir Edward Carson also approved the paragraph, though in a more pragmatic way: "All that seems to me to be as far as we can expect those who follow Mr. Lloyd George to go."[35]

However, it is significant that the Coalition's formal economic program won the support of Conservatives without making reference to the Paris Economic Resolutions or to any other form of Allied economic cooperation. While the Government was definitely worried about Britain's postwar trade position, neither Lloyd George nor Bonar Law were inclined to revive the Paris Resolutions, especially after the verbal encounter with President Wilson in August and September. Also, just before the election campaign began in mid-November, the desire to punish Germany economically was being deflected into a new channel by the appearance of reparation and indemnity as popular issues. Direct compensation from Germany, though not mentioned in the formal program of November 18, soon became the Coalition's leading promise to the electorate.

The emergence of reparation and indemnity as major issues took place during the resurgent anti-German temper at the end of the War. From 1914 to 1918, the two ideas had been marginal, but in the early autumn of 1918 they began to gather popular support as part of the feeling that Germany must somehow "pay" for the way in which she had fought the War. For example, on October 25, the Lord Chancellor, Lord Finlay, gave a strong speech in which he recommended that war crimes trials and reparation be the two principal Allied peace aims.[36] Four days later, the *Daily Express* urged that Germany be made to pay reparation for each maltreated prisoner-of-war.[37] Later, during the election campaign, the connection between German misbehavior and reparation-indemnity became common. On December 6, the *Daily Telegraph* declared, "Germany must pay, and the bill will be colossal. She has willed it so . . . the Germans admitted no scruple. . . Every day that passes brings to light new German infamies."[38]

It was before the Election, however, in September and October, that the main themes of compensation were first explored widely and seriously. In those months, numerous voices were raised in

favor of reparation for damage done in invaded territories. Among
those who led in advocating reparation as an indispensable term
of peace were Attorney General F. E. Smith, Lord Northcliffe,
the *Daily Express* and the *Scotsman*.[39] At the same time, there
appeared a variety of advocates of German maritime reparation
on a ton-for-ton basis. The Germanophobe *Daily Mail* and *National Review* urged this; so did more restrained periodicals,
such as the *Observer* and the *Spectator*.[40] The British shipping
industry was naturally interested in the matter. On October 23,
1918, the Executive Council of the Chamber of Shipping formally
urged the Government to demand the surrender of the entire
German merchant fleet in the terms of peace and to restrict the
growth of German commercial shipping in the postwar years.[41]

The more ambitious idea that Germany should pay the cost
of the War was first proposed by ultra-patriotic journals and
groups. The most emphatic demand for a war costs indemnity
was made by Leo Maxse and the *National Review*. Throughout
1918, Maxse developed the themes of the large indemnity argument: Germany had been the aggressor and ought to pay; German
mineral resources alone were worth many times the Allied cost
of the War; a large indemnity would prevent further German
aggression.[42] In his October issue, Maxse reached a new level
of vehemence in arguing for an indemnity of at least forty billion
pounds sterling:

> . . . just as Germany makes the loser pay whenever she wins a
> war, so she will have to pay when she has lost. This is entirely in
> accordance with Anglo-Saxon ideals, of which the enemy is des-
> tined to hear more before the end. . . . The problem of ways and
> means is a domestic problem which the Germans may settle as they
> please. The Allies must have their pound of flesh.[43]

The first publication to join Maxse in his indemnity campaign was Horatio Bottomley's *John Bull*. In eary October,
Bottomley outlined the peace desired by the "people" as opposed
to the politicians:

> I don't want any more talk about not being out to destroy the Ger-
> man nation—that is just what I *am* out for. And so are you my dear
> reader—or you wouldn't have risked your life or that of someone

dear to you, or be mourning a son or brother or husband today. . . . We will begin, if you please, with that little matter of indemnity. . . We'll have an indemnity—if it takes a thousand years to pay it.[44]

Bottomley felt Germany should pay £10,000,000,000 and, like Maxse, was sure that German coal resources alone were sufficient for the purpose.

Aside from Maxse and Bottomley, there were only a few isolated proponents of indemnity before early November. On October 15, Lord Morris, an ex-Prime Minister of Newfoundland, made a speech in which he warned that a large indemnity was the only way to save the British taxpayer from heavy postwar burdens.[45] On the following day, a minor journalist, W. R. Lawson, published a pro-indemnity article in the *Daily Mail*.[46] In *The Times* of October 24, a letter to the Editor urged that Germany should indemnify Britain after repairing France and Belgium. Most important, the small group of Conservative MPs who called themselves the National Party placed the following advertisement in *The Times* on October 28:

GERMANY CAN PAY
GERMANY MUST PAY

GERMANY forced the war on the world. The crime of Germany has caused the deaths of millions and the crippling and maiming of millions more. She has also wantonly and unnecessarily inflicted great losses in treasure on civilization. Germany must restore the territories she has rendered desolate.

In defence of the world the British Empire has incurred a debt of £ 8,000,000,000.

Are our sons and daughters to carry this load of debt because of the criminal action of Germany?

Germany can pay. The Coal and Potash wealth of Germany alone is valued at £ 190,000,000,000.

THE NATIONAL PARTY, voicing the opinion of men and women of all Parties in the State, demands that Germany, and not our children, shall pay this debt. THE NATIONAL PARTY stands for this definite policy.[47]

This was the first prominent appearance of indemnity in a major daily newspaper.

In early November, the idea of indemnity began to gather momentum. On November 2 at the Albert Hall, Horatio Bottomley chaired a large rally which adopted Bottomley's program for "a people's peace."[48] On the same day, the *Daily Express* hinted at indemnity in proposing that "Germany must be made to pay for her sins: She must pay to the uttermost farthing."[49] On November 6, the *Evening Standard* said that "reparation" should include ". . . the very real damage represented by a high income tax, the increased cost of living, and the loss of the productive services of millions of men and women. In other words . . . indemnity in the fullest sense. . . ." A few days later, an *Evening Standard* columnist suggested a total German payment of £ 50,000,000,000: 25 billion for damages and 25 billion for war costs.[50]

So by the first week of November, the indemnity idea had advanced from the pages of a marginal journal into the leading articles of two daily newspapers and into the program of a small group of militant Conservative MPs. Then, on November 7 and 14, Prime Minister Hughes lent his authority to indemnity. Support by a major political figure provided further momentum. Moreover, just after Hughes' speeches, the election campaign got underway, providing a politically significant outlet for indemnity and the other punitive demands which had been produced by the prisoners-of-war issue, the sinking of the *Leinster*, the destruction on the Western Front, and all the previous frustration of war. At the end of November, the following was a common observation:

> Candidates and speakers say that the predominant feeling is that the peace terms must make the Germans pay heavily; must punish ruthlessly the Huns responsible for crime and cruelty; must send back to their own country the enemy aliens interned here, and must penalise the race for years to come. This sentiment is growing with the return of prisoners, who are now coming back in fairly large numbers.[51]

Equally common by the end of the month were assertions of German war guilt, such as that by Winston Churchill in an election speech at Dundee on November 26:

> Practically the whole German nation was guilty of the crime of aggressive war conducted by brutal and bestial means. It is no use their pretending that their late Government is solely to blame. They were all in it, and they must suffer for it.[52]

Here, clearly stated, was the most basic premise of the anti-German temper, a belief widely shared in Britain at the end of the War.

Nevertheless, there were a few men in all parties who dissented from the severe conclusions drawn from the premise of German war guilt. Most of these dissenters were in the Labour movement. Ramsay MacDonald, Philip Snowden, and other members of the Independent Labour Party continued their wartime campaign against international hatred into late 1918 and 1919. The *New Statesman* treated anti-aliens sentiment with disdain and sarcastic humor.[53] The Fabian George Bernard Shaw wrote a devastating public letter in which he scorned the tendency to make "police court cases out of the incidents of war." Shaw offered a different conception of peacemaking:

> When we break a German's leg with a bullet and then take him prisoner, we immediately set to work to mend his leg, to the astonishment of our idiots, who cannot understand why we do not proceed to break his other leg. We shall have to act on the same principle with the German nation. We have broken its back, and now we have to get its back mended again somehow. The alternative is to kill it, and that is not a practicable alternative.[54]

The Labour Party itself adopted an election manifesto which ignored indemnity, called for increased taxation to pay the cost of the War, and declared against "any form of economic war."[55]

Some Liberals also opposed a severe peace settlement. Liberals who remained faithful to free trade principles were as hostile as ever to economic war after the War. For example, in September, Herbert Samuel told the General Committee of the National Liberal Federation, "We will not continue the war by means of tariffs and boycotts. That is not the way to bring us a lasting peace."[56] As the War drew to a close, ex-Prime Minister Asquith tried to dissociate himself from the Paris Economic Resolutions. In late 1918, he argued that the Resolutions were wartime mea-

sures only, and irrelevant to postwar economic policy.[57] In
the House of Lords and in the daily letter columns, the Liberal
Lord Buckmaster urged caution in the matter of compensation.
During the election campaign, he wrote to Austen Chamberlain:

> I believe the people are being fed on the delusion that the burden
> of the war is going to be lifted from their back and put upon
> Germany. It is such an easy election cry to shout "make the Ger-
> mans pay"; but the mischief that will result when disillusionment
> comes may be far-reaching and serious.[58]

The most eloquent Liberal moderate was C. P. Scott, editor
of the *Manchester Guardian*. Scott was worried by the anti-
German temper, but in contrast to so many others, unafraid of
it. At the end of the War, he devoted much of his leader columns
to graceful pleas for a statesmanlike peace. Scott was especially
anxious that the Allies assist German democracy to a sound
beginning by granting moderate terms of peace. He argued
against a trial of the ex-Kaiser as an unnecessary irritant to Ger-
man-Allied relations.[59] On November 13, he defined his philosophy of peacemaking:

> After conquest must come self-conquest. That, be it said, is a task
> from which none of us is exempt, neither conqueror nor conquered.
> It was said by Prince Max, the flower surely of the old order, that
> in her defeat Germany had still triumphed since she had won a
> victory over herself and had at last learnt the hard lesson that right
> is greater than might. For us perhaps also the greatest triumph is
> yet in store, and it will be ours on the day when we shall have turned
> our military victory to its true and lasting account, and shall have
> buried the wrong and bitterness of the past. . . .[60]

As editor of the nation's most "respectable" Liberal paper, C. P.
Scott laid down a significant challenge to the anti-German temper.

Conservatives were conspicuous for their failure to dissent
from the anti-German mood or to urge moderate attitudes toward
Germany. However, on October 17, the *Evening Standard* prom-
inently displayed an interview with Lord Milner in which the
Secretary for War argued that the Allies should offer Germany
moderate terms of peace. Milner did not believe unconditional

surrender, which Lloyd George was then considering privately, to be worth any additional sacrifice of Allied manpower. Given the favorable military situation, Milner felt that an early armistice would equal victory and enable the Allies to achieve their essential aims. Not only was Germany beginning to recognize defeat, she was also beginning to reject "militarism" and "Prussianism" and Milner felt that the basic instincts of the German nation would continue in the direction of democracy. However, Milner warned that if the Allies talked of war crimes, economic penalties, and drastic territorial changes, they might stiffen Germany's will to resist or push her into a position vulnerable to a Bolshevik revolution. Referring obliquely to President Wilson's armistice diplomacy, Milner especially opposed attempts ". . . to dictate to Germany certain drastic changes in their own government. . . ."[61]

Milner's arguments were quickly attacked from both right and left. The same issue of the *Evening Standard* which carried the interview also included a leading article that disagreed with Milner point by point. Then Lord Northcliffe and his *Daily Mail* castigated the War Secretary for "letting the Hun off."[62] William Morris Hughes sarcastically criticized Milner's concern for Germany's political self-determination.[63] Meanwhile, from the left, Milner was attacked by the *New Statesman* for interfering with President Wilson's attempts to dislodge the Kaiser.[64] In the House of Commons, two Radical Liberals, W. M. R. Pringle and Josiah Wedgwood, called Milner pro-German and "soft" on the Hohenzollerns.[65]

Milner was characteristically surprised at the amount of criticism his interview provoked. He wrote to his private secretary complaining that he had been misinterpreted. He was as anxious as anyone for the demise of the Hohenzollerns, he said, but the Germans themselves must accomplish it. "Certainly they [the Germans] will not be converted by the fulminations of men, who in the same breath that they denounce the Hohenzollerns, also denounce the whole German nation, represent them as monsters of iniquity, etc., etc."[66] Milner also continued to fear that anti-German rhetoric would jeopardize the prospect of an armistice.

The episode of the Milner interview illustrates why dissent

and moderation were weak forces in the debate over Germany in 1918. Dissenters and moderates were too divided over other issues to unite against a punitive peace. The perspectives from which Milner and the *New Statesman*, for example, criticized the anti-German temper were too divorced. Also, there was no strong and popular politician who could lead a campaign for moderation. Asquith's appeal had dwindled by the end of the War and he vacillated about peacemaking. Lord Milner declared for moderation, but he was no man to lead in popular or party politics. He himself recognized this:

> When it comes to settling terms of peace, it is certain that, unless the present hysteria has subsided, I shall feel myself more out of touch with prevalent opinion as represented by the Press than ever. And as I am certainly not going to join hands with the Ramsay MacDonald crowd, I think my chances for a long holiday are improving.[67]

Moreover, there were two further reasons for the weakness of dissent and moderation: the real difficulty of restraining a patriotic emotion and the disabling assumption that the public mood would soon pass.

In fact, by late 1919 the anti-German temper had passed, but in the meantime it had important effects on the Election and on the composition of Parliament, and it placed limits around British diplomacy. At the Peace Conference, Lloyd George was to show that these limits could be pushed outward somewhat, but he also knew that they could not be altogether ignored.

Chapter 8 THE GENERAL ELECTION

IN THE summer of 1918, there were several compelling reasons for an early general election: The House of Commons did not represent current political circumstances; it had been elected in 1910 and was extended three years beyond its five-year term because of the War. Also, the franchise of 1910 was superseded by the Representation of the People Act of June 1918, which more than doubled the electorate by easing residential requirements and granting the vote to women over thirty. Furthermore, the late summer advance of the Allies on the Western Front promised an end of war and, likewise, a safe opportunity to resume party controversy. Most important, the improving military situation enabled the Coalition Government to appeal to the people as the Government that had won the War.

Electoral Arrangements

In July 1918, Coalition Conservatives and Liberals began to make private preparations for an election.[1] They continued planning until early November. Then, on November 2, with an armistice definitely in prospect, Lloyd George and Bonar Law agreed on a formal election program. Three days later, the Prime Minister secured the agreement of the King to a dissolution of Parliament for the purpose of a general election.[2] On November 12, Lloyd George and Bonar Law won the consent of

121

their respective followers to an election and to the program drafted on November 2. The Government formally announced on November 14 that Parliament would be dissolved on November 25. The Coalition program was published on November 18 and serious campaigning began, though many politicians did not face their constituents until the last week of November. The Prime Minister, for example, opened his campaign on November 23 at Wolverhampton. The poll was to be taken on December 14, but the results were not to be known until December 28, because of absentee voting.

The decision to hold an election was accompanied by a decision to extend into peacetime the alliance between Conservatives and Lloyd George Liberals established in December 1916. There was some reluctance about this on both sides of the Coalition,[3] but there is no evidence that either Lloyd George or Bonar Law considered breaking away from the other. The two leaders, although so different in temperament, had developed a close mutual respect and trust by the end of the War. Furthermore, each realized that the other was indispensable to electoral success. As Bonar Law explained to Conservative MPs and candidates on November 12:

> By our own action we have made Mr. Lloyd George the flag bearer of the very principles on which we should appeal to the country. (Hear, hear) It is not his Liberal friends, it is the Unionist Party which made him Prime Minister, (cheers) and made it possible for him to do the great work which has been done by this government. (Hear, hear) . . . If there is to be a coalition it must not be all on one side. Remember this, that in my belief at this moment Mr. Lloyd George commands an amount of influence in every constituency as great as has ever been exercised by any Prime Minister in our political history. (Hear, hear)[4]

Lloyd George was, indeed, as widely popular as a Prime Minister had ever been, but only about 100 of the 260 Liberal MPs in Parliament supported him and he had no well established organization in the constituencies.[5] The Conservatives, on the other hand, were the best organized political party and held 282 seats in the Commons, but no Conservative approached having the electoral appeal of Lloyd George. In these circumstances, coalition made eminent sense.

Lloyd George and Bonar Law also hoped to widen the Coalition into a government of national unity through the electoral cooperation of the Independent Liberals and the Labour Party. On September 24, 1918, with Bonar Law's approval, Lloyd George offered Asquith the Lord Chancellorship and eight other offices for Asquith's followers if the ex-prime minister would join the Government in calling an election and would agree to conscription for Ireland and the exclusion of Ulster from home rule. However, the feud between the two great Liberal leaders had gone too far. Two days after the offer was made, Asquith refused it and the official Liberal Party remained in opposition.[6]

The Coalition also failed to enlist the cooperation of the Labour Party, even though a Labour representative had been included in the War Cabinet since December 1916, and Labour had been granted several secondary ministerial offices. Despite these concessions, the Labour Party, under the skilled guidance of Arthur Henderson, had moved steadily away from the Coalition. Just before the election campaign, on November 14, an Emergency Conference of the Party severed the last ties with the Coalition by requiring Labour men in office to resign. Several Labourites refused to comply, enabling the Coalition to form its own labour group, which enjoyed a modest success in the Election.[7] Nevertheless, the independence of the official Labour Party, and of the Liberal Party, meant the Election would definitely be contested.

Whether contested or not, the coming election presented the Coalition with the major problem of all electoral coalitions: how to divide constituencies. After much bargaining, the party managers agreed in late October that Lloyd George Liberals should be the official Coalition candidates in 150 of the 602 divisions in England, Scotland, and Wales.[8] This would clear the way for Conservatives in 350 to 400 of the remaining constituencies. The bargain naturally disappointed many prospective candidates and local associations, but it nevertheless reflected the balance of assets in the Coalition with fair accuracy. Otherwise, F. E. Guest and Bonar Law would not have described the agreement with such private satisfaction as this:

> I have come to an agreement with Mr. Bonar Law that we should receive their support, where necessary, for 150 Lloyd George Candi-

dates, 100 of whom are our old Guard. This request was generously
acceeded [sic] to by Mr. Bonar Law . . .

As a matter of fact as the net result we have 400 conservative candidates: he [Lloyd George] has less than 150, and if we win the election the result will certainly be the return of a much larger number
of Conservatives than we could reasonably have expected if we had
been fighting the battle on our own account.[9]

Closely related to the private allocation of constituencies was
the problem of publicly designating Coalition candidates. This
was especially necessary because of the confusing party situation
in November 1918. Each of the three major parties contained both
supporters of the Coalition and an independent wing.[10] Also,
there were a host of minor parties and candidates.[11] In these
conditions, Coalition leaders were naturally anxious to indicate
publicly who were and who were not their supporters.

They chose to do this by sending brief public letters of support
to candidates they approved. These letters were derisively compared to ration coupons, first by Asquith and then by other
Coalition opponents; hence the Coupon Election of 1918. The
derision was in answer to Lloyd George's claim that coupons
were sent to men who had patriotically supported the Government during the War and denied to those who had not. The
Commons debate of May 9, 1918, over the veracity of the Government's military figures, the "Maurice debate," was especially
advertised by the Coalition as the test it had applied.[12] However, the connection between the Maurice debate and the coupons
was not so intimate as the Government maintained. While the
debate of May 9 and similar Parliamentary debates may have
determined whether coupons were sent or denied to a minority
of Liberal candidates, the majority of all Liberal and other party
candidates had not voted on May 9, and there were significant
exceptions to the Maurice criterion in the distribution of coupons
to those who had voted.[13] In fact, the main criterion for coupons
was simply the private bargain in constituencies: In close conformity with that bargain, coupons were sent to 364 Conservatives, 159 Liberals, and 18 National Democrats.[14] The Maurice
debate was brought in primarily to give this distribution a patriotic flavor and to justify the proscription of some of Asquith's
followers who also claimed to be supporters of the Government.[15]

Along with constituencies and coupons, the Coalition managers carefully considered issues.[16] Apparently they thought the public anti-German temper would soon disappear, since their plans were to deal with well-established domestic concerns: tariff policy, Irish home rule, social reform, and the Church of England in Wales. The Coalition program of November 2, drafted by Bonar Law and agreed to by Lloyd George, attempted to adjust Conservative-Liberal differences about these matters. As previously mentioned, the program pledged imperial preference, with the reservation that there be no tariff on food and that no duties be enacted for the special purpose of granting imperial preference. The Government reaffirmed its commitment to Irish home rule, but ruled out the coercion of Ulster. Social reform was glossed over with a vague promise of "plenty of opportunity to all." The Church of England was to be dis-established in Wales, but there was a dim promise that the state would assist the Church in making the financial adjustment.[17] Thus, on each point there was compromise, although the program on the whole leaned toward the position of the stronger Coalition partner, the Conservatives.

However, Coalition leaders understood very well that formal pledges do not make election campaigns successful. They intended to appeal to the country mainly on the basis of their effective prosecution of the War and their superior ability to guide Britain through the difficulties of reconstruction. Lloyd George's Chief Whip advised him to fight the election with this theme.[18] Likewise, Bonar Law and Arthur Balfour agreed that the Conservative Party "on the old lines will never have any future in this country."[19] Balfour hoped that the Coalition might become a permanent national party, despite the absention of the Asquith Liberals and Labour.[20] Consequently, the Coalition's formal program was purposely written in the language of national unity:

> The problems with which we shall be faced immediately on the cessation of hostilities . . . cannot . . . be dealt with without disaster on party lines. It is vital that the national unity which has made possible victory in the War should be maintained until at least the main foundations of national and international reconstruction have been securely laid.[21]

In his early speeches, Lloyd George expanded this argument to cast doubt upon the loyalty of the wartime Parliamentary opposition and to question the necessity of opposition during reconstruction.[22]

After the Armistice, the Prime Minister developed a similar theme. In justifying his call for an election, he said, "We must get the mandate immediately. Somebody will have to go to the Peace Conference with authority from the people of this country to speak in their name."[23] Lloyd George did not define his specific peace aims, but on November 12, he told a meeting of Liberals that his diplomacy would not be based on revenge or greed.[24] Two days later, he urged the Allied Governments and peoples not to ". . . behave like small men: Let us have no vengeance, no trampling down of a fallen foe."[25] However, the language of restraint soon all but disappeared from Coalition platforms. As the campaigning got underway, Coalition leaders and candidates discovered that they had failed to anticipate the most important issues, those of the anti-German temper, which seemed to flourish in the midst of an otherwise sluggish election.

The Campaign

"I have never seen so much listlessness in connection with any election," remarked Christopher Addison, the Minister of Reconstruction, after a tour of his constituency in east London.[26] The observation was a common one during an election in which only 58.3 percent of the electorate in contested divisions voted, the lowest turnout in twentieth-century British history. There are a number of explanations for the apathy: war weariness combined with a psychological let down about national affairs after the celebration of the Armistice; the large number of soldiers and war industry workers who were discouraged by the nuisance of absentee voting; confusion produced by the unusual number and variety of candidates; perhaps timidity or ignorance on the part of newly enfranchised voters, who numbered approximately 13,000,000 in an electorate of just over 21,000,000; the inefficiency of the new electoral registers; the rampant influenza, which discouraged all gatherings, electoral and other.

Another important reason for the apathy was the obvious fact that there was to be no close contest between the Coalition and its opponents. The independent Liberals were disheartened by the divisions in their party and lacking a spirited leader. They spent much of their energy in futile denials of the necessity of an election, bickering about the injustice of the coupon, defending their wartime record, and generally responding to Coalition initiatives. Their program of traditional Liberalism seemed outworn. Furthermore, some "independent" Liberals claimed they were Government supporters, trying in this way to associate themselves with the Coalition Juggernaut. Even Asquith himself said on several occasions that there was little difference between himself and Lloyd George.[27] The official Liberals did not present a distinct or attractive alternative to the electors.

Labour, on the other hand, did offer a clear socialist alternative and the Party fielded over 300 candidates, seriously contesting a general election for the first time. Acute contemporaries recognized that this was historic. Yet no one, least of all Labour themselves, dreamed of a Labour Party victory. The Party was financially inferior, in need of experienced candidates, and facing a widespread assumption that Labour could not govern. Moreover, Labour would not seek an alliance with the Asquith Liberals, who, in any case, made no serious offer. The programs of the two parties had become too divorced after Labour's adoption of "the common ownership of the means of production" as a party object in June 1918. The heyday of "Lib-Lab" cooperation was over. Separately, neither Labour nor the official Liberals could provide the drama of a close election.

The absence of such drama had two effects: First, it opened the door to emotional issues that had a seemingly non-partisan, patriotic appeal, such as those of the anti-German temper. Thus, Christopher Addison, who found his district listless, also told a reporter that he was "struck" by his constituents' determination to try the ex-Kaiser and expel German aliens from Britain.[28] Second, the absence of a close contest encouraged press and electors to focus their attention on the governing party and especially on the Prime Minister, the most exciting orator of the day.

The Coalition campaign began on November 18, with the publication of the Lloyd George-Bonar Law program, which was supplemented thereafter by a series of brief manifestos. The first manifesto, given to the press on November 21, repeated the themes of the formal program, referred vaguely to "a just and lasting peace," and added a Government commitment to social benefits for returning servicemen.[29] The Prime Minister opened his campaign with the same ideas, in an address at Wolverhampton on November 23. There it was that he said Britain must become "a land fit for heroes." Reconstruction was the great task and he reminded one questioner that there must be no diversions from it:

> *A voice*—Are you in favour of getting the Germans out of the country?
> *Mr. Lloyd George*: Well, we have had quite enough of them. But you really must allow me to deal with one problem at a time. That may be a very important question, but it is simply a side issue, I can tell you, compared with these big and vast problems. Don't let us be drawn after "stunts." (laughter and cheers) . . . I am all in favour of excluding these people, but if you exclude them all, every one, you will still have to face these great problems.[30]

Other Coalition leaders must also have thought anti-German sentiment "a side issue," given the omission of any appeal to that sentiment in their early programs.

However, at the same time, several important newspapers were beginning to advocate punitive terms of peace. On November 21, *The Times* warned Germany that the terms of the Armistice "may be considerably stiffened in the final document." Six days later, in commenting on the possibility that the German Empire might fall apart, *The Times* said:

> Germany sinned as a whole, she has been beaten as a whole; she will have to negotiate as a whole and to submit as a whole to the terms dictated to her. We are not going to negotiate with chaos.[31]

Meanwhile, the other major Northcliffe paper, the *Daily Mail*, continued its wartime campaign for the exclusion of German aliens. On November 27, its leading article said the "test for candidates" should be "no tenderness to the Hun" on the issues of a trial for the ex-Kaiser, enemy aliens, reparation and indemnity.

Three other influential dailies were moving in the same direction. On November 22, the *Morning Post* asked:

> What, by the way, is the policy of the Coalition on this question of an indemnity? That is a question which the electors should put to their candidates, and especially to the leaders of the parties who are now dividing the electoral coat between them. It seems to us that Mr. Lloyd George, Mr. Asquith, and Mr. Ramsay Macdonald are now in agreement on this subject. None of them porposes to exact an indemnity from Germany for any part of the great loss and damage she has caused to this country.[32]

The *Evening Standard* was also discontented. On November 25, its leading article criticized Lloyd George for calling the aliens question a side issue; several days later the paper began to campaign for a clear Government declaration on the ex-Kaiser, aliens, and indemnity issues.[33] On November 28, the most prominent newspaper in Scotland, the *Scotsman* of Edinburgh, also approved an anti-German election campaign:

> Germany must pay the full penalty. So far as the electoral campaign has gone, a practically unanimous feeling has manifested itself among all candidates in favour of stern dealing with Germany. Further contact with the electorate will confirm this feeling. Candidates will find that they can scarcely put the terms too high for the constituencies.[34]

The *Scotsman's* prediction that constituents would enliven candidates proved accurate. Addison's surprise at anti-German sentiment in east London was experienced by candidates in many other divisions. For example, in West Birmingham, Austen Chamberlain first defined his position on indemnity in response to questions from his audience.[35] In another Birmingham district, Leo Amery made no mention of the anti-German issues in his formal address to electors, but in his first speeches he began to condemn German war crimes and warn about German economic aggression. Just after the campaign, Amery wrote in his diary:

> My experience, like that of most, was that I began talking a good deal about reconstruction and found the people much more concerned with the terms of peace. Whether they will get all they think

> they will get is another story, but at any rate our representatives
> at the Conference will be less timid about making demands either
> for indemnities or for German colonies.[36]

Sir Alfred Mond, Coalition Liberal candidate for Swansea, was
also caught unawares. Privately, he wrote that his long residence
in London during the War had put him out of touch with the
anti-German feeling of his constituents.[37] This was also true
of many others. The press of war work in London and the eight
years which had passed since the last election caused many candidates, especially Coalition incumbents, to misjudge the public
temper.

This was pointed out time and again by the journals that
favored a punitive peace. Leo Maxse's *National Review* charged
that the Coalition was ignorant of the peace terms wanted by
"the man in the street."[38] Lloyd George was especially criticized.
On November 28, a leading article in the *Evening Standard*
said that the country expected the Prime Minister to give "a
plain answer" to the questions of war crimes, aliens, and indemnity.

Lloyd George apparently noticed this expectation. Also, the
political relevance of indemnity was made clear to him by the
Imperial War Cabinet discussion of November 26, and the appointment on that day of the Hughes Committee on Indemnity
must have lessened his fears about raising hopes for large German payments. Thus, in his second major address, at Newcastle
on November 29, the Prime Minister moved toward the anti-
German position.

His personal notes for the Newcastle speech began:

> Deal at this meeting with all controversial matters.
> War Indemnity.
> Exclusion from amongst us of a people who abused our hospi-
> tality to spy on us and to plot against us.
> Personal responsibility of the Kaiser for the crime and the crimes
> of the war.[39]

Early in the speech itself he proclaimed, "It must be a just peace,
a sternly just peace (loud cheers), a relentlessly just peace (renewed
cheers)." Lloyd George kept the enthusiasm alive by reviewing
the perfidies of enemy aliens and asking if such persons could

be tolerated any longer. Answering his own rhetorical question, he cried, "Never again! (Mr. Lloyd George here banged the table in front of him and the audience cheered vociferously)." Then he proceeded to reduce reparation and indemnity to the simplicity of a court case. Germany had lost the War and, like the defeated litigant ". . . must pay the costs of the war up to the limit of her capacity to do so (renewed cheers)." He said the Government had ". . . set up a strong Committee to consider the question of the capacity of the German Empire." However much Germany could pay, the Prime Minister warned that the method of payment must not be the "dumping" of German goods on the British market. Lloyd George concluded his remarks on peacemaking by reminding his audience that Germany had started the War and waged it with barbaric methods, such as the maltreatment of prisoners-of-war. The Government, he revealed, intended to arrange a trial of the ex-Kaiser for these offences.[40]

Like the audience at Newcastle, most of the press reacted favorably to the Prime Minister's remarks. *The Times* Parliamentary correspondent called them "the first touch of realism in the campaign."[41] The *Morning Post* was worried about silent reservations, but thought Lloyd George had "showed himself properly sensitive to the temper of the nation."[42] The Sunday *Observer* agreed:

> Now, on these points [German war crimes], the plain people amongst the Allies feel more profoundly than those who do not move habitually amongst them can realize. When Mr. Lloyd George spoke to his Northern audience upon bringing the Kaiser to justice and making Germany pay to the utmost of her capacity, he suddenly found that deep was calling unto deep.[43]

Only the *Evening Standard* and the *Daily Mail* were critical. The *Standard* wanted a less qualified assurance of indemnity.[44] The *Daily Mail* believed Lloyd George was still "wobbling" on the anti-German issues:

> He began to make his retrieve yesterday. But on the only questions the electors are asking he is still vague . . .
> Is Germany to pay up?
> Are all the Huns to be sent out and kept out?
> Is the Kaiser to be surrendered? . . .

It is not for us to question her capacity. Germany had no consideration for the capacity of France in 1871. There was never
a question of Germany's capacity to make the war. There should
be no question from our side of her capacity to pay for it.[45]

The *Daily Mail* continued hectoring the Prime Minister throughout the campaign.

Despite the dissatisfaction of the most anti-German journals,
the speech of November 29 was the major turning point of the
campaign. Thereafter the anti-German issues became respectable
by virtue of having been the centerpiece of a speech by the Prime
Minister. Not until Lloyd George had spoken on war crimes,
aliens, and indemnity were these matters taken up by several
leading newspapers, such as the *Daily Telegraph*, the *Birmingham Post*, and the *Glasgow Herald*.[46] More important, many
candidates, especially Coalitionists, took their cue from the Prime
Minister. The *Morning Post* noted this with approval:

Following on the Prime Minister's declaration on Friday, Coalition candidates for Parliament are making the demand for the
Kaiser's trial practically an election "cry," and it is significant that
in no case has it yet failed to appeal to an audience.[47]

Conservatives, in particular, switched to the anti-German issues
after November 29. On December 4, the Conservative Central
Office did a study of recent reports from Conservative agents
in 144 constituencies. The study showed that the various election
issues were referred to as leading issues with the following
frequency:

132—Full indemnities and reparation from Germany.
107—Punishment for the Kaiser and other responsible persons
in Germany.
102—Repatriation and exclusion of enemy aliens.
69—Adequate pensions and allowances for soldiers and sailors
and their dependents.
45—Housing reform.
29—Agricultural reform.
25—Safeguarding British industries against unfair competition
and prevention of dumping.[48]

By December 4, reconstruction and the wartime concern about

trade competition had given way to anti-German terms of peace in many divisions. From November 29 until December 14, the latter issues were the main concern of most Coalition candidates.

Coalition manifestos moved in the same direction. That of December 5 gave priority to the prosecution of the ex-Kaiser and his "accomplices," to the expulsion of enemy aliens, and to ". . . the principle that the Central Powers must pay the cost of the War up to the limit of their capacity."[49] The last Coalition manifesto, of December 11, was more succinct:

1. Punish the Kaiser.
2. Make Germany pay.
3. Get the soldier home as quickly as possible.
4. Fair treatment to the returned soldier and sailor.
5. Better housing and better social conditions.[50]

Three days before the polling, the Coalition managers continued to give the anti-German issues precedence over social reforms.

However, many prominent Coalitionists made an important distinction between the three anti-German issues: they used more restraint in their remarks on indemnity than on war crimes and aliens. As previously mentioned, Winston Churchill denounced the entire German nation as guilty of war and yet cautioned his audience that Germany could pay no more than £ 2,000,000,000 reparation. George Barnes, labour member of the War Cabinet, discriminated in a similar way. On November 29, at Netherton, he created a notorious slogan when he said, "I am for hanging the Kaiser."[51] On the other hand, he told his constituents in Glasgow that Germany would never be able to pay a significant indemnity.[52] Likewise, F. E. Smith, the Conservative Attorney General, was emphatic about a trial for the ex-Kaiser and expelling German aliens, but he also reminded an audience that Belgium and France had claims to German compensation prior to those of Britain.[53]

The most prominent Coalition leader to caution the electorate was Bonar Law. The Chancellor of the Exchequer was less concerned with the indemnity agitation than with Britain's fundamental economic problems. By late 1918, British investors had sold the major part of their foreign securities; Britain's gold

reserves had fallen to £ 100,000,000, about one-sixth those of
the United States; the British Government owed the United
States approximately £ 1,000,000,000 and was still spending
£ 7,000,000 daily; much of the British merchant marine had been
lost during the War.[54] The last problem might be lessened by
reparation, but Bonar Law seems to have had little hope that a
German indemnity would be available to help solve the others.
Aware of the "A" Division's pessimism and a careful man by
nature, he chose not to raise expectations. On December 11, at
Mile End, he said that reparation was an imperative necessity,
but warned that the Allies had no certain evidence that Germany
could pay more than reparation. He went on to remark that
whatever Germany could pay, "It would be holding out hopes
which I do not believe if I say they could pay our whole war
debt."[55] That the Chancellor of the Exchequer and Leader of
the Conservatives chose to restrain hopes was significant, though
not generally noticed because Bonar Law's speech was eclipsed
by the Prime Minister's address at Bristol on the same day. However, Law's restraint was not lost upon C. P. Scott, who later
wrote, ". . . the Tory leaders have been careful in their handling
of the 'Make Germany Pay' cry."[56]

Care was also exercised by the major newspapers that supported the Coalition: the *Daily Express*, the *Daily Telegraph*,
the *Observer*, the *Scotsman*, the *Birmingham Post*, the *Daily
Chronicle*, and the *Glasgow Herald*.[57] A leading article in the
Scotsman of December 2 was typical of how the Coalition press
tempered expectations:

> One thing is certain: Germany cannot meet the bill at once. This
> debt can only be settled either in gold which she does not possess
> in near sufficient quantity, or in produce which will require time
> to realise. Many people in this country apparently do not recog-
> nise this fact. Carried away by righteous indignation, they advo-
> cate a policy which, if carried to a logical conclusion, would
> prevent our obtaining any material satisfaction whatever.

A sense of the economic complications of reparation and, especially, of indemnity prevailed in Coalition newspapers.

These complications also inhibited many Coalition leaders.
As men who were ministers, or likely to be ministers, they knew

the dangers of encouraging simple hopes about complex problems. Furthermore, they knew that compensation by Germany
was an international matter: British peacemakers would have
to take the policies of the United States and France into account,
as well as the wishes of the electorate. Compensation also promised to be a continuing diplomatic question, while the war crimes
and aliens issues had the aspect of a temporary hysteria. Emphatic statements about war crimes and aliens were less likely
to result in embarrassing commitments than promises of large
payments from Germany.

It may be, too, that the Coalition was somewhat restrained
by certain criticisms advanced by the main opposition parties.
Lloyd George later claimed that reparation and indemnity
aroused "no distinction between Government and anti-Govern-
ment candidates,"[58] but this was not true. Many independent
Liberals abstained from the agitation for anti-German terms of
peace.[59] Their Leader adhered to "reparation only" for most
of the campaign. At Nottingham on December 10, Asquith said
that to demand more than reparation would place Germany
under an odious servitude. He reminded his audience ". . . that
in any future settlement of Europe and of the world, a place must
be found for our old enemies, as well as for our old friends."[60]

Liberal journals were more pungent and direct in criticizing
the anti-German issues and the Coalition. In the *Manchester
Guardian*, C. P. Scott treated the last Coalition manifesto with
high ridicule:

> We venture to say that in no election within living memory have
> the issues . . . been so paltry, or the mode of their presentation
> been so reckless and vulgar . . . if the Prime Minister has not
> incited he has at least done nothing to restrain the cheap violence
> of his followers. . . . The whole faith of the good Georgian
> . . . is summed up in five brief sentences, and the first two are
> "Punishment for the Kaiser" and "Make Germany Pay." Thus
> are the nations to be regenerated.[61]

Scott and other Liberal editors especially derided the expectation
that Germany could pay more than reparation. A. G. Gardiner,
partisan editor of the Liberal *Daily News*, held the apostate
Lloyd George personally responsible for encouraging false

hopes.[62] One of the better provincial dailies, the Liberal *Nottingham Journal and Express*, said that advocates of indemnity were merely trying to save business wealth from high taxation.[63] The influential *Economist*, which generally favored the Liberals, supported reparation but condemned indemnity as a contravention of the Armistice and the Fourteen Points. On polling day, the *Economist* characterized the campaign as:

> . . . a pretty ending to a war for liberty and justice.
> . . . The gentlemen who are now doing their best to demoralise an economically ignorant public will have a sweet time when they try to fulfill their promises. This is especially so on the subject of collecting an indemnity from Germany.[64]

The weekly *Nation* simply called the indemnity agitation "a farrago of nonsense."[65]

The most effective criticism of indemnity, and other punitive terms of peace, was raised by the Labour Party. Labour's first manifesto, of November 28, opposed the extension of conscription into peacetime;[66] Labour candidates frequently pointed out that a harsh peace would make such conscription inevitable, in the form of an army of occupation. On December 7, in an article in the Labour *Herald*, H. N. Brailsford applied this logic to demands for a large indemnity.[67] The same argument was then taken up by the Liberal press, in leading articles in the *Manchester Guardian* on December 10, and in the *Daily News* on December 12. The election day issue of the *Nation* was entitled, "Peace or Conscription?" There is no doubt that this last minute furor over conscription made some impression on the Coalition; hence, in the last Coalition manifesto, the insertion of "get the soldier home" as a third point after "make Germany pay." Coalition candidates, including the Prime Minister, quickly made similar assurances to the war-weary public.

The Wilsonian character of the Labour campaign may also have reminded the Coalition not to promise terms of peace that would prevent cooperation with the United States at the peace conference. Labour's foreign policy platform derived from the *Memorandum on War Aims*, adopted by the Party in December 1917. This was an almost total commitment to the "new diplomacy" advocated by President Wilson and by Western liberals and socialists.[68] The *Memorandum* was incorporated into *Labour and the New Social Order*, the formal program of the Party, adopted in June 1918; and it was the basis for Labour's election manifestos, which called for "a peace of reconciliation," founded on open diplomacy, international economic cooperation, national self-determination, and the League of Nations.[69] Most Labour candidates and the Labour press urged these objectives rather than a punitive peace.[70] Shortly after the election, the *New Statesman* said indemnity was "electioneering claptrap" which would be dispelled by the arrival of President Wilson.[71]

While Coalition leaders were criticized and perhaps inhibited by the Liberals and Labour, they also faced contrary attempts to "ginger up" their view of peacemaking. The most important of these was the spontaneous expression of anti-German sentiment by electors, which, as previously discussed, was frequently reported by candidates, agents, and newspapers. In addition, there were more specific pressures for punitive terms of peace, and, in particular, for a large indemnity.

From the chauvinistic right, *John Bull*, the *National Review*, and the National Party continued throughout the campaign to scream for a Carthaginian peace. Their influence, however, was not as considerable as their rhetoric. Although they had helped to instigate the anti-German temper, their appeals were adopted and modified by major party candidates during the election campaign and, consequently, their audience dwindled. That was the main reason why the National Party were only able to elect two of their twenty-four candidates.

A more important anti-German pressure was exerted by those who feared deficit spending and high taxation. From 1914 through 1918, the British Government had spent about £ 9,000,000,000. To meet this vast expenditure, new taxes had been created and the income tax had been raised from about one shilling in the pound in 1914 to an average of six shillings in 1918. Nevertheless, increased taxation had only defrayed 28 percent of the wartime expenses; the remainder had been financed by borrowing overseas, principally in the United States, and at home. The domestic borrowing was significant: whereas only 345,000 persons held Government securities before the War, there were approximately 17,000,000 holders of Government war bonds by the end of 1918.[72] Thus, an unprecedented number of private citizens felt at least a small stake in the Government's financial situation, which may help to explain some of the popular interest in the economic terms of peace.

The failure of taxation to keep pace with wartime borrowing had saddled the Government with over £ 6,000,000,000 of debt by December 1918. According to the financial canons of the day, this debt had to be reduced quickly and, if possible, eliminated. A traditional way to do this was to curtail public spending. However, with an election campaign in progress, only a few Conservatives and Liberals were forthright enough to propose this; to do so might mean postponement of the social services and reforms implied in "reconstruction" and "a land fit for heroes." Another obvious way to reduce debt was through continued high and progressive taxation. This was Labour's remedy. The Labour manifesto of December 13, in conformity with the Party's formal program, declared, "Capital has not suffered in the War. The rich must pay for the war (1) by heavier taxation of big incomes, (2) by a levy on capital, with exemption up to £ 1,000. . . ."[73]

Labour's proposal was, of course, anathema to the rich themselves, to businessmen, to most Conservatives, and to many Liberals. They searched for other solutions, such as an adjustment of international war debts. A columnist in the *Evening Standard* expressed the hopes of many when he wrote:

> It is obvious that if every country shoulders its own war debts the advantage will be with those who have sacrificed less. For example, if we have a war debt ten times *per capita* that of America our industry will be immensely handicapped as against American competition. If Germany cannot pay the whole war debt the only just alternative would seem to be a pooling of liabilities by all the Allies, so that each population bears its fair share of a burden incurred for the advantage of all.[74]

Bonar Law suggested a similar adjustment in his public interview with Edward Marshall in early November, noted above. Herbert Gibbs privately represented the same hope in the discussions of the Hughes Committee. In each case, the focus was on the United States, which had become the center of international finance. America's comparatively small sacrifice of lives and her wartime economic growth, both resented in Britain at the end of the War, seemed to oblige the United States to be financially generous after the War, especially in the matter of war debts. During the election campaign this reasoning offered a modest hope for relief from the national debt; during the peace conference, it became an important, though frustrated, argument of British diplomacy.

Indemnity from Germany was more widely and hopefully proposed as an alternative to debt and taxation. The most ardent proponents were the Federation of British Industries, the Associated Chambers of Commerce, the *Morning Post*, and the *Daily Mail*. The *Daily Mail* frequently warned that "the people should realise that if the Germans are not made to pay, then the employers and workers of this country will be put under bondage for a century in order that they may become debt-free."[75] The *Morning Post*, which styled itself a spokesman of business, used similar but more deliberate arguments: ". . . with an indemnity paid by a foreign nation there would at any rate be an addition to the actual resources of the country, which would not be the case in any levy on home capital."[76]

However, it was the business organizations which were most anxious to substitute indemnity for taxation. Lloyd George received an early expression of business opinion on November 7, when Sir Vincent Caillard, a prominent member of the FBI, wrote to him urging the Government to claim an indemnity for all war costs, including pensions.[77] During the heat of the campaign, the FBI notified Bonar Law that they had formed a committee of prominent industrialists, headed by Caillard, to study peace aims. On December 12, this committee produced a long "Memorandum on Peace Aims," which they sent to Bonar Law on the following day. The premise of their document was:

> Unless the enemy countries pay, the burden will have to be borne by this country in the form of immensely increased taxation for many years to come. This taxation, however ingeniously its incidence may be devised, must like all other taxation, fall ultimately upon the industry of the country and form an element in the cost of production.[78]

Therefore, the FBI committee proposed that the Allies demand
an indemnity to cover all war expenses, direct and indirect,
again including pensions. Similar positions were taken by various Chambers of Commerce, and shortly after the election campaign the Associated Chambers of Commerce endorsed the
"Peace Aims" of the FBI and notified Lloyd George.[79] So by
the final days of the campaign, the Coalition was well aware that
the national debt and taxation had—"like the effect of a snake
on a rabbit"—convinced important interests to demand full
indemnity.[80]

Another such pressure was placed on the Government, especially on the Prime Minister, by the most authoritative of British
newspapers, *The Times*. That august journal had greeted the
Armistice with the hope that the Allies would not allow Germany
to lapse into chaos,[81] but as November wore on its leading
articles became more and more anti-German. By the end of the
month *The Times* had taken up the popular cry for war crimes
trials, expulsion of enemy aliens, and a large indemnity. After
Lloyd George's Newcastle speech, *The Times* joined other anti-
German newspapers in rejecting the qualification, "up to the
limit of her capacity. . . . What business at this stage is it of
ours to consider how much Germany could pay? That is not for
the Judge condemning the defeated litigant in costs."[82]

The Times' adoption of the anti-German issues was largely
the result of a feud between its owner, Lord Northcliffe, and the
Prime Minister. Northcliffe believed that during the War his
newspapers had placed Lloyd George at the head of the Government and kept him there. When an election came onto the horizon
in September and October 1918, the press Lord expected to have
a say in the composition of the new Government; he also wished
to be a British peace delegate. Lloyd George, however, did not
practice gratitude and, like many British politicians, he considered Northcliffe arrogant to the point of megalomania. In
early November, he quashed Northcliffe's hopes.[83]

In response, Northcliffe resigned his position in the Ministry
of Information and, having few scruples about editorial freedom,
gradually turned his newspapers around to attack the Government. On the one hand, he urged his papers to portray Lloyd
George as the captive of the reactionary "old gang" of the Con-

servative Party.[84] On the other hand, he bombarded his editors
with dark hints and advice to join the anti-German campaign:

> There are several indications that the Prime Minister is evading
> main issues. He is acting I believe at the instance of . . . people
> . . . who are for the letting loose of interned Germans and who,
> like every other German financier, are trying to prevent Germany
> having to pay for the war. I do not believe that Lloyd George is
> a free agent in this matter and I am determined to bring pressure
> to bear.[85]

This sort of pressure moved *The Times* into a large indemnity
position and soon caused the resignation of the editor of the
paper, Geoffrey Dawson.

Lloyd George regarded the opposition of *The Times* and
its owner as a grave matter. On November 30, he attempted a
private reconciliation through Northcliffe's brother, Cecil
Harmsworth, a Coalition Liberal MP and member of the Prime
Minister's secretariat.[86] In public, the Prime Minister tried to
avoid saying anything that would give Northcliffe grounds
for criticism. However, Lloyd George still refused to satisfy
Northcliffe's personal ambitions and the newspaper owner,
therefore, remained hostile. On December 6, he cabled to Lloyd
George:

> The public are expecting you to say definitely amount of cash
> reparation we are to get from Germany. They are very dissatisfied
> with the phrase "limit of her capacity" which they say may mean
> anything or nothing. They are aware that France has named her
> amount. I am apprehensive of serious trouble in the country on
> this matter. Northcliffe.

Apparently Lloyd George then resigned himself to Northcliffe's
vendetta, for he replied on December 7:

> You are quite wrong about France. No ally has named figure.
> Allies in complete agreement as to demand for indemnity. Inter-
> Allied Commission will investigate on behalf of all on identical
> principles. Dont always be making mischief.[87]

Northcliffe paid no attention. His "mischief" and that of his
papers continued well into 1919.

One of these mischievous doings was to discover and anticipate
the conclusions of the Imperial Committee on Indemnity. By
December 7, some basic facts about that Committee had come into
the hands of the *Daily Mail*. That paper informed its readers
that William Morris Hughes chaired the Committee; that a
provisional report had been made in early December; that the
Committee were unanimous in favor of indemnity; and that Lord
Cunliffe had proposed "an excellent and workable scheme" for
securing payment.[88] Neither the *Daily Mail* nor *The Times*
was mollified by this information. Commenting on the Hughes
Committee on December 9, *The Times* paraphrased Northcliffe:

> To say that a strong British Committee has been appointed to
> consider Germany's capacity may be profoundly misleading. . . .
> There is frankly no basis at present for computing Germany's
> capacity to pay. Moreover, it is not our business to do so. Our
> business is simply to assess our own bill of damages, as the French
> have already done, and then to present it for payment. . . . Mr.
> Lloyd George would do well to make this procedure perfectly
> clear. There is far too much suspicion of influences concerned to
> "let the Germans off lightly". . . .[89]

The Times and its allies wanted an unqualified commitment to
indemnity from the Prime Minister, not a committee report.

Lloyd George, however, continued to hope that the final
conclusions of the Hughes Committee would give him "a leg
to stand on." While he waited for those conclusions, he relegated
the anti-German issues to a secondary role in his speeches. At
Leeds on December 7, he dwelt on his war record and on justifi-
cations for his coalition with the Conservatives.[90] Two days
later, at the Queen's Hall, he called again for "a sternly just
peace," but he also warned that the peace terms ". . . must have
no Alsace-Lorraine. (A voice: Why?) For the simple reason that
if we repeat the error of Germany we shall meet the fate of Germany fifty years afterwards."[91] This prophecy must have an-
noyed the Prime Minister's anti-German critics. If so, Lloyd
George more than redeemed himself in his next major address,
at Bristol, on December 11—he had received the final report of
the Hughes Committee the night before.

The Prime Minister began his Bristol speech by answering

the most significant criticism of the left: The Government, he said, would discontinue conscription "when the emergency has passed."[92] Then Lloyd George moved on to the major subject of his address, reparation and indemnity. He commenced by repeating his court costs analogy: the loser must pay. That was only fair, Lloyd George declared, since Germany was more populous than Britain and had only spent "six or seven thousand millions" on the War whereas Britain's expense, he estimated was £8,000,000,000.

Then the Prime Minister took up that difficult question, "the limit of capacity." Why was this so important? Because, Lloyd George answered, it would be wrong to raise false hopes. The Allied cost of the War was £24,000,000,000 and the Government's financial servants had warned him that Germany might never be able to pay so much. That was why, he continued, ". . . I am not going to mislead the public on the question of capacity until I know more about it, and I am not going to do it in order to win votes." Having said that, the Prime Minister moved deftly on to encourage the expectation of large payments, by reference to the Hughes Committee:

> . . . . I received last night the report of the British Imperial Committee, and you will be glad to hear that they take a more favourable view of the capacity of Germany than do the officials of the Government Department. They think that the assets of Germany have been under-estimated in the past. . . . There is no doubt that Germany herself thinks so. If that is so, you may find that the capacity will go a pretty long way. (Laughter)

However, the Prime Minister attached two conditions to this heartening news: The economic peace terms must not require an army of occupation nor result in the dumping of cheap German goods on the British market. Both reservations were cheered by the audience, especially the first.

Finally, Lloyd George summarized his position in the most well remembered words of the speech:

> First, as far as justice is concerned, we have an absolute right to demand the whole cost of the war from Germany. The second point is that we propose to demand the whole cost of the war. (cheers) The third point is that . . . you must exact it in such a way that

it does not do more harm to the country that receives is than to the country which is paying it. The fourth point is that the Committee appointed by the British Cabinet believe it can be done. The fifth point is that the Allies, who are in exactly the same boat as we are, because they have also got a claim to great indemnities, are examining the proposal in conjunction with us. . . .

The Prime Minister then concluded his speech with a brief repetition of his pledge to try the ex-Kaiser and other German war criminals. He told a questioner that very soon German aliens would be "fired out" of Britain.

The Bristol speech was a paradigm of crowd oratory, a *tour de force* through those skills of which Lloyd George was so much a master. Rhetoric, innuendo, the smooth qualification, and a bantering humor were all there. In content, the speech combined appeals to left and right, with suitable reservations all around. Lloyd George was never more difficult to define. Nevertheless, the contemporary definition was that the Prime Minister had moved closer to his anti-German critics, and they agreed. The *Daily Mail* political correspondent called Lloyd George's remarks "his best speech of the campaign."[93] There was good reason for this satisfaction. Lloyd George had spoken almost exclusively of the anti-German issues and other aspects of peacemaking. Social reform was nowhere in sight. Also, the Prime Minister's peroration on reparation and indemnity leaned toward the punitive view of those questions. His emphatic summary came to represent the entire speech, his last major address of the campaign.

Why did Lloyd George move toward the large indemnity position when other Coalition leaders, notably Bonar Law, were exercising caution? It is doubtful that the Prime Minister personally wanted to encourage anti-German sentiment or expectations of large payments, given the tardiness of his statement at Bristol, only three days before the voting, and considering the ambiguity of the body of his speech. Nevertheless, he had to make some public use of the Hughes report, or Hughes and the members of the Committee on Indemnity would likely feel their efforts had been in vain; that might lead to another public quarrel such as the one with Hughes in early November. Furthermore, the Prime Minister was well aware that most Conservative candidates and voters looked to him for a more emphatic anti-German statement than he had made before December 11; such a statement would please his election partners and solidify the Coalition.[94]

Of course, a less cautious or less sensitive politician might have scorned such considerations. This, however, would have been out of character for Lloyd George, and for any other man who might have gotten to the top of "the greasy pole" in those chaotic times. Leo Amery once wrote of the Prime Minister:

> He was not deliberately inconsistent or untruthful. But living entirely in response to the immediate stimulus, he had no clear memory either of past events or of his own former motives.[95]

The "immediate stimulus" of December 1918 was a general election and Lloyd George was privately worried that he was not responding properly. On December 4, Lord Milner wrote in his diary:

> L. G. asked me to come and see him at 11. I found him alone and had an interview about election matters. He was rather upset about the prospects and the conversation was neither a satisfactory nor an agreeable one.[96]

In this frame of mind, the Prime Minister certainly would have felt a need to be more dramatic on the most popular issues; hence, the Bristol speech. Answering that speech in the *Manchester Guardian*, C. P. Scott wrote, "We could wish the temptations of electioneering were not so strong upon him;"[97] but to wish this of Lloyd George during a general election was not realistic.[98]

The same "temptations of electioneering" were also too strong for most Coalition candidates in 1918. Therefore, the anti-German issues became the only real excitement in a generally desultory election. And the Coalition landslide which the election produced seemed to indicate that the same issues would continue to dominate British politics and diplomacy.

The New House of Commons

The results of the General Election of 1918 could not be tabulated until December 28, because of absentee voting. However,

well before that day it was generally realized that the Coalition
had won a striking victory. For example, on December 17 a high
Conservative Party official privately forecast a Coalition majority
of 255.[99] Even the pessimistic Lloyd George conceded that the
Coalition majority would be at least 150 Members.[100]

These predictions were more than borne out by the results
announced on the 28th. The official Coalition majority in the
new House of Commons was to be 237; more realistically, including "independent" Conservatives and excluding Sinn Feiners,
who never took their seats, it would be 408! The coupon had
been very effective indeed:[101]

	Receiving Coupons	Elected
Conservatives	364	334
Liberals	159	127
National Democrats	18	11

Coalition incumbents had been especially successful, compared
to their counterparts:[102]

	Incumbents Defeated
Coalition Conservative	6
Coalition Liberal	7
Independent Conservative	1
Independent Liberal	65
Labour	15
Irish Nationalist	27
Independent	5
	126

Conversely, as these figures show, the Election was a disaster
for the official Liberals. Among their sixty-five incumbents who
were defeated was practically all the old Liberal talent of Asquith's former governments. Furthermore, Labour's relative
success was a dark omen for the Liberals. Labour became the
official opposition by outrunning the Liberals in Members
elected and popular votes. It was also significant that in three-
cornered contests involving Labour, independent Liberals placed
first only twelve times, second forty times, and third ninety-two
times.[103]

However, more than anything else the Election was a Conservative victory. Conservatives won in many divisions formerly inhospitable to them; for example, they secured eight of the ten seats in Manchester, home of free trade and the *Manchester Guardian*. Even Conservatives who ran without the coupon did well: forty-nine out of eighty-one were elected. So successful was the Party that the new House of Commons would have 101 more Conservative Members than the old. Most important, Conservatives *alone* would have a majority of 132 Members over all other parties, excluding Sinn Fein.

While the new House would be dominated by the Conservative Party, it was a new kind of Conservative Party. Of the 383 Conservative Members elected in 1918, 216 had served in a previous House of Commons, 167 had not. Compared to the former, the latter were older, possessed fewer university degrees, sat for more borough seats, and were distinctly more engaged in business than in landowning.[104] Across the Channel, Elie Halévy remarked, "The Unionist Party is no longer the party of great landowners and country gentlemen, who now struggle against the invasion of modern businessmen, financiers and industrialists."[105] The new Conservatives were also more protectionist. Lord Robert Cecil later wrote, ". . . that the Tariff Reform movements had accelerated the substitution of the commercial for the landowning class [in the Conservative Party], and the war carried this tendency further."[106] The Election reflected these related trends: There were distinctly more tariff advocates in the new House of Commons than in the old.[107]

This new Conservative Parliamentary Party occasioned many regrets. A Liberal, C. F. G. Masterman, wrote:

> The dominant element was far less Land than in any previous Tory victory. Land, for the most part, was either in the House of Lords or at the Front. It was rather the new wealth. . . . It was the new Plutocracy: men who had assisted the Government in the War, who had made their fortunes during the War or who had improved their fortunes during the war.[108]

A Conservative, Stanley Baldwin, was surely thinking of his new party colleagues when he made the most famous comment on the new House of Commons: "They are a lot of hard-faced men who look as if they had done very well out of the war."[109]

Among these hard faces were at least fifty Members, mostly Conservatives, who constantly proclaimed their elections to have been the result of the anti-German campaign they had conducted; they also argued that the over-all election result was a mandate for a punitive peace, a claim examined in the following chapter. During the spring of 1919, these fifty were joined by about 150 other MPs, again mostly Conservatives, in an effort to remind the Government of the anti-German "pledges" made by Coalition leaders during the election campaign. This was one of the few blemishes on the election result, as far as the Government was concerned. Along with the anti-German issues, a Parliamentary agitation for a punitive peace was a development not anticipated by Coalition managers in their careful planning for a General Election.

Chapter 9 THE ELUSIVE MANDATE

EXPLAINING the necessity of an election on November 17, Lloyd George had said, "We must get the mandate immediately. Somebody will have to go to the Peace Conference with authority from the people of this country to speak in their name."[1] The mandate which the Prime Minister sought was doubtless a general and unfettered vote of confidence, and it was not difficult for the Coalition press to portray the results of December 28 as such an expression. On December 31, the *Glasgow Herald* declared:

> With such a majority behind them, Mr. Lloyd George and Mr. Bonar Law will go into the Peace Conference with an irresistable mandate. Their appeal for a strong, just peace has been confirmed, and no country in Europe—least of all Germany—will be able to protest that the voice with which Britain speaks is not an overpoweringly united one.[2]

Likewise, the *Daily Telegraph*, the *Observer*, and the *Scotsman* saw the Coalition victory as a general triumph of the Government over "pacifism and defeatism."[3]

There was, however, another interpretation which admitted that the Coalition had won a vote of confidence but claimed that this confidence was conditional, that it was expressed only because of Coalition commitments to a large indemnity, war crimes trials, and the expulsion of enemy aliens. Here newspapers as dissimilar as the Liberal *Daily News* and the protectionist *Morning Post* agreed:

> The judgement was obtained . . . on three points, hanging the
> Kaiser, punitive indemnities, and "firing out" the Hun.

> The British people desire no sort of truck with Germany. They
> want to see Germany punished; and they want to see Germany made
> to pay to the uttermost farthing. They forced the Coalition to pledge
> itself upon these points before they returned it to power—and woe
> to the British statesman who seeks to evade the pledges which
> have been given.[4]

The experience of Coalition candidates seemed to corroborate
these judgments. As previously mentioned, the Conservative
Central Office found that its agents in all parts of England and
Wales were reporting indemnity, the ex-Kaiser, and aliens to be
the leading issues. On the basis of reports from Coalition Liberal
agents, F. E. Guest told Lloyd George that aside from national
unity and the Prime Minister's personal appeal, the most popular
Coalition policy was "insisting on the complete criminal and
civil liability of Germany."[5]

Also, there were more than fifty Members in the new House
of Commons who believed that their elections and the General
Election represented a mandate on the three anti-German issues.
Conservatives composed about four-fifths of this group and
were most vocal in trying to hold the Government and its negotiators to an anti-German position during the Peace Conference.[6]
On February 12, the day after the new Parliamentary session
began, the Unionist War Committee sent the Government the
following resolution:

> Having regard to the heavy and onerous burdens of taxation . . .
> the losses occasioned by enemy action, and pledges given by Union-
> ist candidates at the recent General Election, the imposition of an
> adequate indemnity from the enemy countries to the full extent of
> such expenditures and loss is an imperative act of justice. . . .[7]

In the following months, Conservatives conducted a "ginger"
campaign on indemnity in the House of Commons. Most
vehement was Colonel Claude Lowther, Member for Lonsdale,
Lancashire, who frequently rose to quote from Lloyd George's
Bristol speech and to accuse the Government of ignoring its
mandate.[8] One of Lowther's associates, Frederick W. Astbury,
Conservative Member for West Salford, complained:

We are in this position, that we gave two definite pledges to our Constituents last December. The first was indemnities from Germany, and the second the bringing to justice of the Kaiser and all his murderous gang. In the majority of cases huge majorities were obtained on these two points, and these two points alone. What authority had we for giving those pledges? We had the authority of the Prime Minister.[9]

Most important, on April 8, 1919, a public telegram sponsored by eight Conservative malcontents was sent to the Prime Minister in Paris, asking for an explicit assurance that the Government would claim a full indemnity from Germany. This claim, the sponsors said, was something "our constituents have always expected—and still expect. . . ."[10] The telegram was signed by no less than 198 Members of the House of Commons. Of these, 164 were Conservatives.[11]

Was there, in fact, a mandate similar to that claimed by the *Morning Post* and the 198 MPs? The historian cannot give an unqualified answer to that question. However, through the use of the local press in specific constituencies, it is possible to obtain a more distinct picture of the role played by the anti-German issues than that provided in the national dailies. And it is important to do so, considering the troublesome impact which the claims to an anti-German mandate had on British diplomacy.

Consequently, the election campaign in nine important constituencies will be described here. The first three were chosen because they received much national attention and, therefore, had an impact on the General Election. The other divisions were successfully contested by six of the forty-three Conservatives who are identified in the Appendix as having participated in the 1919 Commons campaign for punitive terms of peace. This kind of constituency, more than any other, should test the validity of the Conservatives' insistence that the electors had given them an anti-German mandate. The principal criterion for selecting these specific six divisions was that each was different from the others in significant ways, thus affording a variety of social and political environments in which to observe the anti-German issues and candidates.[12]

Three Prominent Constituencies

EAST FIFE

Sprot, Col. Sir Alexander (Cons.)	8,996
*Asquith, H. H. (Lib.)	6,994
Morgan, Pritchard (Independent)	591
	16,581
Conservative plurality	2,002
Conservative majority	1,411 (9% total)
*Incumbent	

The most sensational upset of the campaign was ex-Prime Minister Asquith's defeat in East Fife. Why did a man who had sat for East Fife since 1886 and who had been Prime Minister for eight years lose to an undistinguished, local Conservative? Sir Alexander Sprot, a sixty-five-year-old East Fife landowner, had contested the division against Asquith in the 1910 elections, losing both times by approximately 2,000 votes. His main distinction was four years service in France as a Colonel, where he was decorated several times.

At first it appeared that Asquith might win without a contest. Since no coupon had been allocated for East Fife, the local Conservative association initially decided not to put forward a candidate. The decision was a reluctant one and it was reversed with the appearance of John Chapman, a candidate of the super-patriotic Silver Badge Party, who threatened to capitalize on Conservative sentiment against Asquith. When the Conservatives nominated Sprot, Chapman dropped out of the race, but performed the valuable service of speaking for the Conservative at twenty-one campaign meetings.[13]

Chapman resigned from the race chiefly because Sprot began and continued his campaign on the anti-German themes which enthused the Silver Badge group. In a belated opening address, Sprot declared:

> There must be no tinge of pacifism, "softeeism," or tenderness [toward] Germany on the part of those whom we send to settle this conference. . . . We should insist upon full compensation, by means of an indemnity, from Germany, not only for the damage which she had done in Belgium and France, but also for all the

money we had been obliged to spend and to borrow in order to
carry on the war, which was the direct result of Germany's action.[14]

The Conservative also hoped to restrict German trade. When
Liberal questioners demanded to know how this squared with
the large indemnity, Sprot was evasive, perhaps confused. The
editor of the most important local newspaper came to his rescue:
"The ordinary man may not be able to solve the imports and
exports puzzle, but I think he will be perfectly prepared to run
the risks of getting a big indemnity from Germany."[15]

In the same article, Asquith was condemned for failing to
mention the anti-German issues in his formal address to the
electors. "It is quite evident that Mr. Asquith is not in full
sympathy with the attitude of the country toward Germany.
The duty of East Fife is therefore plain—to return Sir Alexander
Sprot." It was true that Asquith generally avoided the anti-
German issues. Only late in the campaign did the Liberal Leader,
beseiged by antipathetic hecklers, pay his obeisance to the
prevalent mood:

> "Will you make the Germans pay for the War?" asked an elector,
> to which Mr. Asquith replied, "Yes. I am in agreement on that
> matter with what the Prime Minister said yesterday."

> Is it true that for financial and other reasons you are prepared
> to let the Germans down lightly and not repatriate them?—There
> is not a word of truth in it. Are you prepared to hang the Kaiser
> and the commanders of submarines found guilty of crimes?—They
> are to be put on trial, and if they are found guilty no punishment
> can be too severe. (Cheers)[16]

This was no match for Sprot's consistent advocacy of a punitive
peace. Asquith's failure to take a strong stand on the anti-German
issues was an important factor in his defeat.

However, it was not the only factor. In 1918, East Fife was no
longer the safe Liberal seat it had been. Owing to population
changes, the Representation Act of 1918 had redrawn the constituency in such a way as to give the traditionally Conservative
university town of St. Andrews greater electoral weight.[17] There
were other handicaps. The only two local newspapers were

strongly Conservative. More important, Asquith's national speaking obligations prevented him from countering the thorough tour of the division made by Sprot and Chapman. However, aside from the anti-German issues, the most important factor in Asquith's defeat was the backlog of resentment against his conduct of the War:

> Asquith had to be chucked to win the war; are you going to send him back to spoil the peace?

> Vote for Sprot and support the Government that has Won the War. Don't wait and see.[18]

These Conservative cries against Asquith had their effect. Along with the anti-German issues, they prevented the ex-Prime Minister from overcoming his other handicaps in East Fife.

CAMBRIDGE BOROUGH

*Geddes, Sir Eric (Co. Cons.)	11,553
Williams, Rev. T. R. (Labour)	3,789
	15,342
Conservative majority	7,764 (51% total)

None of Asquith's disadvantages hampered Sir Eric Geddes in Cambridge. Geddes was one of Lloyd George's most outstanding recruits to the war effort from the business world. As First Lord of the Admiralty at the end of a successful war, Geddes was bound to be popular throughout Britain and especially in a constituency where a strong Liberal association had stepped aside in his favor. Geddes' progress to an easy victory might have been placid and unnoticed but for certain remarks he made in his opening speech.

The First Lord's conscientious devotion to his work had kept him out of touch with Cambridge. When on November 27, he left the Admiralty for a few hours to speak to the Central Conservative Club of Cambridge, he showed himself unaware of the mood of the electorate on reparation and indemnity. Sir Eric was all in favor of German compensation in principle, but was completely sceptical of the idea that significant payments could be made without harming British trade and employment. Most alarming to local and national audiences was the First Lord's dissent from "ton for ton" maritime reparation. He warned of the effect such reparation would have on the very considerable British shipbuilding industry, a *caveat* all too rare in 1918. And, in general, the tone of his remarks showed an unwelcome degree of pessimism:

> He was all in favour of indemnities. Everyone was. But he had never yet found anyone to tell him how, without hurting ourselves, an indemnity of that kind could be received. (A voice: Spread it over years) Fifty thousand millions! How many years, how many centuries would it take her to pay that?[19]

Geddes' remarks of November 27 set off an outcry in the pro-indemnity press. Faced with public criticism and receiving, in all probability, some advice from his more experienced political colleagues, Geddes did an about face. On December 5, he sent a public letter to the Chairman of the Cambridge Conservative association:

> In case there should be any doubt in Cambridge as to my attitude on indemnities, as I said at the meeting at the Conservative Club on Wednesday, November 27, I am entirely for Germany paying every cent of the cost of the war. Of course she should and must absolutely pay to her full capacity not only present but future. If I have anything to do with it, I shall see that she does. . . . I shall make my view abundantly clear on December 9. . . . Believe me, tenderness for the Hun is not, and never has been, one of my faults.[20]

Geddes' did, indeed, make his views "abundantly clear" on December 9. In very strident terms, he assured his audience that he was as anti-German as anyone in the Government. Though he mentioned the difficulties of German compensation, his main emphasis was elsewhere. " 'I would strip her [Germany] as she stripped Belgium,' declared Sir Eric, amidst cheers."[21] The following day he reinforced his new position with the most famous remarks of the campaign on reparation and indemnity:

> The Germans, if this Government is returned, are going to pay every penny; they are going to be squeezed as a lemon is squeezed

—until the pips squeak. My only doubt is not whether we can squeeze hard enough, but whether there is enough juice. (Laughter) It is right that they should pay. They brought this war on, they asked for it, and they have got it, and now let them pay the bill for the goods they have asked for. (Applause)[22]

In this manner, Geddes retrieved his patriotic reputation.

However, his conversion to large indemnity payments was not crucial for his election, though undoubtedly it helped. His opponent was only a local minister who suffered from his membership in the Independent Labour Party and had to fight off charges that he was a conscientious objector.[23] Furthermore, Reverend Williams adhered to radical social reform, which probably did him little good in relatively prosperous Cambridge.[24] On the issues of peacemaking, he supported the League of Nations and "reparation only," and refused to pledge the expulsion of enemy aliens.[25] This impressed few Cambridge electors. Williams and his program went down in utter defeat before the lemon metaphor.

WEST LEICESTER

Green, J. R. (Co. N.D.P.)	20,570
*MacDonald, J. Ramsay (Labour)	6,347
	26,917
Co. N.D.P. Majority	14,223 (53% total)

Reverend Williams could take some comfort from the fact that his most illustrious colleague in the Independent Labour Party experienced a defeat as humiliating as his own. Moreover, if Asquith in East Fife suffered from his wartime record, Ramsay MacDonald in West Leicester bore the personal burden of being almost a devil figure.

In part, MacDonald's trials resulted from the general opinion that Leicester was a crucial test of the Coalition's drawing power among working-class voters. Leicester was an industrial town, though a fairly prosperous one. The primary occupations of the city were dressmaking and textile working, in which women outnumbered men by six to one. Most Leicester men were employed in the boot and shoe industry and in metal working.[26]

Before 1918 Leicester had been a two-member constituency, which had gone "Lib-Lab" by a large margin. The Representation Act of 1918 reapportioned the city into three single-member districts, South, East, and West. Every variety of Coalition candidate stood in the three Leicester contests, each of which was fought by the Labour Party. A Coalition Conservative ran in South Leicester; Gordon Hewart, a prominent Coalition Liberal, ran in East Leicester; and a member of the Coalition labour group, J. R. Green, was assigned West Leicester.

Green had no previous parliamentary or party political experience, but he chose the right issues with which to defeat Mac-Donald. Green was wholehearted in his call for war crimes trials, for the expulsion of enemy aliens, and for getting ". . . every farthing out of Germany to pay for the war."[27] The other Coalition candidates and the local newspaper, of Conservative sympathies, shared Green's enthusiasm.[28] In contrast, MacDonald's campaign adhered to Labour's social reform attitude toward the cost of the War. *The Pioneer*, a struggling, local weekly owned by the ILP, rejected indemnity as "humbug" and a diversion from the only proper method of paying the cost of the War, a levy on capital.[29] On the hustings, MacDonald made courageous but unsuccessful attempts to turn back the anit-German temper:

> "Does he agree that the mongrels of Germans should pay for the war, and what does he think of the swine who tortured our men who were prisoners?" Mr. MacDonald replied that, as to making the Germans pay for the war, he wanted to see an authoritative Commission investigate the damage and assess it. He wanted to divide that damage up into three sections: first, the ordinary military damage; secondly, the destruction done by Germany in Belgium and France to factories and houses; thirdly, ordinary war costs. The industrial damage done must be paid for, at 20s. in the pound. As to indemnities, let them not be carried away by a word. The economics of an indemnity was one of the most difficult things in the world. . . . He did not come to that conclusion from sentimental feelings about Germany, but for economic reasons only.[30]

These defensive qualifications made a poor impression on most of Leicester.

However, the main point of discussion in Leicester was Mac-Donald's recent opposition to the War. The *Leicester Mail* frequently mentioned MacDonald's efforts at

> peace by negotiation, which would have meant a peace dictated by Germany. Are the men and women of West Leicester whose sons and other relatives have fought and bled for the victory we have achieved, going to support a politician with a war record such as Mr. MacDonald has?[31]

Green's speeches were more violent and personal. MacDonald was not "a true Britisher," Green said. The ILP Member was trying to pretend that the War was history, but "they would not forget the traitorous and wicked things MacDonald said" in the last four years. MacDonald had admitted he had "German friends." He was a blot on the patriotic name of Leicester.[32] Green's local hate campaign against MacDonald received distinguished assistance. F. E. Smith, in referring to enemy aliens, said, "We have no friends among them though Mr. Ramsay MacDonald has."[33] The Prime Minister himself, in a brief speech at Camberwell on December 12, used MacDonald to smear the entire Labour Party:

> Mr. Ramsay MacDonald and Mr. Snowden—(hisses)—are no manual workers. The Labour Party is not being run by real labour; it is being run by Pacifists and Bolsheviks. . . . If they had their way we would to-day be the slaves and bondsmen of Germany.[34]

The results in Leicester City and County must have pleased Coalition leaders and others who looked to that area for a test of working-class affections. Labour ran six candidates in the three borough and three county seats which were contested. All went down to crashing defeat. The vote for the entire County was Coalition, 56,750; Labour, 17,220. Though only two of these Labour candidates were members of the ILP, the unpatriotic image of that organization and of its leader, Ramsay Mac-Donald, doubtless was the main factor in all their defeats. As the *Leicester Mail* trumpeted, "When the industrial character of certain portions of the county is considered it can fairly be claimed that the election proves that the I.L.P. has little right to speak for 'the workers'."[35] Patriotism and the related anti-German issues were the main factors in the Labour debacle. In the absence of such issues at the General Election of 1922, Green lost his seat to Labour by more than 4,000 votes.

Six Punitive Constituencies

LONSDALE, LANCS.

Lowther, Col. Claude (Co. Cons.)	9,662
Hunter, David (Labour)	4,472
*Bliss, Joseph (Liberal)	4,276
	18,410
Conservative plurality	5,190
Conservative majority	914 (5% total)

Claude Lowther put the anti-German issues in the forefront of his campaign in the northernmost division of Lancashire.[36] In fact, he may have made the first campaign statement on indemnity when he told the Lonsdale Conservative association on November 7, that ". . . he was in favour of compelling Germany to pay a heavy share towards the cost of the war and of making full restitution and reparation. It was a rich country and could well afford to do so."[37] However, Lowther's early mention of indemnity was not really in anticipation of a popular issue. Indemnity was an old idea for Claude Lowther. During the Boer War, he had proposed that the Transvaal pay an indemnity![38] So, in 1918, it was natural for him to urge that Germany should be compelled to pay "if not the whole, at least three-quarters of the cost of the war."[39]

Lowther's opponents did not share his anti-German prescriptions for the peace settlement. Joseph Bliss put more emphasis on the League of Nations. As a free trader, he rejected the prevalent view that imports from Germany would be "dumping."[40] Late in the campaign, he agreed to indemnity in principle, but emphasized the prior claims of the Continental Allies.[41] David Hunter did favor the expulsion of enemy aliens, probably as part of his attempts to dissociate himself from the ILP, Bolshevist stigma.[42] On the other hand, Hunter supported the League of

Nations and rejected indemnity in favor of the nationalization of British railways and mines as the proper way to pay for the War.[43] And he offered the electorate a needed reminder: "Do you agree to allowing the Germans at the peace table?—There can be none without the Germans being there. You cannot make terms if there is nobody to make terms with."[44]

Certainly the differences between Lowther and his opponents on the anti-German issues was important in the Conservative's victory. So also was the simple fact that he faced a divided opposition. Lonsdale constituency was a working class division where the principal occupations were farming, mining, and metal working.[45] In the past, Conservative candidates had won the seat only by narrow margins against a Liberal with strong labour sympathies.[46] Hunter was the first Labourite to contest Lonsdale, and his appearance was resented by Liberals:

> *Questioners:*—Why . . . do you come in opposition to a man well acquainted with the Labour movement? If you had not come there would have been a better chance for a Labour-Liberal vote than the Conservative. As it is, you have come into the field and neither Liberal nor Labour will get there. (Hear, hear)[47]

Given the very marginal nature of the contest, Hunter's candidacy almost ensured the defeat of Bliss and the election of Lowther.[48] This fact, in addition to Lowther's anti-German views on peace-making, accounted for his victory.

Elland, West Riding, Yorkshire

Ramsden, Capt. G. T. (Co. Cons.)	8,917
Dawson, H. (Liberal)	7,028
Hardaker, D. (Labour)	5,923
*Trevelyan, C. P. (ILP)	1,286
	23,154
Conservative plurality	1.889
Conservative majority (negative)	-5,320 (-23% total)

Even more than Claude Lowther, George Ramsden faced a badly divided opposition in a constituency that had traditionally been Radical Liberal.[49] Elland was one of those Yorkshire constituencies composed predominantly of textile workers, enjoying less than the national standard of living, residing for the most part in the mill towns of the West Riding.[50] In the two 1910 elections, Ramsden had lost to the Radical Liberal Trevelyan by 20 percent of the total vote. In 1918, their positions were strikingly reversed. The presence of an independent Liberal and a Labourite in a constituency where recent history had seen only straight fights had much to do with this. However, Ramsden also enjoyed a split opposition in 1922, but he finished last.[51] Therefore, the character of the issues in 1918 was probably very important in producing a Conservative plurality in Elland.

Ramsden began his campaign on November 27:

> . . . he went straight on to a question which he intends to put in the forefront of his programme.
>
> "Germany has to pay for it all," he declared amid cheers. "There is a good deal of talk about a blank cheque. . . . The only thing I want to see in that way is a cheque which we shall fill in to the amount of what the war has cost us, and make Germany sign it. . . ."[52]

True to his word, Ramsden made indemnity the most prominent issue in every speech he gave. His last program was "1. Full Indemnities; 2. Punishment of the Kaiser and the War Lords; 3. The return of all enemy aliens to their own countries."[53]

Ramsden taunted his opponents with the same issues: "My opponents are beginning to mention indemnities now. Second thoughts are sometimes best. (Laughter)"[54] The Liberal, Dawson, apparently did have second thoughts on indemnity. He made several statements in favor of the principle and practicality of an indemnity, perhaps as part of his effort to associate himself with the Coalition.[55] Hardaker, on the other hand, adhered to the official Labour policies of social reform, a Wilsonian peace, accepting reparation, but rejecting indemnity.[56] Charles Trevelyan provided an even more clear alternative to Ramsden. Trevelyan had been one of the prominent Radical leaders of the Union of Democratic Control during the War. Gradually, he had become convinced that the Independent Labour Party was a more likely vehicle of social reform than the Liberal Party. Faced with Ramsden's hackneyed gibe, "What did you do in

the Great War?'', Trevelyan did not flinch. He refused to repent
his wartime activity, and stated that he would vote with the ILP
if elected. Like Hardaker, Trevelyan hoped a League of Nations
would be the principal feature of the peace. He rejected Ramsden's
indemnity and proposed instead a capital levy to defray the cost
of the War.[57]

Thus, the anti-German issues, especially reparation and
indemnity, were the principal difference between Ramsden and
his fragmented opposition. Probably more than any other
factor, these issues provided the Conservative with the rare
opportunity of winning the working-class constituency of Elland.

FROME, SOMERSET

Hurd, Percy (Co. Cons.)	11,118
Gill, Captain E. (Labour)	10,454
*Barlow, Sir J. E. (Liberal)	2,004
Kincaid-Smith, Col. (Nat'l Party)	258
	23,834
Conservative plurality	664
Conservative majority (negative)	-1,598 (-7% total)

Percy Hurd's situation in Frome was similar to Ramsden's in
Elland, with the important exception that the fourth candidate
was a member of the National Party, not the ILP.[58] Frome
was mainly a mining constituency where recent political history
had seen very even fights between a Conservative and a Liberal
with labour sympathies, with the latter holding a slight edge.[59]
In 1918, the Conservative candidate benefited greatly from the
fact that both parties of the left had entered a candidate. Barlow
won just enough votes to ensure Hurd's plurality over Labour's
first candidate in Frome's history. When Hurd eventually lost
the seat in 1923, it was in a straight fight with Labour.

In 1918, Hurd's divided opponents provided him with the
further advantage of the initiative on the anti-German issues.
Both Barlow and Gill concentrated on domestic reforms and,
when they mentioned peacemaking, proposed a Wilsonian settlement.[60] In contrast, Hurd began and maintained his campaign
on a strong anti-German note. He especially stressed the need for

a clear mandate on peacemaking with which the Coalition Government could go to the Peace Conference. His prescription for the content of that mandate was:

> *Justice and Indemnities.*—Stern justice for the Kaiser and all German criminals, high and low. Germany must "make good" and must pay. The Allied taxpayers cannot be left to bear the full burden of a War so wantonly thrust upon a peaceful world by Prussian arrogance and greed. . . .the Alien evil must finally be removed. . . .[61]

Hurd's anti-German position was reinforced by his opponent on the right, Colonel Kincaid-Smith. The campaign of the National Party's candidate was strongly anti-German and pro-indemnity. Hurd believed this to be a threat to his own support and tried to persuade Kincaid-Smith to withdraw.[62] Hurd may have overestimated the appeal of the National Party in Frome. On the other hand, had he been less anti-German, Kincaid-Smith might have won enough votes among Conservatives to enable the election of the Labourite. Hurd probably would have campaigned on an anti-German platform in any case, but the presence of Kincaid-Smith ensured this. In Frome, the key factors in Conservative victory were divided opposition and an anti-German campaign, bolstered by the presence of the National Party.

CANTERBURY, KENT

*McNeill, Ronald (Co. Cons.)	11,408
Palmer, E. T. (Labour)	2,719
	14,127
Conservative majority	8,689 (61% total)

Canterbury was a world removed from those precarious divisions of Lonsdale, Elland and Frome, where Conservatives struggled to sway working-class audiences. In the town of Canterbury and in the outlying areas which made up Canterbury constituency, agriculture, commerce, finance and domestic service were the principal occupations. Housing was relatively plentiful and the population was growing.[63] The constituency had, within living memory, always been a safe Conservative seat. In 1918, the only opposition was a young, inexperienced Labour candidate.

In these conditions, Ronald McNeill might well have remained in London and still held his seat.[64] Yet he conducted a vigorous campaign in Canterbury, on violently anti-German and anti-Labour lines. The two directions of attack were related in McNeill's speeches. The election of "pro-German, pacifist Labourites" would mean a "rotten peace" with "the Hun." McNeill, on the other hand, was having "no truck with Fritz." Britain was to remain for the British. The enemy aliens were to be turned out "neck and crop."[65] Terrible, unspecified punishment was to be meted out to German war criminals. Germany was to pay large indemnities, including the cost of pensions, and there would be no difficulties in collecting:

> "How are we to make Germany pay for the war if we do not trade with that country?" McNeill: "The way I would make Germany pay for the war is to occupy her territory and take her mines, her potash, her iron and coal, and earmark, if necessary, the revenue from her State railways and Customs duties, and take what we require. I would do that with as little trade with Germany as possible. So far as the actual ordinary commerce is concerned, I would . . . boycott Germany if I could."[66]

According to McNeill, Palmer shared none of these anti-German intentions. Palmer belonged to "the party of conchies and shirkers" and would embrace "Brother Boche" if he could.[67]

The anti-German fury of McNeill's campaign kept Palmer on the defensive. His appeals for social reform fell on deaf ears. Most of his audiences came to hear him retract, usually with some ambivalence, his supposed sympathy for Germany:

> Is it correct that you are in favour of friendship with the Huns, after their blood-thirsty murders on land and sea?
> I want to say positively that the restoration of friendship with the Hun is neither possible to me or my party, except on the terms laid down in President Wilson's 14 points, or such modifications

On another occasion, Palmer gave in to a heckler's demand for the cost of the War from Germany.[69] Throughout the campaign he was forced to defend the Labour Party from being labelled "un-British." However, none of Palmer's defensive efforts made a dent in McNeill's super-patriotic campaign.

Why did McNeill mount such a furious assault against his hapless opponent? Perhaps he found the anti-German issues a convenient mask for his rather paternal views on social reform.[70] Yet we should not doubt that McNeill was personally sincere in his Germanophobia, since he was a leading parliamentary advocate of anti-alien legislation during the War. Likewise, anyone who could liken the Labour Party to the anti-Christ must have been genuinely fearful of the "evils" of socialism. No doubt McNeill honestly considered himself the recipient of an anti-German, anti-Labour mandate, just as there is no doubt that he would have won on practically any platform in Canterbury.

CHELSEA

*Hoare, Sir Samuel (Co. Cons.)	9,159
Phipps, Miss E. (Independent)	2,419
	11,578
Conservative majority	6,740 (58% total)

Like Canterbury, the West End division of Chelsea was definitely safe for the incumbent Conservative, Sir Samuel Hoare.[71] Chelsea was both a middle-class and a working-class division, but the primary occupation of the latter was residential female domestic service.[72] In these favorable conditions, Hoare's only opponent was an independent woman candidate, an ex-President of the National Federation of Women Teachers, who was interested mainly in the rights of her sex.

There was little difference between the two candidates on the anti-German issues, except in emphasis. Miss Phipps paid little attention to these matters, but in reply to questions ". . . said she was in favour of Germany paying for the war to the utmost of her capacity."[73] While Miss Phipps treated peacemaking as secondary, Hoare put it in the forefront of his campaign. He favored a League of Nations that would not interfere with British colonial affairs, supported imperial preference, called for war crimes trials—especially for those who had maltreated prisoners-of-war—and proposed tighter immigration laws which would exclude "undesirable aliens" from Britain.[74] However, reparation and indemnity were Hoare's favorite subjects. His position on these issues became more punitive throughout the campaign:

> He did not deny that it [indemnity] might take time, but if it took ten or twenty or even fifty years and if Germany had to surrender to the allies one-half or even three-quarters of the whole of her wealth, the expiation she made would be far less than she deserved. (Loud applause).

His final advertisement read, "Vote for Hoare who is pledged to 1.—Make the Germans pay. 2.—Judge the German criminals. 3.—Keep the Germans out of England."[75]

In retrospect, it is interesting to note the degree of anti-Germanism in the campaign of a man who was to play a large role in British foreign relations between the Wars and who eventually became known as an appeaser of Germany. Moreover, circumstances in Chelsea did not require Hoare to adopt the anti-German issues. Like McNeill's views on Germany, Hoare's punitive outlook was more an act of free choice than of local political necessity.

East Islington

Raper, Lieut. Alfred B. (Co. Cons.)	9,352
*Smallwood, E. (Liberal)	5,968
Lewer, Major A. J. (Labour)	3,122
Copplestone, C. E. (Natl. Party)	575
Wickhart, F. A. (Independent)	147
	19,164
Conservative plurality	3,384
Conservative majority (negative)	-460 (-2% total)

Alfred Raper's situation in East Islington resembled those three-way contests for working-class votes in Lonsdale, Elland, and Frome.[76] The north London borough of Islington was a crowded dormitory for transport workers, metal workers, clerks, draftsmen, salesmen, shop assistants, female domestics, dressmakers, and charwomen—a microcosm of the city's working

class.[77] Electoral conditions in East Islington were very uncertain. In the six elections from 1910 to 1924, the constituency
elected a Liberal three times and a Conservative three times,
with Labour making progressively greater inroads.

In normal times, the main issues in East Islington would have
been social and economic policy, with foreign policy playing a
secondary role. In 1918, Raper reversed the formula, as did Coalition Conservatives throughout the country. The Conservative
candidate usually began his speeches with an anti-German
prescription for peacemaking. The ex-Kaiser and his associates
were to be tried and punished. Enemy aliens were to be expelled,
which Raper artfully noted would mean additional jobs for
Britons. "Germany would have to pay full indemnities, and she
had the wealthiest mines in Europe from which the money could
be obtained."[78] Housing, pensions and related subjects came
at the end of Raper's speeches.

In contrast, the incumbent Liberal, Smallwood, kept the attention of his audience focused on social reform, free trade, and
pensions for ex-servicemen. He declared that as long as the
Coalition Government pursued these objects he would support
it. Peacemaking was secondary for the Liberal candidate. He
favored a League of Nations and the payment of the cost of the
War—by British "profiteers" as well as by Germany.[79] The
Labour candidate's campaign was similar to Smallwood's,
except that Major Lewer placed greater emphasis on a progressive peace settlement that would abolish conscription, secret
treaties, and foreign capitalist concessions in the less developed
areas of the world.[80] On the subject of reparation and indemnity,
he agreed with his Liberal competitor, but he came down harder
on the "profiteers":

> He would make the Germans pay all that they were physically
> capable of paying for the damage they had wrought. The work
> of reconstruction of society must, however, in the main be paid
> by the capitalists (especially the profiteers) who had fattened upon
> the people during the war.

> He warned them against the false political cries which they
> heard on all sides. The people who had to pay for the cost of the
> war were the men who had made fortunes out of the war.[81]

Lewer's remarks put him at the opposite extreme from the National Party candidate, Copplestone, who demanded full indemnity and other punitive terms of peace.[82] Alfred Raper, like Percy Hurd, worried about the National Party candidate. Noting that Copplestone had said that he supported the Coalition program and, in addition, full indemnity, Raper replied:

> The words "in addition" are superfluous, as the Coalition Government has definitely pledged itself to secure indemnities from Germany to the limit of her capacity. In view of these facts I fail to understand why the National Party are opposing Coalition candidates in some constituencies and supporting them in others. Recent utterances by Mr. Lloyd George and his colleagues make it absolutely clear that they intend to make the Huns pay, as well as to punish those responsible for the war, however high their positions. I pledge myself to support all action taken in this direction.[83]

Raper enjoyed a split opposition, which was an important aspect of his victory, but he was not so confident as to overlook the possibility that Conservative voters might defect to the National Party if he was not sufficiently anti-German.[84]

Conclusions

In each of the nine constituencies discussed above, the successful candidate preferred to emphasize the anti-German issues rather than other concerns. This preference was a matter of strategy as well as of belief. Conservatives, in particular, welcomed the appearance of the anti-German temper and used it to divert attention away from social reform, for which they had little enthusiasm and on which they had little appeal. F. E. Guest wrote to Lloyd George that "the Coalition policy of insisting on the complete criminal and civil liability of Germany was intensely popular—this undoubtedly brought votes which would otherwise have gone to Labour."[85] This was understood very well by Conservatives in precarious divisions such as Lonsdale, Elland, Frome, and East Islington, where patriotic issues were needed to attract electors who did not traditionally vote Conservative.[86] Moreover, Conservatives in safe constituencies such as Cambridge, Canterbury, and Chelsea, who did not need the anti-German issues for success, apparently still felt that the general requirements of their Party obliged them to assist with the most expediential issues. Therefore, Conservatives from all sorts of divisions felt that the success of the Party in the Election was largely due to the strategy of attracting non-Conservative voters with the anti-German issues. Many Conservative MPs translated this into political rhetoric, to mean that the Party and the Coalition had received an anti-German mandate for the Peace Conference.

However, our nine constituencies indicate that the anti-German issues were not the only reason for Conservative success. The war record of opponents, divided opposition, the editorial position of the local press, the Coalition coupon, and the Conservative Party label were also important. When these things are taken into account, the content of the electors' mandate becomes vague. And if this was so for the more punitive Conservatives, surely it was also true for Coalition candidates in general. Therefore, the Coalition's vote of confidence was not so clearly dependent on the anti-German issues as many Conservatives claimed in 1919.

Nevertheless, there is no reason to doubt the personal sincerity of Conservatives who claimed a mandate for punitive terms of peace. They genuinely believed in such a peace and would naturally exaggerate the "mandate" they had received. Furthermore, they believed that Lloyd George, in his speeches at Newcastle and Bristol, had made anti-German pledges similar to their own. This gave many Conservatives confidence in their own anti-German predilections and in the value of Lloyd George as a coalition partner. Then, in 1919, this confidence was shaken by the behavior of the Prime Minister at the Peace Conference, where he became preoccupied with matters other than those discussed during the election campaign, and where he moderated his views on reparation and indemnity. Hence, the exaggerated anxiety of statements such as that by Sir Edward Nicholl on April 2, 1919:

> I had no Parliamentary ambitions until the war-cry went throughout the land to support the Prime Minister in making Germany pay for the War. Then I came into the arena. . . . I shall be very disappointed, indeed, if when the Prime Minister returns from

France we hear that he has consented to any reduction of the bill
. . . the Prime Minister [should realize] that if this country does not
get that indemnity, that they will want to know the reason why. And
the life of the Government, I contend, will be a very short one.[87]

It seemed to backbench Conservatives that the Prime Minister
had decided to ignore the mandate of the Election.

In fact, Lloyd George did not purposely ignore his election
promises. As Leo Amery put it, "He was not deliberately inconsistent or untruthful," but lived "in response to the immediate
stimulus." At Paris in 1919, the awful magnitude of making
peace dwarfed the themes of the Election, which had so affected
Lloyd George in November and December 1918. Gradually he
moved away from the mentality of the hustings to grapple with
the complexities of a ravaged Europe. Even so, he did not dissociate himself from the assumption of German war guilt and
the theoretical liability of Germany for the entire cost of the
War. To that extent, Lloyd George and the British Empire
Delegation obeyed the "mandate" of 1918.

Chapter 10 FROM WAR TO PEACE

WITH THE passing of the General Election, the leaders of the British Government and Empire were able to turn their attention to more deliberate preparations for peacemaking. Though not fully agreed among themselves about the important subject of compensation from Germany, they were able to define their basic aims—principally that the British Empire should have its just share of whatever Germany was able to pay—and to marshall the ideas and arguments with which these aims might be pursued. During the Peace Conference itself, their intentions and thoughts were somewhat modified by the need to cooperate with President Wilson, by an apparent shift back toward Liberalism in British politics, and by an intense and growing desire for demobilization among the British public. These influences, however, were not strong enough to deflect British policy from its war-generated *sine qua non*: that Germany should pay at least some of the significant costs, as well as damages, of the War, and that this was justifiable since Germany had caused what seemed the most barbarous conflict in modern history.

* * *

In preparing for the Peace Conference, a first logical consideration for the members of the Imperial War Cabinet was the report of their own Committee on Indemnity. Discussion of the report began on December 23, when several members of the Imperial Cabinet pointed out the differences between the con-

clusions reached by Hughes' Committee and those produced by
the Treasury. The Cabinet then decided to discuss the two
reports fully on the following day, and at the same time to com-
pose instructions that would guide the British Empire reparation delegates at the Peace Conference.[1]

On December 24, Hughes and Walter Long undertook to
defend the work of their Committee against rival memoranda
and opinions. Hughes continued to argue that reparation and
indemnity were equally valid claims. A war costs indemnity, he
said, was necessary to reduce taxation and bolster the relative
economic position of Britain and the Dominions. He admitted
that Germany might not be able to pay the entire Allied cost of
the War, but argued that "it was not for us to limit our demand,
but for Germany to prove to our satisfaction that she could not
pay all that she ought to do."[2] Long agreed with Hughes,
adding that the Federation of British Industries and Associated
Chambers of Commerce had recommended full indemnity and
that there would be "a very awkward situation" if the Government did not demand the entire cost of the War.

Long's reference to the national business organizations was
timely. Only the day before the ACC had notified Lloyd George
that they endorsed the FBI "Peace Aims" memorandum of December 12.[3] That memorandum, as we have seen, stressed the
desirability of a large indemnity. It also made a clear and precocious suggestion as to how such an indemnity could be collected: the payments should be in cash and kind over a long
period of years and the collection should be supervised by a
permanent Allied reparation commission in Germany. The commission would make an army of occupation unnecessary, according to the FBI memorandum. "Such a course would probably be preferred even in the enemy countries themselves to the
constant interference and friction caused by a prolonged and
extensive military occupation."[4] This suggestion foretold one
of the central features of the Treaty of Versailles. However, on
December 24, the specific suggestion was less important than the
fact that two important business groups supported Hughes' view
of peacemaking.

Hughes and Long, nevertheless, encountered stiff resistance
in the Cabinet. Sir George Foster repeated his argument that the

emphatic conclusions of Hughes' report were not warranted by the existing evidence on German capacity. Sir Robert Borden, the Canadian Prime Minister, agreed with his Minister of Finance. Borden said that indemnity was outside the Fourteen Points and would harm Anglo-American relations. George Barnes, soon to be a British Delegate to the Peace Conference, added that to demand an indemnity would appear a contradiction of the Armistice agreements. Like Foster and Borden, Barnes doubted Germany's capacity to pay an indemnity and urged that Britain concentrate on her more realistic claim for maritime reparation.[5]

The most discouraging opposition Hughes faced was that of Bonar Law. On December 24, the Conservative Leader brought to bear some of the considerations which had influenced his restraint during the election campaign. He doubted that Germany could pay more than reparation, "nor did he see a way of our getting more than reparation without being damaged ourselves." Until some expert opinion—presumably in the Treasury—contradicted his assumptions, Bonar Law thought "it was foolish to quarrel about indemnities."[6] Furthermore, he shared Borden's concern about the effect of this question on Britain's relations with the United States. Then Lord Milner and Winston Churchill, who would shortly replace Milner at the War Office, joined in the scepticism with an argument that was to reappear at the Peace Conference: a large indemnity might prevent German economic recovery from the War and thereby encourage a Bolshevik revolution in Germany.

Faced with a divided Cabinet, Lloyd George did not commit himself to either side. On the one hand, he joined Hughes in the Australian's dislike for American policy. Reasoning as he would again many times in 1919, the British Prime Minister said,

> it was important to remember that we had been fighting for four and a half years, whereas the United States had had to bear the cost of only a year and a half of war. . . . Unless President Wilson was prepared to pool the whole cost of the war, and for the United States to take its share of the whole, he was not in a position to reject our claim for indemnity.[7]

However, Lloyd George also doubted whether the entire cost of

the War could ever be paid by Germany. Then he brought forward the formal instructions which he believed should be given
to the three British Empire reparation delegates to the Peace
Conference, Hughes, Lord Cunliffe, and Lord Sumner:

> To endeavour to secure from Germany the greatest possible in-
> demnity she can pay consistently with the economic well-being
> of the British Empire and the peace of the world, and without
> involving an army of occupation in Germany for its collection.[8]

There was no objection to this vague compromise, one which
would cover any adjustment of British aims to further developments.

One immediate development which affected British aims was
the arrival of President Wilson in Britain on December 26. Lloyd
George, perhaps counting on his personal charm, hoped that he
could persuade the President of the justice of the British position
on indemnity.[9] However, Wilson soon dealt this hope a sharp
blow. After a long, confidential talk with the President, Lloyd
George was compelled to relate Wilson's intransigence to the
Imperial Cabinet on December 30.

> With regard to indemnity, Mr. Lloyd George reported that he found
> the President, on the whole, stiffer than on any other question. The
> utmost concession he seemed inclined to make was that the claims
> for pure reparation should be tabled first, and that then other
> claims might possibly be considered afterwards. Mr. Lloyd George
> had pointed out that that practically ruled the British Empire out
> in spite of the enormous burdens it had borne, and that France and
> Belgium, who had borne a lesser burden, would get practically
> everything. . . . Similarly, he had pointed out that Australia at
> this moment owed 75 pounds sterling for every man, woman, and
> child of her population, a loss which was just as real as any loss
> represented by destroyed houses. He had, however, failed to make
> any impression on the President.

This report brought forth a bitter response from Hughes, who
said,

> that if we were not very careful, we should find ourselves dragged
> quite unnecessarily behind the wheels of President Wilson's chariot.
> . . . The United States had made no money sacrifice at all. They

had not even exhausted the profits which they had made in the
first two and a half years of the war. In men, their sacrifices were not
even equal to those of Australia. . . .

Taking a cue from Hughes, Lord Curzon added that "it might be
necessary, on some issues at any rate, for Mr. Lloyd George to
work at the Conference in alliance with M. Clemenceau."[10]
Walter Long agreed.

Hughes' remarks probably surprised no one, but Curzon's
comment disturbed several members of the Cabinet. Lord Reading, Ambassador to the United States, hoped that Curzon was not
suggesting a British-American rupture. Winston Churchill reminded the Cabinet that if President Wilson would agree to a
readjustment of war loans, "we might go some way towards
meeting his views in the matter of indemnity. For the rest, we
should be civil and insist upon our essential points."[11] Lord
Robert Cecil, only recently appointed British League of Nations
Delegate, remarked that Anglo-American understanding was the
best guarantee of lasting peace.

More important, at the Imperial Cabinet of December 31,
Lloyd George himself spoke against the impression that had
been created by his comments of the day before. He emphasized
that "there was only one point [indemnity] where they were up
against a really hard resistance from President Wilson." On other
issues, the Prime Minister said, Wilson showed signs that he
would be flexible if he got his way on the League of Nations.
"In any case, the British representatives were not going to leave
the Peace Conference without securing the things which mattered most to us, though he was inclined to doubt whether
Germany could actually pay all the indemnity we had a right
to demand."[12]

So by the last day of 1918, Lloyd George had once again come
up against the reality of Wilson's principles and, as in September, the Prime Minister gave way. Neither he nor the majority
of the Imperial Cabinet believed indemnity worth the risk of
losing American cooperation in other aspects of peacemaking,
such as colonies and naval limitations. Likewise, only a minority
of the Cabinet would ever contemplate an alignment with France
against the United States over indemnity or, for that matter, over
any other question.

This did not mean, however, that the Imperial Cabinet would surrender their basic economic aims, but only that they intended to "be civil and insist on our essential points," as Churchill put it. Why, for example, provoke President Wilson when the United States had the power to grant an adjustment of war loans favorable to Great Britain? Was it not "foolish to quarrel over indemnities," as Bonar Law remarked, when they were unsure whether Germany could pay more than reparation? The main point was to insist on a significant British share of whatever could be obtained, whether it was called reparation or indemnity. Moreover, taking this practical view, there was a good hope for American cooperation. On January 17, 1919, Jan Smuts reported to Lloyd George the views of Sir William Wiseman, who knew American thinking as well as any British observer: "He thinks the Americans will agree to Germany paying to her utmost capacity and that the distinction between reparations and indemnities should be avoided."[13] It was in this spirit, avoiding distinctions of principles, that American and British negotiators were to find their *modus vivendi* on economic peacemaking. The Imperial Cabinet discussions of late December, though acrimonious and resentful of the United States, clearly pointed in this direction.

The practical concern about share of compensation was, indeed, central to British policy, not only toward the United States but also toward the other parties to the economic peace. We have already seen how his consideration prompted the British to insert "aggression" into the momentous Allied reservation of November 5, 1918. It continued to preoccupy British thinking, and naturally engendered tension between Britain and her Allies. As Leo Amery wrote in a spirited vein to Arthur Balfour on December 26, ". . . the most important aspect of the whole question [is] how to ensure that whatever sum is available from the Enemy Powers, we should get our fair share and not be done in the eye by our more pushful Allies."[14]

These words were part of a letter that covered a memorandum of considerable insight, "Notes on Indemnity," written by Amery on December 26.[15] This essay dealt with German capacity and with the criteria for determining the total Allied claim and the distribution of payments among the Allies. Amery thought that if internal German consumption were curtailed over the next 30 years, Germany would be able to make cash payments of £ 3,800,000,000 to the Allies. Counting the value of territory ceded and of payments in kind by all the enemy powers, he estimated a grand total of £ 10,000,000,000—a middle position between the optimism of Hughes and the pessimism of Keynes.

On the criteria for Allied claims, Amery was closer to Hughes. Like the Australian, Amery thought Germany should be responsible for war costs as well as for direct damage. However, Amery did more than Hughes, or anyone else, to define a clear basis for Allied claims and for the eventual distribution of whatever Germany could pay. This basis was to be "total net loss," by which Amery meant physical damage plus war costs minus increased production resulting from the War, foreign expenditure in home territory during the War, and the economic value of territory ceded by Germany. The formula was clear and comprehensive, and, accepting the premise of German liability to pay, it was more fair to Germany and to the Allies than any other formula for claims and distribution proposed in 1918-19. Amery believed that its application would ensure a just division of compensation between France and the British Empire. Although France had suffered great damage, Amery reminded his readers that she had also enjoyed the benefits of great British and American expenditure on her soil. France would also receive Alsace and Lorraine, which were much more valuable, economically, than the colonies Britain was likely to annex. "Total net loss" would take these things into account.

Amery sent copies of his memorandum to Arthur Balfour, Bonar Law, and Jan Smuts on December 26, and to Lloyd George and William Morris Hughes on January 1.[16] Sir Maurice Hankey circulated the paper to the entire Imperial Cabinet on December 31. Thus, the memorandum may have influenced the Cabinet discussions of December 30 and 31. This is likely, since the private response of the readers was complimentary.[17] Bonar Law noted on his copy, "I have read it with much care and interest," and Hughes praised the memorandum in a letter to Amery of January 3.[18] That Law and Hughes could agree on the merit of Amery's writing signified the importance of his

objective: a considerable British Empire share of German payments. Amery presented some of the best tactical arguments for
attaining that goal. His thoughts doubtless went with his
superiors to the Peace Conference along with the memoranda
by the Hughes Committee, the FBI, the Treasury's "A" Division,
and the Board of Trade.

Memoranda, of course, were not all that the British took to
Paris. They also made peace under the influence of an enormous,
new Parliamentary majority. On the eve of the Peace Conference, Lloyd George and other members of the Government
seemed to realize that this majority was not to be an unmixed
blessing. Austen Chamberlain wrote to his sister on January 1
that "the Govt. would do better if it had a stronger opposition
in front of it."[19] C. P. Scott told Woodrow Wilson that "the
greatness of the majority was no real strength to the Government,
perhaps the reverse." Wilson replied, "Yes; when he saw Ll.G.
and Balfour before leaving London they were overwhelmed and
could not get their bearings."[20] One source of this consterna-
tion was apprehension about how an unchecked Conservative
House of Commons might hamper British peacemaking.
Throughout the Peace Conference, Lloyd George and Bonar
Law had to make constant efforts to free their diplomacy from
the embarrassing Parliament elected at the end of the War.

Nevertheless, the two Coalition leaders largely succeeded in
holding their Conservative critics at bay. At Westminster, Bonar
Law dealt manfully with their anxious and sometimes hostile
enquiries. At Paris, Lloyd George felt free enough of backbench
influence to urge politic concessions to Germany, as in his Fontainebleau Memorandum of March 25.[21] Later, on April 9, he
replied to the telegram from 198 MPs by warning them that he
would not flinch from an electoral test of the issue they had
raised:

> My colleagues and I mean to stand faithfully by all the pledges we
> gave to the constituencies. We are prepared at any moment to sub-
> mit to the judgement of Parliament and, if necessary, of the country
> our efforts loyally to redeem our promises.[22]

More important, Lloyd George returned to London where he
confronted his anti-German critics in the House of Commons on

April 16, and put them to ridicule with a devastating speech, after which there were no more querulous telegrams to Paris.[23] Then in late May and early June, the Prime Minister worked for several last-minute concessions that would enable Germany to sign the Treaty. These were acts of courage. They fulfilled C. P. Scott's prediction of December 30: "We have good reason to believe that Mr. George is better than his speeches, and that he will do much better and greater things than his speeches presaged."[24]

However, the moderate policies of March to June were not conceived solely or independently by the Prime Minister. He and the British Empire Delegation were also responding to certain political and diplomatic developments. At home during the Conference, journalistic opinion was beginning to turn away from the spirit of the Election. The March issue of the *Round Table* commented:

> Seen at a two-month's interval these war-cries [of the Election] seem not only utterly unworthy of the situation in which the country then found itself, but also somewhat unreal; since in the intervening period the punishment of the Kaiser has receded into the background, indemnities have been whittled down to reparation and referred to an International commission which is not likely to put the British claims in the forefront.[25]

The *Round Table*'s assessment was not altogether accurate, but the monthly was right in detecting the beginnings of a shift away from the anti-German temper. This tendency was also expressed in party politics, by a swing back toward Liberalism. At the West Derby, Liverpool by-election of February 27, 1919, the Conservative General Election majority was strikingly reduced. More important, independent Liberals displaced Conservatives in by-elections at West Leyton on March 1, at Central Hull on March 29, and at Central Aberdeen on April 16.[26] These developments bolstered Lloyd George's courage to negotiate according to his own lights and enabled him to frighten the anti-German MPs on April 9 with the threat of an early election.

Another domestic opinion which moved the Prime Minister to conciliate Germany, especially late in the Conference, was the clear, insistent desire for peace and demobilization. By June

1919, most British citizens had come to realize that further sacrifices might be required of themselves and of their relatives in the
military, especially if Germany collapsed into a proletarian
revolution or if the German Government refused to accept the
Allied terms. Lloyd George tried to prevent both developments
by urging moderation in early June, especially regarding German
boundaries in the East, the admission of Germany to the League
of Nations, the length of the Allied occupation in the West, and
the method of fixing a total sum of reparation. If the French
would not agree to concessions in these areas, the British Empire Delegation was prepared to withdraw the British Army and
the Royal Navy from Allied service.[27]

The early success of British diplomacy at the Peace Conference
also enabled Lloyd George to be moderate from March to June.
Well before the Fontainebleau Memorandum, the German fleet
had been interned at Scapa Flow and the British Empire Delegation had achieved their basic aims in the matter of colonial
mandates. In March, the anxieties of British negotiators were
further relieved by a compromise with the United States on
reparation and indemnity: Although Germany was to be liable
in theory for reparation *and* indemnity, only categories of
reparation would be considered within Germany's capacity to
pay. This would satisfy most American scruples. The British
desire for a healthy share of German payments would be met by
including pensions and separation allowances as categories of
reparation. As Lloyd George told the British Empire Delegation
on March 13:

> Colonel House had said that, if the exaction could be framed as to
> exclude the cost of the war, the United States would stand aside.
> We should be able, under such a scheme, to include the capitalised
> cost of our pensions in our claim. He had succeeded in getting the
> Americans to support his view on the question of distribution.[28]

Indeed, the inclusion of pensions and separation allowances
promised to raise the British portion of German payments from
about 17 percent to the more respectable neighborhood of 25
percent, at least half of what France would receive.[29] But were
pensions and separation allowances really "damage done to the
civilian population of the Allies . . . by the aggression of Ger-

many?"[30] On the last day of March 1919, Jan Smuts convinced President Wilson that they were, thereby clinching the British case on distribution.[31] The President also agreed, on May 9, to a division of maritime reparation proportionate to British losses.[32] In these discreet ways, British negotiators were able to secure the consent of the United States to the essential economic aims of the British Empire, just as the Imperial Cabinet had hoped in late December. This success was another reason why Lloyd George was willing and able to conciliate Germany late in the Conference. Or, as Clemenceau cynically remarked about the Fontainebleau Memorandum, the "maritime peoples who had not known invasion" and who had achieved their most important objectives were willing to "appease" Germany at the expense of the Continental Allies.[33]

Even so, the appeasement Clemenceau spoke of was appeasement through expedient concessions, not through genuine negotiation. The latter was rendered impossible by the still prevalent consciousness of war, which could not have dissolved so early as June 1919. Thus, while urging concessions on June 1, Lloyd George could also say, "By every principle of justice, by the principles of justice which were recognized as applicable between individuals, the Germans were liable for the whole of the damages and the cost of recovering them;" and later, "Somebody had to pay. Those who ought to pay were those who caused the loss."[34] Six months after the Election, the themes of the campaign still interlaced the Prime Minister's thinking. Also, he was still under pressure from William Morris Hughes. Hughes was nearly eclipsed by the galaxy of statesmen at Paris, but, with a characteristic single-mindedness, he followed his campaign for war costs through to its bitter conclusion. On June 9, for instance, Hughes, Cunliffe, and Sumner addressed to Lloyd George one of the last of many vigorous recommendations they sent to him during the Conference. They wrote, "Substantial concessions on our part would not hasten the signing of peace but would encourage the Germans to make further demands."[35] They especially urged Lloyd George to rebuff the German offer to assume a definite, total obligation of £5,000,000,000, which was very near the sums then being discussed in Allied councils.[36] The Allied rejection of this German proposal was counted by the three British reparation delegates as one of their important achievements.

They were also pleased with the Reparation Articles themselves, especially with the first, Article 231:

> The Allied and Associated Governments affirm and Germany accepts the responsibility of Germany and her Allies for causing all the loss and damage to which the Allied and Associated Governments and their nationals have been subjected as a consequence of the war imposed upon them by the aggression of Germany and her Allies.[37]

To Hughes and the like-minded, the stark premise of aggression and the inclusive liability seemed a fitting recognition of their efforts.

It is true, of course, that some such form of words was logically necessary to justify the demands for "reparation" that followed in Article 232 and in Annex I to the Reparation Articles. It is also true that the German Government itself seized upon the implication of war guilt in order to stimulate German national unity and bolster their position in the National Assembly.[38] However, these two considerations should not obscure the fact that the Allies sincerely believed in the truth and justice of their declaration. They made this clear in the reply they gave to the German counter-proposals of May 29. The Allies carefully discussed their response from May 30 to June 16, when they sent a public reply to the Germans in the form of a long memorandum and covering letter.[39] These granted several concessions to Germany, but their language was also replete with terms such as "barbarity," "criminal," and "lust for tyranny." The basic assumptions of the covering letter were that

> the war which began on August 1st, 1914, was the greatest crime against humanity and the freedom of peoples that any nation, calling itself civilised, has ever consciously committed. . . . Germany's responsibility, however, is not confined to having planned and started the war. She is no less responsible for the savage and inhuman manner in which it was conducted.[40]

Thus, the Germans were right to claim that Article 231 was more than a drafting premise. The Allied condemnation was intended to be moral as well as logical.

This was also the prevalent interpretation in the British press. Referring to Article 231 as published in the Allied preliminary terms of May 7, the *Daily Telegraph* said, "the principle is laid down with all desirable rigour. . . . To have that admitted in set terms is the indispensable moral foundation for all that follows."[41] The *Spectator* agreed:

> On the whole, we believe that the Allies have taken the right course. They intend, as we have continually urged that they should, to make Germany admit her full responsibility for the whole cost of the war. That is a moral responsibility which Germany must acknowledge before the bar of the world.[42]

Later, *The Times* ridiculed the German delegates because "they writhe at the obligation imposed upon them to confess their guilt."[43] One of the few aspects of the Treaty which the jingo *National Review* felt "left little to be desired" was Article 231, which editor Maxse called "an unimpeachable statement of an undeniable fact."[44] Those who had demanded a punitive peace were also pleased with Article 232 and Annex I, which spelled out the categories of "reparation" demanded of Germany. The indirect damage done by the cost of pensions was included there; so was "damage caused by any kind of maltreatment of prisoners of war."[45] This seemed to redress one of the major grievances of the British public. Here and elsewhere in the Reparation Articles the wartime campaign to recover at least some of the costs of the War had found a dramatic, official expression.

Moderate opinion was not yet strong enough nor sufficiently general in June 1919 to resist that expression. Almost another year was required for a Conservative MP to be able to say to the House of Commons,

> I was elected, as so many others were, on the ticket of "Hang the Kaiser and make the Germans pay." What I wish to point out is that at the time we were elected we were extraordinarily ignorant of the position of Germany. We thought even when she was beaten that she was still a very powerful nation, and we hated her because we feared her, and fear is the basic principle of hatred.[46]

Fear of Germany's economic and military strength, and hatred of her arrogance—these were the origins of Reparation and war

guilt in Britain. Both emotions stretched back well into the war
years; both took various forms, inspiring trade war and then indemnity, focusing first on enemy aliens and later on German war
crimes; both were given a final impetus by the General Election
and by the fiscal worries of Britain at the end of the War. They
survived into the months of Peace Conference and saddled the
Treaty of Versailles with its fateful mixture of economic penalty
and moral censure. That decent men and sensible politicians
could not avoid this outcome was a final testimony to the strain of
war.

Appendix

PUNITIVE MEMBERS
OF PARLIAMENT

Punitive Members of Parliament

Members of the House of Commons elected in December, 1918 who advocated a large indemnity, war crimes trials, or expulsion of enemy aliens during the months from the opening of Parliament in February to the debate on the Versailles Treaty in July, 1919. (Name, constituency, source of punitive speech or similar activity.)

Conservatives

1. Archer-Shee, Sir Martin. Finsbury. 113 HC Deb 1310, March 13.
2. Astbury, Frederick W. West Salford. 114 HC Deb 1325, April 2.
3. Balfour, Gerald. Hampstead. 112 HC Deb 1122, February 20.
4. Burgoyne, Col. Alan. N. Kensington. *The Times* (hereafter *TT*), March 31, p. 6.
5. Burn, Col. Charles R. Torquay, Devonshire. 113 HC Deb 538, March 5.
6. Butcher, Sir John G. York City. *TT*, July 3, p. 7.
7. Carter, R. A. D. Withington, Manchester. 114 HC Deb 2800, April 15.
8. Coates, Maj. Sir Edward. West Lewisham. Initiated telegram of April 8, *TT*, April 9, p. 13.
9. Craik, Sir Henry. Scottish Universities. *TT*, February 19, p. 9.
10. Davies, Alfred T. Lincoln City. 114 HC Deb 867-8, March 31.
11. Doyle, N. Grattan. N. Newcastle. 112 HC Deb 1122, February 20.
12. Fell, Sir Arthur. Great Yarmouth. *TT*, May 16, p. 13.
13. Goulding, Sir Edward. Worcester. Initiated telegram of April 8, *TT*, April 9, p. 13.

14. Greene, Lt.-Col. W. R. N. Hackney. 114 HC Deb 2745, April 15.
15. Gretton, Col. John. Burton, Staffs. 112 HC Deb 198, February 12.
16. Griffiths, Col. Sir John Norton. Central Wandsworth. 112 HC Deb 265, February 13.
17. Guiness, Maj. Walter E. Bury St. Edmonds, Suffolk. 112 HC Deb 179, February 12.
18. Gwynne, R. Eastbourne. 112 HC Deb 265, February 13.
19. Hailwood, Augustine. Ardwick, Manchester. 114 HC Deb 1332, April 2.
20. Hall, Lt.-Col. Sir Frederick. Dulwich. 114 HC Deb 1062, April 1 and 114 HC Deb 867, March 31.
21. Hambro, Capt. Angus V. S. Dorset. Initiated telegram of April 8, *TT*, April 9, p. 13.
22. Hoare, Col. Sir Samuel. Chelsea. 114 HC Deb 1327, April 2 and 118 HC Deb 1038, July 21.
23. Hurd, Percy. Frome, Somerset. Initiated telegram of April 8, *TT*, April 9, p. 13.
24. Jones, Kennedy. Hornsey, Middlesex. Initiated telegram of April 8, *TT*, April 9, p. 13.
25. Joynson-Hicks, William. Twickenham, Middlesex. TT, February 14, p. 12.
26. Lonsdale, James R. Mid Armagh. Initiated telegram of April 8, *TT*, April 9, p. 13.
27. Lowther, Col. Claude. Lonsdale, Lancs. Initiated telegram of April 8, *TT*, April 9, p. 13.
28. Lyle, C. E. Leonard. Stratford, West Ham. *TT*, May 19, p. 13.
29. Macmaster, Donald, Chertsey, Surrey. 112 HC Deb 202, February 12.
30. McNeill, Ronald. Canterbury. 112 HC Deb 136, February 12.
31. Meysey-Thompson, Lt.-Col. Ernest. Handsworth, Birmingham. 114 HC Deb 3008, April 16.
32. Nicholl, Commander Sir Edward. Penryn and Falmouth. 114 HC Deb 1310, April 2.
33. Nield, Sir Herbert. Ealing. *TT*, February 13, p. 9.
34. Prescott, Maj. W. H. N. Tottenham. 112 HC Deb 1188, February 20.
35. Raeburn, Sir William H. Dumbartonshire. *TT*, May 9, p. 13.

36. Ramsden, Capt. George T. Elland, West Riding. 113 HC Deb 1087, March 11.
37. Raper, Lt. Alfred B. East Islington. 112 HC Deb 559, February 17.
38. Stewart, G. Wirral, Chester. *TT*, July 3, p. 7.
39. Surtees, Brig.-Gen. H. C. Gateshead. *TT*, May 9, p. 13.
40. Weigall, Lt.-Col. W. F. G. Horncastle, Lincs. Initiated the telegram of April 8, *TT*, April 9, p. 13.
41. Wild, Sir Ernest. Upton, West Ham. 114 HC Deb 2774, April 15.
42. Winterton, Col. Lord. Horsham and Worthing. 112 HC Deb 1124, February 20.
43. Yate, Col. Charles E. Melton, Leicestershire. 112 HC Deb 265, February 13.

Coalition Liberals

44. Dalziel, Sir J. H. Kirkcaldy Burghs. 114 HC Deb 2811, April 15.
45. Greig, Col. J. W. W. Renfrew. 113 HC Deb 551, March 5.
46. Warner, Sir Thomas C. Lichfield, Staffs, 116 HC Deb 2456, June 6.

National Democrats

47. Edwards, A. Clement. East Ham, South. 112 HC Deb 81, February 11.
48. Loseby, Capt. Charles E. East Bradford. 116 HC Deb 354, May 21.
49. Seddon, J. A. Hanley. 118 HC Deb 980, July 21.
50. Stanton, C. B. Aberdare. 114 HC Deb 2745, April 15.

National Party

51. Cooper, Sir Richard. Walsall. 117 HC Deb 322, June 26.
52. Croft, Brig.-Genl. Henry Page. Bournemouth. 112 HC Deb 88, February 11.

Independents

53. Billing, N. Pemberton. Hertford, Herts. 114 HC Deb 1210, April 2.
54. Bottomley, Horatio. S. Hackney. 112 HC Deb 130, February 12.

Notes

Chapter 1 INTRODUCTION: Paying for the war

1 Less attention was given to the guilt of Germany's allies, almost none to their economic capacity to pay for the War. This study, therefore, concentrates on economic attitudes and policies toward Germany and on the economic peace of Versailles.

2 "Reparation" and "indemnity" had distinct technical meanings. Reparation meant compensation for damage done to civilian population and property by military action. Indemnity meant compensation for all other expenses related to the war effort. The contemporary usage was not so distinct. Each term was frequently used to mean all manner of compensation. Indemnity was especially liable to this misuse. Here, contemporary misnomers will be noted as they are presented. In the text of this study, the two terms will be used according to their technical meanings.

Chapter 2 ANTI-GERMAN ECONOMICS

1 Figures from R. J. S. Hoffman, *Great Britain and the Anglo-German Trade Rivalry, 1875-1914* (Philadelphia, 1933), pp. 102 ff.

2 Ernest E. Williams, *Made in Germany* (London, 1896), p. 169.

3 See the excellent account of the prewar Tariff Reform League in Bernard Semmel, *Imperialism and Social Reform* (New York, 1968), pp. 91-117.

4 From "The War and Economic Policy," a memorandum in the Papers of W. A. S. Hewins, formerly in the possession of Mr. Richard Hewins, now at the University of Sheffield Library. Hewins was a former Director of the London School of Economics, a leading historical economist, and an avowed imperialist. As Conservative MP, Chairman of the Unionist Business Committee, Secretary of the Tariff Commission, Under-Secretary at the Colonial Office, and a member of many Government economic committees, he spread his views widely.

5 See Carson's memorandum of January 21, 1918 at the Public Record Office, paper no. G 190 in Cabinet Papers, class 24, volume 4 (hereafter G 190, CAB 24/4); and the speech by Algernon Firth of March 7, 1916 in *Monthly Proceedings of the Associated*

Chambers of Commerce of the United Kingdom, March 1916, Appendix I, p. 18.

6   "German Post-War Economic Policy," a memorandum by the Reconstruction Committee, paper no. G.T. 307, a copy in the Hewins Papers.

7   For example, his speech of January 10, 1916 in *Parliamentary Debates.* House of Commons. (Fifth series) Volume 77, column 1300. (Hereafter 77 HC Deb 1300.)

8   July 20, 1917, p. 7.

9   "The Prevention of War," a 1918 memorandum in the Papers of Leopold S. Amery, in the possession of Mr. Julian Amery.

10   September 28, 1916, p. 4.

11   In a speech at Glasgow, April 28, 1916, quoted in the *War Notes* of the Tariff Reform League, May 15, 1916, No. 18, p. 276.

12   De F. Pennefather, Member for Kirkdale, Liverpool, 77 HC Deb 1353.

13   Charles S. Henry, Member for Wellington, Shropshire, 78 HC Deb 799. January 21, 1916.

14   January 12, 1916. Leading article. This three-level scheme was a common suggestion.

15   "Notes on Possible Terms of Peace." April 11, 1917, paper no. P. -17 in Cab. 29/1. On the theme of self-sufficiency, see Sir Keith Hancock, "Problems of Economic Policy, 1919-1939," *Survey of British Commonwealth Affairs* (Oxford Press, 1940), vol. 2, part 1, chap. 5. Hancock describes the British wartime mentality as the "economics of siege."

16   pp. 115 and 5.

17   No. 20, p. 753.

18   Article by Cox in the *Sunday Times,* February 6, 1916, p. 6.

19   *Daily Chronicle,* February 1, 1915, p. 6.

20   Speech of February 29, 1916, quoted in the *War Notes* of the Tariff Reform League, no. 14, p. 223.

21   The vote was 988 against the resolution, 527 in favor. *War Notes* of the Tariff Reform League, March 1, 1916, no. 13, pp. 195-96.

22   *Round Table,* September 1916, no. 24, p. 757.

23   Member for Mansfield, Nottinghamshire, March 23, 1916. 81 HC Deb 513-4.

24   Member for Calmachie, Glasgow. January 10, 1916. 77 HC Deb 1335-6. See the sketch of Mackinder in Semmel, *Imperialism and Social Reform,* pp. 157-168.

25   "Rough Preliminary Note on Trade War," October 8, 1917, at the Public Record Office in Foreign Office Papers, class 800, volume 214. (Hereafter, FO 800/214).

26   "Trade Policy After the War," June 18, 1918, EDDC 18, CAB 27/44. Mond was a leading organizer of the chemical industry (he later founded the Imperial Chemical Industries), and it may be

that his interest in that "key" industry prompted his change of view.

27 "Imperial Trade Relations," n.d., GT 385, FO 800/214.

28 In fact, the McKenna duties remained in force until 1924, when the Labour Government removed them. In 1921, they were supplemented by the wider range of tariffs enacted by the Safeguarding of Industries Act.

29 August 2, 1916. 85 HC Deb 333-342.

30 August 2, 1916. 85 HC Deb 418.

31 "Rival Economic Systems in Europe," *Contemporary Review* 109 (February 1916): 196.

32 Diary entry of October 22, 1917, Amery Papers.

33 For example, see its praise of Prime Minister Hughes in April 1916, vol. 46, p. 293; and of the Paris Economic Resolutions in July 1916, vol. 47, pp. 61-62.

34 For a complete list of the initial members see W. A. S. Hewins, *The Apologia of An Imperialist*, 2 vols. (London, 1929), 2:11.

35 Committee documents in the Hewins Papers show that 114 Conservatives attended, out of a Conservative Parliamentary Party which varied in size from 270 to 282.

36 For example, Sir Frederick Banbury, Director of the Great Northern Railway and of the London and Provincial Bank, and MP for the City of London; and Sir George Younger, owner of the Scottish brewing firm and Chairman of the Conservative Party from 1917 to 1923.

37 Shirley Benn and De F. Pennefather were prominent members of the ACC. George Terrell was important in the NUM.

38 Hewins, *Apologia*, 2: 102-04.

39 Ibid., p. 9. The Commission had been set up at Joseph Chamberlain's initiative to make an "objective" study of tariffs, but its political activities were definitely protectionist.

40 *Tariff Reformer*, November 1917, no. 9. This publication succeeded the *War Notes* of the Tariff Reform League in 1917.

41 Annual Report of the Unionist Business Committee for 1916-17. Hewins Papers.

42 John Gretton, a member of the UBC Executive, to W. A. S. Hewins, October 16, 1915. Hewins Papers.

43 Hewins, *Apologia*, 2:111. Long had disliked Bonar Law since 1911 when the Conservative Leader had won his position at Long's expense.

44 Ibid., p. 112.

45 See the long letter from Lord Hugh to Lord Robert Cecil in the Viscount Cecil of Chelwood (Robert Cecil) Papers in the British Museum. January 10, 1915. Vol. 51157. Hugh Cecil was MP for Oxford University; Robert Cecil for Hitchin, Hertfordshire.

46 pp. 2-3. Bentinck was MP for South Nottingham.

47 February 13, 1918. 103 HC Deb 161, 163-64.
48 The War Committee and the Business Committee were not wholly distinct groups, since some Conservative MPs belonged to both.
49 87 HC Deb 249.
50 87 HC Deb 304 ff, 314 ff, 328 ff.
51 87 HC Deb 259 ff.
52 87 HC Deb 351.
53 87 HC Deb 355.
54 87 HC Deb 278 ff., 332 ff. Baldwin was Member for Bewdley, Worcester.
55 Entry for November 13, 1916, Hewins Papers.
56 Trevor Wilson ed., *The Political Diaries of C. P. Scott, 1911-1928* (Ithaca, New York, 1970), diary entry for November 20-22, 1916, p. 235.
57 See Neal Blewett, "Free Fooders, Balfourites, Whole Hoggers. Factionalism within the Unionist Party, 1906-10," *The Historical Journal*, 11, no. 1, 1968, pp. 95-124.
58 Hughes' speech of March 9, 1916, to the Empire Parliamentary Association. *The Times*, March 10, 1916, p. 7.

Chapter 3 TWO WARTIME POLICIES

 1 For example, Sir Llewellyn Woodward's profound history, *Great Britain and the War of 1914-18* (London, 1967), neglects the Resolutions. Existing treatments are fragmentary; for instance, Laurence Martin's excellent *Peace without Victory* (New Haven, 1958), pp. 32-33, 69-71, and *passim.*
 2 *Monthly Proceedings* of the ACC, December 1915, no. 615, pp. 180-85.
 3 The *Sydney Morning Herald*, July 28, 1915, and a letter from the Agent-General of British Columbia to the *Morning Post*, October 25, 1915.
 4 Memorandum by Lord Granville and a covering letter by Lord Bertie, September 14, 1915. CAB 37/141, no. 15.
 5 CAB 37/142, no. 29.
 6 Privately, he was successful. Prime Minister Asquith and Walter Runciman, President of the Board of Trade, assured him on separate occasions that an Allied commercial conference was being arranged. Hewins Papers, 1915 correspondence and Hewins Diary, December 11, 1915.
 7 77 HC Deb 1299.
 8 Ten of the eleven Conservatives were members of the Unionist Business Committee, and seven of these ten were on the UBC Executive.
 9 77 HC Deb 1367.
10 *War Notes* of the TRL called the discussion "an epoch-making debate." January 15, 1916, no. 11, p. 161.

11 Letter of January 12, 1916, Hewins Papers, 1916 correspondence. Sir Alfred Mond was one of the Liberals who spoke for the motion. For an essay on Cunningham, see Semmel, *Imperialism and Social Reform*, pp. 180-93.

12 A meeting called at the suggestion of.the London Chamber of Commerce and attended by the President and prominent members of the Associated Chambers of Commerce, several members of the Unionist Business Committee, Agents-General for most of the Canadian and Australian provinces, and representatives of many other business associations. *The Times*, February 1, 1916, p. 5.

13 *Monthly Proceedings* of the ACC, March 1916, no. 618, pp. 3 ff.

14 A copy is in the Hewins Papers, 1916 correspondence.

15 80 HC Deb 1771-4.

16 Unofficial memorandum, March 10, 1916, Papers of Herbert Henry Asquith, Lord Oxford and Asquith, Bodleian Library, Oxford University, vol. 29, fol. 219.

17 For example, when Briand proposed that economic collaboration would shorten the War and prevent postwar German dumping, "Asquith and Grey were rather reserved on this subject." Lord Bertie's minutes for the meeting of March 27, 3:30 p.m., Bertie Papers, FO 800/175.

18 *Procès-verbaux* of the conference in CAB 37/145, no. 39.

19 CAB 37/147, no. 3.

20 A copy of these draft resolutions, dated June 5, 1916, is in the Asquith Papers, vol. 30, 116 ff.

21 The Board of Trade exaggerated only slightly in saying that the British draft resolutions ". . . were practically adopted without serious amendment." From an unofficial memorandum of June 30, 1916, drawn by the Board for Asquith's use in the House of Commons. This is the best record of the Conference, and the following account is based largely on it. A copy is in the Asquith Papers, vol. 30, 116 ff.

22 This preamble was interpreted as the Allied response to the economic aspects of Frederich Naumann's *Mitteleuropa*, published earlier in the year. See J. A. R. Marriott, "Mitteleuropa and the Meaning of the Paris Pact," *War Notes* of the TRL, January 1, 1917, and a leading article in *The Times*, August 14, 1917.

The text of the Resolutions used here is the official translation in the Public Record Office, Treasury Papers, class 172, volume 371 (hereafter, T 172/371).

23 Board of Trade memorandum of June 30, 1916.

24 Llewellyn Smith regarded the Italians and Russians as the "main difficulty" at the Conference. Telegram of June 16, 1916, FO 368/1669.

25 Board of Trade memorandum of June 30, 1916.

26 83 HC Deb 500-502.

27 The Conservative Party's *Gleanings and Memoranda* printed the same slogan in a similar way.

28 CAB 37/151, no. 23. No discussion recorded.
29 85 HC Deb 332-450.
30 CAB 37/143, no. 19.
31 From a copy of the terms of reference in the Hewins Papers, 1916 correspondence.
32 John Gretton, a member of the UBC, to Hewins, October 10, 1916, Hewins Papers, 1916 correspondence.
33 Copies of the Committee's reports are in FO 800/214.
34 *War Notes* of the TRL, November 1, 1916, no. 29, p. 65.
35 On December 18, 1916, Walter Long told Hewins, ". . . the failure of the B. of B. Committee was one of the causes of the downfall of the late Ministry as I had told Asquith it would be. I pointed the moral for the new Ministry." Hewins, *Apologia*, 2:99-100.
36 George Terrell in a letter to the *Morning Post*, January 11, 1917.
37 Hewins, *Apologia*, 2:140.
38 A copy of the letter, dated July 5, 1917, is in the Hewins Papers, 1917 correspondence.
39 In a letter from Hewins to Walter Long, July 24, 1917, ibid.
40 *Tariff Reformer*, November 1917, no. 9, p. 287. In the autumn of 1917, the Government blunted some of the discontent of the two backbench committees. They appointed Hewins Under-Secretary for the Colonies and assigned Sir Edward Carson, First Lord of the Admiralty and former Chairman of the War Committee, to the Chairmanship of the new Economic Offensive Committee. However, neither man remained content.
41 Conversation of April 11, 1917, described by Hewins in *Apologia*, 2:133-34.
42 November 8, 1916, 87 HC Deb 273.
43 Minutes of the first meeting of the Committee on Economic and Non-Territorial Desiderata in the Terms of Peace, April 16, 1917, in CAB 21/78. The Committee members were distinctly sceptical of the Paris Resolutions. Their deliberations are discussed further in chap. 4.
44 Speaking in the House of Commons on May 16, 1917, 93 HC Deb 1956. After the War, Mackinder turned against the Paris Resolutions. In his famous explanation of the "heartland" theory, *Democratic Ideals and Reality* (New York, 1919), he said on p. 194 that an economic "war after the war" was impractical and would encourage another world war.
45 The Board of Trade memorandum of April 12, 1917 on the Paris Economic Resolutions was a typical comment. CAB 24/10.
46 "Memorandum on Recent German Pronouncements on Economic Policy," June 14, 1918, Papers of Sir William Wiseman, folder 91-6, Yale University. Wiseman was chief of British intelligence in the United States, a friend of Colonel House, and an important,

informal liaison between London and Washington. See W. B.
Fowler, *British-American Relations, 1917-18: The Role of Sir
William Wiseman* (Princeton, 1969).

47 "Memorandum on Trade War," June 27, 1917, Wiseman Papers,
folder 91-6.

48 Memorandum of September 28, 1917, FO 800/214, G.-159.

49 Spring-Rice also said that the Resolutions had confirmed the
American suspicion that ". . . England had entered the war in
the spirit of commercial rivalry and for the purpose of putting an
end to German commercial competition." CAB 37/151, no. 812.

50 Two Foreign Office memoranda circulated among the Cabinet on
October 30, 1916, CAB 37/158, no. 3.

51 Final Report of the Committee on Economic and Non-Territorial
Desiderata in the Terms of Peace, CAB 21/78.

52 Memorandum of July 20, 1917, G.T. 1492. Balfour Papers, FO
800/214.

53 The anonymous American's views described in a letter of February 7, 1918, from Cecil to F. S. Oliver, Chelwood Papers, British
Museum, vol. 51090.

54 Hewins to Walter Long, May 21, 1918, Hewins Papers, Trade
Relations Committee file.

55 This British-American quarrel of 1918 is discussed further in
chap. 5. A brief account of the American reaction to the Paris
Resolutions may be found in Carl P. Parrini, *Heir to Empire:
United States Economic Diplomacy, 1916-28* (Pittsburgh, 1969),
pp. 15 ff.

56 For an excellent discussion of imperial preference, see Hancock,
"Problems of Economic Policy," pp. 84 ff.

57 From 1884 to 1894 the proportion of total colonial and Dominion
imports from foreign countries increased from one-quarter to
one-third. Hoffman, *Anglo-German Trade Rivalry*, p. 198.

58 Of the self-governing Dominions, these two traded most with
Germany before the War. In the years 1906 to 1910, Australia
received 8.8 percent of her imports from Germany and sent 9.2
percent of her exports to that country. From 1909 to 1913, South
Africa imported 8.6 percent of her total imports from Germany and
sent 3.1 percent of her exports to Germany. "Trade of Germany
with the Self-Governing Dominions," November 2, 1917, CAB
27/15.

59 *The War and British Economic Policy* (London, 1915), pp. 3-4.
Probably written by Hewins.

60 Papers of Arthur J. Balfour, Lord Balfour, at the British Museum,
vol. 49779.

61 Hewins diary, March 22, 1917.

62 From a copy of the resolutions in the Hewins Papers, 1917
correspondence.

63 Command Paper 8462. There is a good discussion of this Commission and its Report in Hancock, "Problems of Economic Policy," pp. 98-103.
64 Minutes of the Imperial War Cabinet, IWC 11, CAB 23/40.
65 Minutes of the Imperial War Cabinets of April 24 and 26, 1917, IWC 11 and 12, CAB 23/40.
66 Meeting of April 26, IWC 12, minute 16, CAB 23/40.
67 Ibid. A second point was the venerable policy of encouraging emigrants from Britain to go to some British, rather than foreign, country.
68 The Commerical Department expressed these reservations again in a memorandum of July 1917. A copy is in the Hewins Papers, 1917 correspondence.
69 Letter of March 7, 1917, from Amery to Henry Page Croft, to be read at a Tariff Reform League dinner. Amery Papers, E. 60.

Chapter 4 PREPARING TO NEGOTIATE
1 Runciman's memorandum in CAB 37/139. Members of the Committee were Bonar Law, Arthur Henderson, Austen Chamberlain, Lord Crewe, Edwin Montagu, Lord Selbourne, and Runciman. A full discussion of the Reconstruction Committee may be found in Paul B. Johnson, *Land Fit for Heroes* (Chicago, 1968), pp. 10 ff.
2 G.T. 307, also quoted at the beginning of chap. 2. This memorandum and the papers upon which it was based are in the Balfour Papers in FO 800/214.
3 Memorandum P. 12 in CAB 29/1, one of the very important "P" series of memoranda written in preparation for the coming peace conference.
4 Meeting of the Imperial Cabinet, March 23, 1917, IWC 3, minute 6, CAB 23/40. Milner's support is recorded in the diary of his private secretary, Sir Hugh Thornton, entry for March 24, 1917 in the Papers of Alfred Milner, Lord Milner, New College, Oxford University, vol. 301.
5 *My Political Life* (London, 1953), 2:103. Amery was a secretary of the Imperial Cabinet.
6 Other members of Milner's committee were Smuts, Arthur Henderson, Walter Long, H. A. L. Fisher, Sir Robert Borden, Sir Joseph Ward, Sir Edwin Morris, Sir J. Meston, The Maharaja of Bikaner, Sir Eyre Crowe, Sir Hubert Llewellyn Smith, and Edwin Montagu. Leo Amery's diary entry for April 16, 1917, indicates that members were chosen according to a free trade-tariff reform criterion. Sir Hugh Thornton made a similar remark on April 16 in his journal.
7 Minutes of the Committee meetings are summary and reveal little more than the final report. CAB 21/78.
8 ". . . any too comprehensive or ambitious project to ensure world

peace might prove not only impracticable, but harmful. . . .
The Treaty of Peace should provide that none of the parties who
are signatories to that treaty should resort to arms against one
another without previous submission of their dispute to a Conference of the Powers."

9   Minutes of meetings on April 26 and May 1, 1917, IWC 12 and 13,
    CAB 23/40.
10 G. 156 in the Balfour Papers, FO 800/214. Carson drew from a
    memorandum by Ernest M. Pollock of the Foreign Office, G.T.
    1447, June 27, 1917, Wiseman Papers, mentioned in chap. 3.
11 Memorandum of October 4, 1917, G. 158, Balfour Papers, FO
    800/214.
12 "Rough Preliminary Note on Trade War," October 1917, ibid.
13 Other members of the Committee were Walter Long and W. A. S.
    Hewins from the Colonial Office; Lord Robert Cecil and Arthur
    Steel-Maitland of the Foreign Office; Albert Stanley, President
    of the Board of Trade; Stanley Baldwin, financial secretary to the
    Treasury; Christopher Addison, Minister of Reconstruction; and
    George N. Barnes, Labour member of the War Cabinet.
14 EOC 1, October 17, 1917, CAB 27/15.
15 These are in CAB 27/15-16.
16 EOC 3, CAB 27/15.
17 G. 190, CAB 24/4. Carson's emphases.
18 Carson said he suggested the new title because "Economic Of-
    fensive is a rather German-sounding phrase, not very pleasant
    to British ears, and not very easily understood by the man-in-the-
    street."
19 G. 196, February 23, 1918, CAB 24/4.
20 WC 429, CAB 23/6.
21 EDDC minutes and memoranda in CAB 27/44.
22 *The Great Illusion* (New York, 1910), p. 33.
23 "The Indemnity Futility," pp. 85-105, ibid.
24 *After All: The Autobiography of Norman Angell* (New York,
    1951), p. 150.
25 Ibid., p. 164.
26 Ibid., p. 169.
27 *The Franco-German War Indemnity and its Economic Results*
    (London, 1913).
28 p. 122.
29 p. 134.
30 Jones subsequently wrote fourteen books on economics from
    1915 to 1941.
31 Speech at the Guildhall, *The Times*, November 10, 1914, p. 10.
32 Labour Executive resolution at the annual Conference, *The
    Times*, August 11, 1917, p. 4.
33 Conservative Party *Gleanings and Memoranda*, vol. 44, May
    1915, pp. 476-480.

34   *The Times*, December 20, 1916, p. 10.
35   Leading article, October 30, 1916, p. 9.
36   *Daily Chronicle*, November 16, 1914, p. 6.
37   Ironically, Angell remembered Money as having been sympathetic to *The Great Illusion* before the War. *After All*, p. 169.
38   Francis Gribble, "How Germany Can Pay." Like Money, Gribble continued to advocate an indemnity throughout the War. See his "Germany and the Day of Reckoning," *Daily Chronicle*, September 15, 1916.
39   *The Times*, August 1, 1916, p. 11.
40   A copy of this scheme was sent to W. A. S. Hewins by Sir John Pilter, President of the British Chamber of Commerce in Paris on December 17, 1916. Hewins Papers.
41   T 172/639. This volume also contains an article by A. G. Gardiner, the radical Liberal columnist, in which he advocated paying for the War by a "conscription of wealth." *Daily News*, September 8, 1917.
42   Speech in the House of Commons, July 26, 1917, *The Times*, July 27, 1917, p. 10.
43   103 HC Deb 181-2.
44   p. 135.
45   For example, the Commons speech by Sir John Simon, August 2, 1916, 85 HC Deb 354.
46   Speech to the Royal Colonial Institute, Milner Papers, 147 IX.
47   *The Times*, July 31, 1917, p. 8.
48   Angell mentioned Keynes' sympathy in *After All*, p. 169. However, there is no mention of Angell, *The Great Illusion*, or J. H. Jones' rejoinder in the Royal Economic Society's 1971 edition of Keynes' writings for the period 1910-19. See *The Collected Writings of John Maynard Keynes*, vol. 15, *Activities: 1906-14*, and vol. 16, *Activities: 1914-19*.
49   The pamphlet is attached to memorandum P. 12, CAB 29/1.
50   See Semmel, *Imperialism and Social Reform*, pp. 194-207.
51   Attached to P. 12, CAB 29/1. See also *Collected Writings of Keynes*, 16: 313-334.
52   "If an indemnity . . . were paid in part in material wealth, it would be necessary for a valuation to be made of the objects transferred, and for the particular ally which acquired them to make itself responsible for putting an equivalent amount of wealth at the disposal of the territory to be restored."
53   Vol. 1, p. 295.
54   In the *Sunday Times* of October 23, 1938, Keynes himself stressed these two points in replying to Lloyd George's recently published memoirs. *Collected Writings of Keynes*, 16: 335.
55   P. 12, CAB 29/1. Also discussed in the first section of this chapter.
56   P. 15, CAB 21/78.
57   Ibid.

Chapter 5 BRITAIN, WILSON, AND REPARATION

1   A typical complaint was made by Sir Alfred Mond, a member of the Economic Defence and Development Committee, in July 1918. Mond resented the fact that the War was forcing British firms out of export markets which were being captured by American businessmen. "Trade Policy After the War," EDDC 18, CAB 28/44.
2   CAB 21/108.
3   *Tariff Reformer*, August 1918, no. 18, p. 131.
4   *The New York Times*, August 2, 1918, p. 1.
5   Leading article, August 2, 1918, p. 2.
6   IWC 32, CAB 23/43.
7   IWC 33, CAB 23/43.
8   Cable 703, Reading correspondence, FO 800/225.
9   Cable 751, Reading correspondence, FO 800/225.
10 *The Times*, September 13, 1918, pp. 7-8.
11 Philip M. Burnett, *Reparation at the Paris Peace Conference*, 2 vols. (New York, 1940), 1:379-80.
12 Quoted in Martin Gilbert, *The Roots of Appeasement* (London, 1966), pp. 38-9. The minutes were shown to Gilbert by Lord Beaverbrook; the present writer found no record of them in the PRO. Milner made his views public on August 17 in the *Evening Standard*, an interview discussed further in chap. 7.
13 WC 491B, CAB 23/14.
14 Balfour, Bonar Law, Lord Curzon (the Lord President), and Sir Eric Geddes (First Lord of the Admiralty) each spoke in favor of an armistice. Ibid.
15 Ibid. Smuts was a member of the British War Cabinet from June 1917 to December 1918.
16 WC 491A, CAB 23/14.
17 British minutes of the Inter-Allied Conference, IC 83, CAB 28/5.
18 Quoted in WC 495A, CAB 23/14.
19 IC 88, CAB 28/5.
20 IC 92, CAB 28/5.
21 IC 83, CAB 28/5.
22 IC 88, CAB 28/5.
23 My emphasis. British minutes of a meeting of Allied Prime Ministers, Burnett, *Reparation*, 1:407.
24 Note attached to the final reservation, ibid.
25 Letter from Lothian to a South African historian, probably E. A. Walker, quoted in Gilbert, *Appeasement*, p. 31. See also J. R. M. Butler, *Lord Lothian* (London, 1960), pp. 72-73. Butler refers to a letter along the same lines written to Walker on March 18, 1931. Butler also notes that one of Kerr's British colleagues at the Paris discussions, Edgar Abraham, first thought of "aggression."
26 Meeting of November 3, IC 92, CAB 28/5.
27 Burnett, *Reparation*, 1:415.
28 IC 91, CAB 28/5.

29   IWC 36A, CAB 23/44.
30   *Collected Writings of Keynes,* 16:338-343.
31   FO 373, box 7.
32   P. 33, CAB 29/1.
33   Britain had lost 7,684,000 tons of merchant shipping due to naval warfare, or 74.3 percent of total Allied and Associated tonnage lost. (Figures from "The Ton for Ton Policy," an undated and unsigned paper attached to the Board of Trade memorandum.) The Board was specifically interested in acquiring a large share of the 1,378,000 tons of German shipping detained in Allied and neutral harbors at the outbreak of war. The United States had interned over half of these ships. (702,000 tons) At the Peace Conference, the two nations quarrelled over the disposition of the ships and then compromised: The United States kept the ships and paid Britain their cash value through the general reparation fund.
34   P. 33, CAB 29/1.
35   The memorandum is undated. A copy, designated P. 46, is in CAB 29/2. See also *Collected Writings of Keynes,* 16:344-383.
36   The Division also included Andrew MacFadyean, Frank Nixon, Dudley Ward, Geoffrey Fry, and Rupert Trouton. R. F. Harrod, *The Life of John Maynard Keynes* (New York, 1951), pp. 203, 219, and 229. The case for Keynes' authorship is persuasively made in *The Collected Writings of Keynes,* 16:344.
37   *Collected Writings of Keynes,* 16:380.
38   Treasury emphasis. Ibid., p. 382.

Chapter 6 BRITAIN, HUGHES, AND INDEMNITY

1   Meeting of June 26, 1918, CAB 32/1, part 2.
2   Speeches at Cardiff, July 21, 1918, *Daily Mail,* July 22, 1918, p. 2; at Derby, September 2, 1918, *The Times,* September 3, 1918, p. 8; at the Baltic Exchange on October 9, *Daily Telegraph,* October 10, 1918, p. 5; and before the Tariff Reform League on October 16, *The Times,* October 17, 1918, p. 8.
3   Hughes planned to visit the United States on his way home. To prevent this and the inevitable speeches, Wilson wanted to bar the Australian's entry. Secretary of State Lansing convinced the President to send, instead, a strong warning that a Hughes speech in America would be met by a public disavowal. Sir William Wiseman transmitted this message on August 31 to Ambassador Reading, who informed Lloyd George shortly thereafter. Telegrams no. 723, 761 and 769 in Reading correspondence, FO 800/225. In 1919, Hughes returned to Australia direct.
4   WC 484, CAB 23/8.
5   Letter copy in the Amery Papers, E. 61.

6 Sir Maurice Hankey to Lloyd George, October 18, 1918, describing a Cabinet meeting for which no official minutes were taken. Papers of David Lloyd George at the Beaverbrook Library, London, F 23/3/17.
7 A copy of the itinerary is in the Lloyd George Papers, F 23/3/17.
8 Leo Amery wrote in his diary on November 8, 1918, that British ministers found Hughes ". . . irritating . . . on account of his deafness and aggressive manners." Amery Papers.
9 IWC 36A, CAB 23/44.
10 Ibid.
11 Ibid. Hughes adroitly replied that in that case the third point was worthless.
12 Ibid.
13 *Morning Post*, November 8, 1918, p. 8.
14 Lloyd George Papers, F 28/2/9.
15 Lloyd George Papers, F 28/2/10. This assurance had been drafted by Lloyd George, Balfour and Amery, and released to the press the day before, November 8. Amery's diary entry for November 8, 1918.
16 *Morning Post*, November 13, 1918, p. 9.
17 Amery to Hankey, November 13, 1918. In the Papers of Philip Kerr, Lord Lothian at the Scottish Record Office, GD 40/17, 57.
18 *Daily Telegraph*, November 15, 1918, p. 9.
19 Leading articles, respectively, of November 8, 1918, p. 7; November 9, 1918, p. 4; and November 9, 1918, p. 4. *The Times* leader majestically reminded Hughes that in immediate situations Britain must act as the "Imperial Government." Hughes shot back that there was no such Imperial Government: "There is a British Government, and there are Governments of the various Dominions." Letter to the editor of November 9, 1918, p. 7.
20 December 1918, no. 430, pp. 399-400.
21 Leading articles of November 8, 21, 22, and 27, all on p. 4.
22 Speeches by Major Newman, Donald Macmaster, and Claude Lowther, *Daily Telegraph*, November 13, 1918, p. 7.
23 W. Lane-Mitchell, Conservative candidate for Streatham, Wandsworth, to Bonar Law, November 8, 1918, in the Papers of Andrew Bonar Law at the Beaverbrook Library, London, 95/4.
24 Ibid.
25 In *My Political Life*, 2:91, Amery claims that he originated the idea of the Imperial Cabinet.
26 Memorandum of November 14, 1918, Lothian Papers, GD 40/17, 57.
27 Letter copies in the Amery Papers, E. 61.
28 Lloyd George Papers, F 5/2/28.
29 This and the following discussion based on Imperial War Cabinet minutes, IWC 39, CAB 23/43.

30   Vol. 1, pp. 303-06.
31   Later, John Maynard Keynes privately recalled, ". . . who that knows [Cunliffe] could suppose that his opinion as to Germany's capacity to pay was of the slightest value. He was brought in for electioneering and parliamentary purposes; and for parliamentary and press purposes he and Lord Sumner [a British Reparation Delegate] were retained. The Prime Minister was never under the slightest illusion as to the value of their advice." Keynes to Austen Chamberlain, December 28, 1919, Papers of Austen Chamberlain at Birmingham University, A/C/35/1.
32   Verbatim, shorthand notes were taken of most Committee discussions. Unless otherwise indicated, the following account is based on these notes, which are in CAB 27/43.
33   IWC 38, CAB 23/43.
34   A typed copy of the proposal, dated December 1, is in the Hewins Papers, Indemnity Committee file.
35   P. 38, CAB 29/2.
36   Hewins, characteristically, claims credit for the basic ideas of the report. Combined diary entry for October 1918-May 1919. Hewins Papers.
37   IC 97, CAB 28/5.
38   IC 98, CAB 28/5.
39   Meeting of 10:30 a.m., IWC 40, CAB 23/42.
40   Meeting of 11:15 a.m., December 3, 1918, IC 100, CAB 28/5. Lloyd George's emphasis.
41   The change was retrospectively inserted into the minutes of December 2, IC 98a, CAB 28/5.
42   See cable from House to Wilson, December 5, 1918, Burnett, *Reparation*, 1:431.
43   IWC 40, CAB 23/42.
44   Smuts to Lloyd George, December 4, 1918, Lloyd George Papers, F 45/9/25.
45   Again, this account of Committee discussions, unless otherwise indicated, is based on the verbatim notes in CAB 27/43.
46   Lloyd George Papers, F 28/2/15.
47   This and the following account from the "Report of the Committee on Indemnity," P 39 in CAB 27/43. The Committee held all the enemy powers responsible, although they and everyone else realized that only Germany was relevant, given the dissolution of Germany's allies.
48   Along with the Report, Hughes sent extensive notes he hoped Lloyd George would use at Bristol. Lloyd George did not, however, use them. Hughes to Lloyd George, December 10, 1918, Lloyd George Papers, F 28/2/13.
49   Minutes of December 11, 1918, CAB 27/43. W. A. S. Hewins was bitter at not being chosen. "I was indignant about this, as I was mainly responsible for the report." Combined diary entry for November-December 1918, Hewins Papers.

50 Lloyd George Papers, F 28/2/17.
51 There is no record of why this decision was made. Gibbs was
    perhaps omitted because he was one businessman too many,
    perhaps because of his anti-American sentiments. Lloyd George
    later said he chose Sumner because he mistakenly thought the
    justice would temper Hughes and Cunliffe. *Memoirs of the Peace
    Conference,* 1:314.

Chapter 7 THE ANTI-GERMAN TEMPER

1   For an interesting and somewhat paradoxical comparison, see
    Kipling's "Recessional" (1897).
2   Arthur Marwick, *The Deluge* (Boston, 1965), p. 31 ff. provides an
    excellent discussion of British attitudes toward Germany early in
    the War.
3   Ibid., pp. 131-32.
4   At one time, about 32,000 enemy aliens were interned. From April
    1918 to July 1919, 26,090 were deported, usually to their country
    of origin. About 80 percent of those interned and deported were
    German nationals. 114 HC Deb 1091 and 117 HC Deb 1635.
5   The campaign had an anti-Semitic flavor, since many German
    aliens were also Jewish. *The Times,* as well as the extremist press,
    often used "German" and "Jew" interchangeably. C. C. Arons-
    feld, "Jewish Enemy Aliens in England during the First World
    War," *Jewish Social Studies,* October 1956, p. 275.
6   Crowe was attacked in *Brittania,* a militant suffragette publi-
    cation, as "a nephew of Kaiser Wilhelm in the Foreign Office."
    His wife received threatening letters. Near the end of the War, a
    mob almost attacked his London home. From press clippings in
    FO 800/243. Ironically, Crowe was one of the most anti-German
    policy makers in the Foreign Office before and during the War.
7   Reginald Pound and Geoffrey Harmsworth, *Northcliffe* (New
    York, 1960), pp. 646 and 669.
8   Billing was brought to trial for libel by one of the 47,000, but
    was acquitted after proceedings that were "grossly mishandled"
    by the presiding Justice. Robert Blake, *Unrepentant Tory: The
    Life and Times of Bonar Law* (New York, 1956), p. 379.
9   Henry Page Croft, *My Life of Strife* (London, 1948), pp. 130-31.
    Croft was the Leader of the Party.
10 Pound and Harmsworth, *Northcliffe,* pp. 649, 653, 654-55, and
    The History of The Times, 4 vols. (London, 1952), *4,* part one,
    pp. 270, 364.
11 Marwick, *Deluge,* pp. 51, 131-32, 211-14. After the War, the con-
    verted corpses were discovered to have been horses rather than
    human beings. The memory of this fiasco later caused scepticism
    of the stories about Nazi gas chambers.
12 *The Times,* October 12, 1918, p. 2. The sinking encouraged

opposition to an armistice in Britain and America. See Harry Rudin, *Armistice, 1918* (New Haven, 1944), chap. 5.

13 The *Daily Mail* was especially descriptive. See, for example, the issue of October 16, 1918.

14 October 19, 1918, p. 7.

15 October 26, 1918, pp. 6-7.

16 November 20, 1918, p. 3.

17 November 23, 1918, p. 207.

18 November 20, 1918, p. 6.

19 *The Times*, October 30, 1918, p. 8.

20 WC 484, CAB 23/8. The 28 day warning was an obligation under a Hague convention of 1917 governing the treatment of prisoners-of-war.

21 IWC 37, CAB 23/43. The Government also considered bombing five publicly designated towns in reprisal, but decided against this on October 15, because of command problems and the armistice negotiations. Balfour Papers at the British Museum, vol. 49748; and at the PRO, WC 484, CAB 23/8.

22 WC 484, CAB 23/8.

23 See *John Bull*, October 26, 1918, p. 6; *Daily Chronicle*, November 11, 1918, p. 4; *Birmingham Post*, November 11, 1918, p. 6; *Spectator*, November 16, 1918, p. 542; *New Statesman*, November 16, 1918, p. 129.

24 Speech at East Ham, *Daily News*, November 16, 1918, p. 6.

25 WC 488, CAB 23/8 and Lord Beaverbrook, *Men and Power* (London, 1956), pp. 386-87.

26 IWC 37, CAB 23/43.

27 IC 98a, CAB 28/5. Premier Clemenceau was enthusiastic about such a tribunal, before and during the London conference.

28 *Monthly Proceedings of the ACC*, October 1918, p. 110.

29 October 1918, pp. 387 ff.

30 Balfour Papers at the British Museum, vol. 49693.

31 Impatient questions were asked on October 17, 21, 22, and 24. The interrogators were George Terrell, W. M. R. Pringle, Col. C. E. Yate, De. F. Pennefather, George Lambert, Claude Lowther, and Richard Cooper. *Tariff Reformer*, November 1918, p. 171. All but Pringle were members of the Unionist Business Committee and/or the Unionist War Committee.

32 Lloyd George Papers, F 42/4/4.

33 A typed copy of the resolutions is in the Bonar Law Papers, 84/3/5.

34 Bonar Law Papers, 95/1. The Coalition program was, in fact, drafted by Bonar Law and his private secretary, John C. Davidson. On November 2, Lloyd George agreed to issue the draft over his name. Information supplied the author by Lord John Davidson in August 1966. Leo Amery corroborates this claim in his diary entry for November 2, 1918. Amery Papers. Furthermore, all the

drafts of the Coalition's formal program are in the Bonar Law Papers, 84/7/96 and 95/1.
35 Shorthand notes of the meeting in the Bonar Law Papers, 95/3.
36 Speech to the Inter-Allied Parliamentary Committee, *Morning Post*, October 26, 1918, p. 7.
37 Leading article, October 29, 1918, p. 2.
38 Leading article, December 6, 1918, p. 8.
39 Speeches by Smith and Northcliffe in *The Times*, September 19, 1918, p. 3 and September 20, 1918, p. 3. Leading articles in the *Scotsman*, October 10, 1918, p. 4, and in the *Daily Express*, October 18, 1918, p. 2.
40 Respectively, November 5, 1918, p. 2; October 1918, p. 144; October 13, 1918, p. 6; October 12, 1918, p. 381.
41 *The Times*, October 24, 1918, p. 7.
42 *National Review*, March 1918, p. 5; July 1918, p. 555; August 1918, p. 675; September 1918, p. 33.
43 *National Review*, October 1918, p. 153.
44 Bottomley's emphasis. *John Bull*, October 12, 1918, pp. 6-7.
45 *Morning Post*, October 15, 1918, p. 8.
46 October 15, 1918, p. 2.
47 Ten column inches on p. 8. All emphases those of the National Party.
48 *The Times*, November 4, 1918, p. 3.
49 November 2, 1918, p. 2.
50 "Phoenix," November 12, 1918, p. 4.
51 Analysis of electoral feeling in Sussex, *Morning Post*, November 29, 1918, p. 5.
52 *The Times*, November 27, 1918, p. 10. However, in the same speech, Churchill emphasized penalizing Germany through loss of territory and colonies rather than through reparation and indemnity. He said £2,000,000,000 was the limit of German capacity; to demand more would damage the German economy in ways that would encourage Bolshevism. This remained his attitude toward the economic peace throughout the campaign and in 1919.
53 "On Being an Alien," in the issue of July 13, 1918, pp. 287-78.
54 *Manchester Guardian*, November 21, 1918, p. 10.
55 *The Times*, November 28, 1918, p. 8.
56 *The Times*, September 27, 1918, p. 3.
57 For example, his speech to the National Liberal Federation, September 27, 1918, *The Times*, September 28, 1918, p. 4.
58 Letter of December 7, 1918, Austen Chamberlain Papers, AC 15/1/1-35.
59 *Manchester Guardian*, leading articles of November 11, 12, 13, 28, and December 6, 1918.
60 *Manchester Guardian*, November 13, 1918, p. 4.
61 *Evening Standard*, October 17, 1918, pp. 1-2.
62 Speech by Northcliffe, October 22, 1918, *History of The Times*,

4, part one, p. 376. The *Daily Mail* also attacked with leading articles on November 4 and 6, 1918. *The Times* made a more restrained criticism on October 22, 1918, p. 9. *Times* Editor Geoffrey Dawson was a close friend of Milner's. Dawson was already embroiled in a dispute with Northcliffe that soon led to the Editor's resignation.

63   Speech of October 22, 1918, *The Times*, October 23, 1918, p. 8.
64   October 26, 1918, p. 64.
65   Respectively, October 24, 1918, 110 HC Deb 1071-9; and October 28, 1918, 110 HC Deb 1114.
66   Letter to Sir Hugh Thornton, October 31, 1918, Milner Papers, 145 VII.
67   Ibid.

Chapter 8 THE GENERAL ELECTION

 1   Trevor Wilson, *The Downfall of the Liberal Party, 1914-35* (London, 1966), pp. 141 ff., and Bonar Law Papers, 95/1.
 2   Harold Nicolson, *King George V* (London, 1953), pp. 328-29.
 3   F. E. Guest, the Chief Coalition Liberal Whip, for a time advised Lloyd George to fight the election independently. On August 16, 1918, Guest told Lloyd George he could and should win the election on a purely Liberal program of domestic reconstruction and Wilsonian peace aims. Lloyd George Papers, F 21/2/31. Some Conservatives warned Bonar Law that Lloyd George intended to destroy the traditional principles of the Conservative Party. Walter Long to Law, July 17, 1918, Bonar Law Papers, 83/5/17, and Sir George Younger, Conservative Party Chairman, reporting on Conservative opinion in Newcastle, September 6, 1918, Bonar Law Papers, 84/1/9.
 4   Shorthand notes of the meeting in the Bonar Law Papers, 95/3.
 5   On July 20, 1918, F. E. Guest estimated that 98 Liberal MPs (25 ministerial, 73 backbenchers) supported the Prime Minister. Guest to Lloyd George, Lloyd George Papers, F 21/2/28.
 6   The offer was made through the mediation of Alexander Murray of Elibank, a former Chief Liberal Whip. Arthur C. Murray, *Master and Brother* (London: 1945), pp. 175-78. Three ministries and six under-secretary positions were offered. Letters of Arthur Murray to Sir William Wiseman, September 21 and October 8, 1918, Wiseman Papers, fols. 91-87, 91-88.
 7   George N. Barnes, G. H. Roberts, and G. J. Wardle stayed with the Coalition. Labour's position is well described in Arno Mayer, *Politics and Diplomacy of Peacemaking*, (New York, 1967) pp. 140 ff.
 8   Guest to Lloyd George, October 29, 1918, Lloyd George Papers, F 21/2/46. The agreement did not cover the 105 divisions in Ireland because of the Irish political situation, dominated in the South by Sinn Fein and in the North by Unionist Conservatives.

9   Respectively, ibid., and Bonar Law to Archibald Salvidge, promi-
    nent Liverpool Conservative, November 23, 1918, Bonar Law
    Papers, 95/4.
10 There were 81 independent Conservative candidates in the 1918
    election, but they were independent only in the sense that they
    did not have formal Coalition approval of their campaigns.
    Thirty six of the 81 were candidates in Ulster, where Coalition
    leaders thought approval was neither desirable or necessary. Most
    of the remainder were candidates of local Conservative associations
    which refused to stand aside for a Coalition Liberal. A few were
    denied Coalition approval because such approval would have
    been thought in bad taste; for example, Asquith's Conservative
    opponent was denied approval out of respect for the wartime
    service of the ex-prime minister. Almost all of the nominally inde-
    pendent Conservative candidates supported Coalition programs
    and those elected voted with the Government in the new House of
    Commons. See John McEwen, "The Coupon Election of 1918 and
    Unionist Members of Parliament," *Journal of Modern History,*
    34 (September 1962): 295.
11 Most important were the National Party (24 candidates), the
    National Federation of Discharged Soldiers and Sailors (23 candi-
    dates), the British Socialist Party (12 candidates), and the Cooper-
    ators (10 candidates). Also, there were 120 candidates of no party
    affiliation. *The Times,* December 6, 1918, p. 10.
12 The Maurice debate resulted from an allegation by Major-General
    Sir Frederick Maurice, Director of Military Operations in the War
    Office, that Lloyd George had exaggerated British military
    strength with inaccurate statistics. Asquith asked for an enquiry.
    Lloyd George, instead, insisted on a vote of confidence, which the
    Government won, 293 to 106. Asquith's support came mainly
    from independent Liberals. A few anti-war Labourites and one
    Conservative, Aubrey Herbert, also voted with Asquith. Several
    prominent Conservatives abstained, including Lords Robert and
    Hugh Cecil. 105 HC Deb 2401 ff.
13 Edward David argues that the Maurice debate was a real criterion,
    in "The Liberal Party Divided, 1916-1918," *The Historical
    Journal,* vol. 13, no. 3, 1970, pp. 521-522. However, Trevor Wil-
    son's more general and more persuasive analysis of the coupons
    minimizes the importance of the Maurice debate. See *Downfall of
    the Liberal Party,* chap. 6.
14 Wilson, *Downfall of the Liberal Party,* p. 157.
15 W. A. S. Hewins recalled a ministerial breakfast in mid-November
    1918, at which Lloyd George said, ". . . he wanted some test
    that would separate the sheep from the goats among the Liberals
    who were offering their support." Hewins, *Apologia,* 2:174.
16 Discussion of issues began as early as July 24, 1918, and was con-
    stant thereafter, as indicated by Conservative and Liberal cor-
    respondence in the Bonar Law Papers, 95/1 and 83/6/9.

17 Printed program in the Bonar Law Papers, 95/3.
18 Guest to Lloyd George, August 3, 1918, Lloyd George Papers, F 21/3/30.
19 Bonar Law to Balfour, October 5, 1918, Balfour Papers at the British Museum, vol. 49693.
20 Balfour to Bonar Law, October 11, 1918, ibid.
21 Bonar Law Papers, 95/3.
22 On November 23, Lloyd George referred to the Maurice debate as "a Parliamentary conspiracy to overthrow the Government." A week earlier he had said, "When you have great, gigantic tasks . . . you really do not want a strong opposition. (cheers)" *The Times*, November 25, 1918, p. 13, and November 18, 1918, p. 4.
23 Speech at Central Hall, November 17, *The Times*, November 18, 1918, p. 4.
24 *The Times*, November 13, 1918, p. 4.
25 Speech to employers and trade unionists at Caxton Hall, November 14, *The Times*, November 15, 1918, p. 8.
26 Addison, *Four and a Half Years* (London, 1934), 2 vols., 2:598.
27 Speeches of November 13 and December 7, *The Times*, November 14, 1918, p. 7 and the *Morning Post*, December 9, 1918, p. 9.
28 *The Times*, November 28, 1918, p. 8.
29 *Morning Post*, November 22, 1918, p. 5.
30 *The Times*, November 25, 1918, p. 13. "Stunts" was a transparent reference to the promotional habits (e.g., sponsoring airplane marathons) of the Northcliffe press.
31 Leading articles of November 21 and 27, 1918, p. 7.
32 Leading article, p. 4. Similar leaders appeared on November 27, 1918, p. 4 and on November 28, 1918, p. 7.
33 Leading articles of November 25, 27, and 28, 1918, p. 4.
34 Leading article, p. 4.
35 Chamberlain hoped for a large indemnity, but warned that this might have harmful side effects. *The Times*, November 29, 1918, p. 10.
36 Formal address, speeches, and diary in the Amery Papers.
37 Mond to Arthur Balfour, December 4, 1918, Balfour Papers, British Museum, vol. 49866.
38 November 1918, pp. 330 ff. and December 1918, pp. 487 ff.
39 Lloyd George Papers, F 237.
40 This account of the speech in *The Times*, November 30, 1918, p. 6. The reference to the Hughes Committee was the first public mention of its existence. However, Lloyd George did not reveal the Committee's membership.
41 *The Times*, November 30, 1918, p. 9.
42 Leading article, November 30, 1918, p. 4.
43 Leading article, December 1, 1918, p. 6.
44 Leading articles of November 30 and December 2, 1918, p. 4.
45 Leading article, November 30, 1918, p. 2.

46 The editors of these papers first wrote leading articles on the anti-German issues on November 30, 1918. The *Glasgow Herald* was sceptical about Germany's ability to pay large sums.

47 Leading article, Monday, December 2, 1918, p. 7.

48 Bonar Law Papers, 95/2. The 144 reports came from every part of England and Wales. Each report referred to at least two or three issues. Only in Yorkshire and the East Midlands were the anti-German issues challenged by social reform and even there indemnity was referred to most often.

49 *The Times*, December 6, 1918, p. 9.

50 *Morning Post*, December 12, 1918, p. 4.

51 *The Times*, December 2, 1918, p. 10.

52 Speech at Gorbals, Glasgow, December 10, *The Times*, December 11, 1918, p. 12.

53 *Morning Post*, December 2, 1918, p. 7.

54 In early November, Bonar Law revealed all these concerns in an interview with the owner of an Anglo-American news service, Edward Marshall. Law reminded the American and his subscribing newspapers that America had sacrificed many fewer lives than the British Empire, while the American economy had been stimulated by the War; the Chancellor clearly implied that the United States ought to cancel or reduce the sums Britain owed her. Bonar Law probably thought this a more hopeful remedy for Britain's problems than indemnity. The interview was printed in the *Observer*, November 10, 1918, 9.

55 *Morning Post*, December 12, 1918, p. 8.

56 *Manchester Guardian*, March 18, 1919, p. 6.

57 The first five papers were known as Conservative. The editor of the *Scotsman*, J. P. Croal, and the owner of the *Daily Express*, Lord Beaverbrook, were confidantes of Bonar Law. Lloyd George and his friends held controlling interest in the *Daily Chronicle*. The *Glasgow Herald* was independent of party.

58 *Memoirs of the Peace Conference*, 1:311.

59 Reginald McKenna, a prominent Liberal ex-minister, wrote to a friend, "Anti-Germanism and the desire for revenge were strong amongst the masses of the people. . . . The Liberals are not thought as a party to be sufficiently venomous . . ." Letter of December 29, 1918, Wilson, *Downfall of the Liberal Party*, p. 175.

60 *Nottingham Journal and Express*, December 11, 1918, p. 1.

61 Leading article, December 11, 1918, p. 4.

62 Leading article, December 6, 1918, p. 4.

63 Leading article, December 4, 1918, p. 2.

64 December 14, 1918, p. 799.

65 December 21, 1918, p. 344.

66 *The Times*, November 28, 1918, p. 8.

67 "The Folly of Indemnities," p. 12. Brailsford was a prominent member of the ILP and of the Union of Democratic Control. He

was one of the foremost socialist writers on war aims during the War.

68   See Arno Mayer, *Wilson versus Lenin* (New York, 1963), pp. 315-21, 388-89.

69   *The Times*, November 28, 1918, p. 8 and the *Daily Mail*, December 13, 1918, p. 2.

70   Although many Labourites, anxious to eliminate "Prussianism," joined in the attack on the ex-Kaiser. For example, J. R. Clynes' speech of November 22, *The Times*, November 23, 1918, p. 8.

71   Leading article, December 21, 1918, p. 231.

72   Figures on expenditure and taxation from Marwick, *Deluge*, p. 40 and A. J. P. Taylor, *English History, 1914-45* (Oxford, 1965), p. 41. Government security and war bond figures from "Democratic Finance," *Daily Telegraph* leading article, November 16, 1918, p. 6. The *Telegraph* remarked, ". . . since the State is now the debtor to about half the population of Great Britain, there are more persons interested in promoting its stability than ever before."

73   *Daily Mail*, December 13, 1918, p. 2.

74   "Londoner's Diary," *Evening Standard*, November 28, 1918, p. 4.

75   Leading article, December 2, 1918, p. 4. The newspaper's argument reflected the views of its owner, Lord Northcliffe. "The threat of high taxation to pay for the war was one of his prime motives for pressing the policy of a high indemnity from the Germans." *History of The Times*, 4, part one, p. 495.

76   Financial Editor's column, December 12, 1918, p. 2.

77   Lloyd George Papers, F 6/1/25. Caillard and the FBI were among the very few who advocated pensions, specifically, as a legitimate category of compensation before the Peace Conference, where the matter became crucial.

78   Bonar Law was informed of the committee on December 6; he received its memorandum on December 13. T 172/903.

79   The endorsement was made on December 18; Lloyd George was notified on December 23. *Monthly Proceedings of the ACC*, December 1918, pp. 150-51. On December 10, about 1,000 members of the London Chamber of Commerce sent Lloyd George a resolution for full indemnity. *Morning Post*, December 11, 1918, p. 6.

80   "The National Debt had the effect of a snake on a rabbit: it deprived even the most educated of sense." Taylor, *English History*, p. 124.

81   Leading article, November 12, 1918, p. 9.

82   Leading article, December 7, 1918, p. 9.

83   For a full description of this quarrel, see *History of The Times*, 4, part one, pp. 386-7 and 393-96; Henry Wickham Steed, *Through Thirty Years* (London, 1924) p. 241 ff.; John Evelyn Wrench, *Geoffrey Dawson and Our Times* (London, 1955), p. 177 ff., and Blake, *Unrepentant Tory*, p. 391.

84   See Northcliffe to Dawson, December 1, 1918, *History of The Times*, *4*, part one, pp. 455-56. The *Daily Mail* assisted the attack on Lloyd George from the left, by providing free space in its columns for the Labour Party. The Northcliffe papers were the only ones to combine domestic progressivism with punitive terms of peace.

85   Northcliffe to Dawson. November 30, 1918, ibid., 454-55.

86   According to Cecil Harmsworth's diary entry for November 30. Lloyd George "urgently" sent for him to ask the reasons for Northcliffe's displeasure. Diary in the possession of Harmsworth's son, the present Lord Harmsworth. Other details of the mediation in a letter from Harmsworth to Lloyd George, December 2, 1918, Lloyd George Papers, F 84/1/19.

87   Copies of both telegrams are in the Lloyd George Papers, F 41/8/30-1.

88   December 6, 1918, pp. 4-5 and December 7, 1918, p. 5.

89   Leading article, p. 9.

90   *Evening Standard*, December 7, 1918, p. 8.

91   *Morning Post*, December 10, 1918, p. 8.

92   The following account based on a careful comparison of *The Times*, December 12, 1918, p. 6 and the *Morning Post*, December 12, 1918, p. 8.

93   December 12, 1918, p. 5.

94   Roy Harrod touched on this explanation when he wrote of Lloyd George, "At heart he was still a Liberal, but at the end of 1918 the solid phalanx of official Liberalism was opposed to him. He was not a Conservative. Somehow he must seek to win the greatest possible number of votes." *Keynes*, p. 266.

95   *My Political Life*, 2:94.

96   Milner Papers, vol. 281.

97   Leading article, December 12, 1918, p. 6.

98   A less generous view of Lloyd George may be found in Wilson, *Downfall of the Liberal Party*, pp. 149-56, which slights the considerations presented above. American scholars have often indulged in a superficial indignation. For example, Thomas A. Bailey condemns ". . . the enormity of his [Lloyd George's] crime. Like a pyromaniac scattering firebrands around England, he deliberately whipped up passions at a time when peacemaking demanded a subsidence of passion . . ." *Wilson and the Lost Peace* (Chicago, 1963), p. 244.

99   Sir John Boraston, Secretary of the National Unionist Association, to Lloyd George, Lloyd George Papers, F 48/5/1.

100 *Lord Riddell's Intimate Diary of the Peace Conference and After* (London, 1933), p. 8.

101 "Receiving Coupons" from Wilson, *Downfall of Liberal Party*, p. 157.

102 *The Times*. December 30, 1918, p. 10.

103 Wilson, *Parliamentary Liberal Party*, p. 107.
104 McEwen, "Coupon Election and Unionist MPs," pp. 297, 298, 300-02.
105 "Apres les Élections Anglaises," *Revue de Paris*, March 1, 1919, p. 208.
106 *A Great Experiment* (London, 1941), p. 102.
107 *Tariff Reformer*, February 1919, pp. 231-32. However, the figures presented to support this were slightly exaggerated.
108 "Rise and Fall of the Coalition," *Nineteenth Century*, June 1919, p. 1238.
109 John Maynard Keynes, *The Economic Consequences of the Peace* (New York, 1920), p. 145.

Chapter 9 THE ELUSIVE MANDATE

1 *The Times*, November 18, 1918, p. 4.
2 Leading article, p. 4.
3 Respectively, in leading articles of December 30, 1918, p. 6; December 29, 1918, p. 6; and December 30, 1918, p. 4.
4 Both leading articles of December 30, 1918, p. 4 and 6 respectively.
5 Letter of no date in the Lloyd George Papers, F 21/2/57.
6 See "Appendix: Punitive Members of Parliament." A thorough study of House of Commons debates and *The Times* for the months January to July 1919 shows that 54 MPs continued to agitate the election issues in ways critical of the Government during the Peace Conference. Of these, 43 were Conservatives, three were Coalition Liberals, four were National Democrats, two were Members of the National Party, and two were Independents.
7 *The Times*, February 13, 1919, p. 9.
8 For example, his speech of March 17, 1919: ". . . we who have pledged ourselves up to the hilt to endeavour in our own humble way to exact from Germany and from our enemies the very utmost they can pay, have a right to demand why the Government have suddenly turned a political somersault . . ." 113 HC Deb 1871.
9 Speech of April 2, 1919, 114 HC Deb 1325.
10 The text of the telegram was fully printed in *The Times* on April 9, 1919, p. 13. The sponsors were Sir Edward Coates, Sir Edward Goulding, Angus Hambro, Percy Hurd, Kennedy Jones, J. R. Lonsdale, Claude Lowther, and Col. W. F. G. Weigall. Kennedy Jones, formerly a journalist for Lord Northcliffe, was acting on Northcliffe's advice. Harmsworth and Pound, *Northcliffe*, p. 710.
11 Among the other signatories were 21 Coalition Liberals, nine National Democrats, two National Party MPs, one independent Liberal, and one Labourite. The full list of 198 is in the Lloyd George Papers, F 214/1. There may have been more signatories since newspaper accounts referred to 300, 370, and 380; and since

Lloyd George once remarked that 203 Conservatives alone signed. R. B. McCallum, *Public Opinion and the Last Peace* (Oxford, 1944), p. 118n. However, there are no lists other than that of the 198 in the Lloyd George Papers.

12   The selection was based on these differences: 1. *Class*. Two of the constituencies were primarily middle class, the other four mainly working class according to occupation and housing/person as shown in the most approximate census, that of 1921. 2. *Safeness or marginality of the seat*. Two of the Conservatives won easily, the other four were hard pressed, with a majority of less than ten percent of the total vote. (Majority rather than plurality is the fairest test of safeness/marginality where the Conservatives' major opponents were both to the left and splitting a vote which, if consolidated, might bring Conservative defeat.) 3. *Kinds of opposition*. Two were straight fights; four included both Liberal and Labour candidates, three of these four also having minor party candidates. 4. *Location*. All were in England, where 322 of the 383 successful Conservatives were elected. Two were in the North of England, one in the West Country, one in a Home County, and two in London. Claude Lowther's prominence as an indemnity agitator also influenced the choice of his district.

13   John Chapman, "In East Fife," *National Review*, February 1919, pp. 764 ff.

14   *St. Andrews Citizen*, December 7, 1918, p. 2. Speech of December 2, 1918.

15   *St. Andrews Citizen*, December 14, 1918, pp. 2-3.

16   Speeches of December 12 and 13. The *Manchester Guardian*, December 13, 1918, p. 8 and *The Times*, December 14, 1918, p. 12.

17   J. M. Hogge, a prominent Liberal, stressed this in a letter of consolation to Asquith. Letter of December 30, 1918. Asquith Papers, vol. 33.

18   *St. Andrews Citizen*, December 14, 1918, pp. 2-3.

19   *Cambridge Chronicle and University Journal*, December 4, 1918, p. 8.

20   *Morning Post*, December 6, 1918, p. 5.

21   *Cambridge Daily News*, December 10, 1918, p. 4.

22   *Cambridge Daily News*, December 11, 1918, p. 3.

23   In one speech he explained how 1914 had converted him from pacifism. He had sent three sons to the War. One, "a beautiful boy of 24," was killed. *Cambridge Daily News*, December 7, 1918, p. 4.

24   A high proportion of males were employed in commercial, financial and professional occupations. Whereas one out of every five women employed in England and Wales was a domestic servant, in Cambridge this ratio was one out of three. The national average number of rooms per person in dwellings occupied (not necessarily owned) by private families was 1.10. In Cambridge, it was

1.47. *Census of England and Wales, 1921*, general tables 2, 4, and 20-21; and Cambridgeshire tables 10, 11, and 16.

25 *Cambridge Daily News*, November 28, p. 4; December 3, p. 4; December 6, p. 4; and December 10, p. 3.

26 *Census, 1921*, Leicester County, p. 54. Private families lived in 1.26 rooms per person. Ibid., p. 19.

27 *Leicester Mail*, December 11, 1918, p. 1.

28 For example, the speech of A. T. Blane, Coalition Conservative, on a common platform with Green, on December 4. *Leicester Mail*, December 5, 1918, p. 1. See also leading article of the *Leicester Mail*, November 30, 1918, p. 2.

29 Leading article of December 13, 1918, p. 2.

30 Speech of December 7 at Leicester. *The Times*, December 9, 1918, p. 10, col. 3.

31 Leading article, December 6, 1918, p. 2.

32 *Leicester Mail*, December 3, p. 1; December 4, p. 1; and December 6, p. 1. In a speech to a local Labour dinner, MacDonald had referred to German socialists as the friends of British labour.

33 *Leicester Mail*, December 5, 1918, p. 2.

34 *Leicester Mail*, December 13, 1918, p. 1.

35 Leading article, December 30, 1918, p. 2.

36 Claude Lowther, 1872-1929. Conservative MP, 1900-06 and 1910-22. Educated Rugby. Diplomatic service in Spain. VC for gallantry in South Africa. Chairman of the Anti-Socialist Union. *Dod's Parliamentary Companion*, 1919, p. 322 and *Who Was Who*, 1929-40, p. 831.

37 *Northwestern Daily Mail*, November 8, 1918, p. 4.

38 A delightful discovery made by R. B. McCallum: "So he was at it even then?" *Public Opinion and the Last Peace*, p. 45.

39 *Northwestern Daily Mail*, November 28, 1918, p. 7. His position on the other issues of peacemaking was at times grotesque: "He would put the Kaiser in an iron traveling cage and show him in every town and village." *Northwestern Daily Mail*, November 29, 1918, p. 7.

40 *Northwestern Daily Mail*, December 9, 1918, p. 4.

41 *Barrow Guardian*, December 14, 1918, p. 3.

42 There was also some republicanism in Hunter's feelings against enemy aliens: "One half of the Royal Family were German. Clear them out. (Applause)" *Barrow Guardian*, December 14, 1918, p. 3.

43 *Barrow Guardian*, December 7, 1918, p. 3.

44 *Barrow Guardian*, December 14, 1918, p. 2.

45 *Census*, 1921, Lancaster County, table 10.

46 In the 1910 elections. Bliss lost to a Conservative by only 69 and 74 votes! *Dod's*, 1910, p. 188 and 1915, p. 203.

47 *Northwestern Daily Mail*, December 13, 1918, p. 5.

48 Significantly, when the Labour Party stood aside from the Liberals in 1923, the result was a Liberal majority—of ten votes! *Dod's*, 1924, p. 237.

49 George Taylor Ramsden. Born 1879. Educated Eton and Trinity College, Cambridge. Owner of a Halifax brewery. Mayor of Halifax, 1911-12, and other local offices. Served in the Army as lieutenant and captain, 1914-19. *Dod's*, 1919, p. 355.

50 *Census*, 1921, Yorkshire, tables 16-18. Rooms per person in Elland was 0.96, below the national average of 1.10 and the Yorkshire average of 1.01. Tables 10-11. Furthermore, the population of Elland was declining over the years 1911-21.

51 *Dod's*, 1923, p. 231. Conservatives didn't even contest Elland in the 1923 General Election.

52 *Halifax Daily Guardian*, November 28, 1918, p. 3.

53 *Halifax Daily Guardian*, December 7, 1918, p. 3.

54 *Halifax Daily Guardian*, December 9, 1918, p. 3.

55 *Halifax Evening Courier*, December 2, p. 6 and December 5, p. 3.

56 *Halifax Evening Courier*, November 26, p. 6 and December 12, p. 3.

57 *Halifax Evening Courier*, November 25, 1918, p. 3, November 20, 1918, p. 3, and December 6, 1918, p. 3.

58 Percy Hurd. Born 1864. Son of local solicitor and farmer. Well known in Frome as a local businessman. Author of several books on imperial unity. Had four sons, two of whom were killed in the War. *Dod's*, 1919, p. 308 and the *Somerset Standard*, November 15, 1918, p. 2.

59 *Census*, 1921, Somerset, table 17. In 1910, Barlow had retained Frome by majorities of 779 and 578 votes. *Dod's*, 1919, p. 200 and 1915, p. 215.

60 *Somerset Standard*, November 29, 1918, p. 2 and December 6, 1918, p. 4. *Somerset and Wilts Journal*, December 13, 1916, p. 1.

61 *Somerset Standard*, December 6, 1918, p. 2.

62 On December 2, Hurd promised Kincaid-Smith that he would adopt the National Party program if Kincaid-Smith would retire. The Nationalist refused. *Somerset Standard*, December 20, 1918, p. 3.

63 *Census*, 1921, Kent, tables 10-11 and 16-17. Private families occupied 1.37 rooms per person.

64 Ronald McNeill. Born 1861. An Ulsterman. Educated Harrow and Christ Church, Oxford. A barrister. Editor *St. James's Gazette*, 1900-04. Author of books on home rule, socialism, and the empire. First elected to House of Commons in 1911. *Dod's*, 1919, p. 332.

65 *Kentish Gazette and Canterbury Press*, November 30, p. 5, December 14, p. 2.

66 Ibid., December 7, 1918, p. 2.

67 Ibid., December 21, 1918, p. 5.

68 Ibid., December 14, 1918, p. 3.

69 Ibid., December 7, 1918, p. 1.

70 For example, his reminder to agricultural laborers that their prosperity depended on how much the land produced. Ibid., November 30, 1918, p. 2.

71 Sir Samuel Hoare. 1880-1959. Second Baronet, 1915. Educated
    Harrow and New College, Oxford. MP for Chelsea, 1910-44.
    Chairman Coalition backbench committee on Foreign Affairs,
    1919. Secretary of State for Air, 1922-3, 1924-29, 1940. Secretary of
    State for India, 1931-35. Foreign Secretary, 1935. First Lord of the
    Admiralty, 1936-7. Home Secretary, 1937-39. Ambassador to Spain,
    1940-44. *Who Was Who,* 1951-60, and *The Times,* February 14,
    1919, p. 9.
72 Commercial, financial and professional occupations were the
    dominant male activities, followed closely by transport work. *Census,* 1921, London County, p. 86. Private families lived in 1.17
    rooms per person. Ibid., p. 26.
73 *West London Press and Chelsea News,* December 6, 1918, p. 3.
74 Nevertheless, Hoare would not expel naturalized Germans who
    had fought for Britain, and warmly defended a local man named
    Meinertzhagen who was socially suspect despite being a third
    generation British citizen. Ibid., November 29, p. 3; December 6,
    p. 3; December 13, pp. 3-4.
75 Speech and program in ibid., December 13, 1918, p. 3.
76 Alfred B. Raper. Born 1889. Educated Merchant Taylors and in
    Brussels. A timber merchant in East London. Served in the Royal
    Air Force as a pilot during the War. *Dod's,* 1919, p. 356.
77 Male transport workers were by far the largest group. Housing
    was very bad in Islington. Candidates referred frequently to the
    problems of slum housing. Private families lived in 0.85 rooms
    per person, a condition far below the national average and more
    crowded than any other area studied here. *Census,* 1921, London
    County, pp. 28, 95.
78 *Daily Gazette* (of Islington), December 9, 1918, p. 3.
79 Ibid., December 2, p. 3; December 4, p. 3; and December 11, p. 3.
80 Ibid., December 4, p. 3; December 5, p. 3; December 10, p. 3; December 12, p. 3; December 13, p. 3.
81 Ibid., December 4, p. 3, and December 10, p. 3.
82 Ibid., November 28, 1918, p. 3.
83 Letter to the *Daily Gazette* (of Islington), December 5, 1918, p. 3.
84 The "ginger" effect of the National Party candidates in Frome and
    East Islington should not leave the impression that this tactic had
    an important impact on the Election, since only 21 National Party
    candidates contested divisions up to polling day.
85 Letter of no date in the Lloyd George Papers, F 21/2/57.
86 Although as a group, the 43 punitive Conservatives were not more
    (or less) from marginal, borough seats than were other Conservatives:

	punitives	*other Conservatives*
marginal	25.6% (11/43)	25.0% (85/340)
borough	53.5% (23/43)	48.5% (165/340)

Marginality defined as winning with less than a majority of 10

percent of the total vote. Percentages determined by a survey of *Dod's*, 1919, and *The Times* Election Supplement of December 30, 1918.
87   114 HC Deb 1310-11.

Chapter 10 FROM WAR TO PEACE

1   IWC 45, CAB 23/42.
2   IWC 46, CAB 23/42. Lloyd George gave an almost full account of the Imperial Cabinet minutes of December 24 in his *Memoirs of the Peace Conference*, 1:315 ff. However, his omissions were unfairly selective.
3   *Monthly Proceedings of the ACC*, December 1918, pp. 150-51.
4   T 172/903.
5   IWC 46, CAB 23/42.
6   Ibid.
7   Ibid.
8   Ibid.
9   On December 24, Lloyd George had argued, disingenuously, that ". . . he did not think it could be argued that President Wilson had ruled out indemnities. It was in his speeches and was covered by his use of the term reparation." Ibid. These remarks Lloyd George omitted from his *Memoirs*.
10   IWC 47, CAB 23/42. See also Lloyd George, *Memoirs of the Paris Conference*, 1:114 ff.
11   IWC 47, CAB 23/42.
12   IWC 48, CAB 23/42.
13   Lloyd George Papers, F 45/9/27.
14   Balfour Papers, FO 800/215.
15   GT 6573, T 172/905.
16   Dated copies of the covering letters are in the Amery Papers, E 61.
17   Except for that of John Maynard Keynes, who wrote to Amery on January 6. Keynes said that Amery's hope for reduced German consumption was unrealistic; that France would never consent to treating Alsace-Lorraine as part of reparation (an accurate prediction); and that Amery's notions would offend the United States. On the last point, Amery replied that American policy was secondary: "The tussle must necessarily be between ourselves on the one side and our European Allies on the other for a fair partition of whatever the Germans can pay." Both letters are in the Balfour Papers, FO 800/215. Amery sent them to Balfour, presumably to prompt a verdict from the Foreign Secretary, but Balfour took no recorded interest.
18   Bonar Law's notation of December 28, in T 172/905 and Hughes' letter in the Amery Papers, E 61.
19   Austen Chamberlain Papers at Birmingham University, AC 5/1/1-762.

20 J. L. Hammond, *C. P. Scott* (London, 1934), p. 249.
21 Formally, "Some Considerations for the Peace Conference before they finally draft their terms, by David Lloyd George." For the text, see Gilbert, *Roots of Appeasement*, p. 189.
22 Published in *The Times*, April 10, 1919, p. 13.
23 One of the most spectacular and successful defenses of policy ever made by a Prime Minister in the House. For its full effect, compare 114 HC Deb 2936 ff. with the interjections recorded in *The Times*, April 17, 1919, p. 16.
24 *Manchester Guardian*, leading article, p. 6.
25 "The General Election," March 1919, p. 356. In fact, indemnity had not been "whittled down" to reparation.
26 At Central Hull the Liberal, Comdr. J. M. Kenworthy, turned a Conservative General Election majority of 10,371 into a Liberal by-election majority of 917!
27 See the minutes of the British Empire Delegation of June 1, 5:30 p.m., reproduced in Lloyd George, *Memoirs of the Peace Conference*, 1:478-81.
28 BED minutes no. 13, FO 374/22.
29 As Keynes explained in a letter to Lloyd George on March 28, 1919. Lloyd George Papers, F 213/5/14. However, the distribution eventually fixed at Spa in July 1920 was British Empire, 22 percent and France, 52 percent. The final distribution agreement of April 1931 was British Empire, 23.58 percent and France, 56.14 percent. U.S. Department of State, *The Treaty of Versailles and After* (Washington, 1947), pp. 441-42.
30 Only a few Britons had thought so before the Conference. Most important, pensions were part of the FBI "Peace Aims" and the program of the Comrades of the Great War, a Conservative veterans group. The program of the latter was published by the *Glasgow Herald*, October 30, 1918, p. 8.
31 Though later in the Conference, the South African decided that pensions would mean too great an increase in the total reparation bill and urged the deletion of this category of damage. See Sir Keith Hancock, *Smuts: The Sanguine Years* (Cambridge: Cambridge University Press, 1962), pp. 515-16, 541-42.
32 Text of the agreement, also signed by Clemenceau, in the Department of State, *Treaty of Versailles and After*, p. 845. For an excellent discussion of British-American relations concerning reparation and indemnity, see Seth P. Tillman, *Anglo-American Relations at the Paris Peace Conference of 1919* (Princeton: Princeton University Press, 1961), pp. 229-59.
33 Copy of Clemenceau's counter-memorandum, March 31, 1919, FO 800/215.
34 British Empire Delegation minutes no. 34, June 1, 5:30 p.m., FO 374/22. In 1938, perhaps out of regard for his German readers, Lloyd George omitted the second comment from his quotation of these minutes in *Memoirs of the Peace Conference*, 1:474.

35 Lloyd George Papers, F 28/3/40.
36 The Germans also offered to repair the devastated areas with their own labor and materials, similar to a suggestion made by Lloyd George in early June. At the Council of Four on June 3, President Wilson said he thought the German proposals would "form a good basis" for a reparation settlement. CF 44, CAB 29/38. Why, then, was there no agreement? First, because the Germans did not offer to pay interest on their total obligation. Second, because the Germans asked for related Allied concessions that would have upset the delicate compromises already worked out by the Allies among themselves. Third, because the Germans were not able to negotiate in person, whereby they might have adjusted more readily to Allied objections. Finally, because the Germans, ironically, offered too much. An agreement would probably have given the impression that the Allies had accepted a German suggestion with little modification. This was still anathema in 1919. The total obligation fixed by the Allied Reparation Commission in 1921 was £ 6,600,000,000. By 1937, Germany had paid just over £ 2,000,000,000, far less than the German offer of 1919.
37 The basic form of Article 231 was first drafted by the American expert, John Foster Dulles, who hoped that a declaration of theoretical liability for war costs would make it politically possible for the Allies to demand less than war costs in practice. However, Lloyd George and Clemenceau strengthened the Dulles draft on April 5, by insisting that there be an explicit German acceptance, as well as Allied affirmation, of aggression and consequent liability to pay. The American negotiator, Norman Davis said, "The American delegation had no special interest in the first Article. In drafting it we attempted to meet the views of Great Britain and France." See Tillman, *Anglo-American Relations at the Paris Peace Conference*, pp. 235-36, 246-48.
38 Hajo Holborn, *History of Modern Germany*, 3 vols. (New York, 1969), 3:571-74.
39 These were signed by Clemenceau, but they had been drafted from June 13 to 16 by an Allied committee composed of André Tardieu, Philip Kerr, and representatives of the United States, Italy, and Japan. Kerr had already been assigned to this task by Lloyd George on June 2, and most historians, therefore, assume that Kerr was the principal author of the Allied reply. However, that reply also bears the imprint of Tardieu's passionate anti-German views. On June 10, Tardieu wrote to President Wilson, "When dealing with Germany it is France that must be heard. . . . I would not have the moral position of the Allies sacrificed to the Brockdorff memorandum." Tardieu, *The Truth About the Treaty* (Indianapolis, 1921), pp. 121-22. See also Sir Maurice Hankey, *The Supreme Control at the Paris Peace Conference 1919* (London, 1963), pp. 173-74.
40 Department of State, *Treaty of Versailles and After*, pp. 44-45. The

only major concessions were a plebiscite for Upper Silesia and the Allied assurance about commercial non-discrimination mentioned in Chap. 3. No total sum of reparation was fixed, as requested by the Germans and recommended by the Americans, but a procedure for determining a sum before the end of the year was promised. After an Allied ultimatum of June 22, the German National Assembly voted on June 23 to accept the Treaty on the basis of the Allied reply; two German delegates signed the Treaty at Versailles on June 28.

41 Leading article, May 8, 1919, p. 10.
42 Leading article, May 10, 1919, p. 584.
43 Leading article, June 24, 1919, p. 13.
44 Leading articles of June 1919, p. 474 and of July 1919, p. 861.
45 Department of State, *Treaty of Versailles and After*, p. 457.
46 Lt.-Col. J. T. C. Moore-Brabazon, Member for Chatham, Rochester, 127 HC Deb 681.

Bibliography

Plan of the Bibliography:
1 Unpublished Documents at the Public Record Office
  Records of the Cabinet Office
  Records of the Foreign Office
  Records of the Treasury
2 Unpublished Papers, Letters, and Diaries
3 Published Documents, Debates, and Statistics
4 Newspapers and Periodicals
  London and Major Provincial Publications
  Local Newspapers
5 Articles
  Scholarly
  Contemporary
6 Principal Works Consulted
7 Supplementary Sources

1 UNPUBLISHED DOCUMENTS AT THE PUBLIC RECORD OFFICE

Records of the Cabinet Office

Class 21, volumes 73, 77, 78, 108, 109. Minutes and memoranda of several of the wartime economic committees.

Class 23, volumes 6, 8-10, 14-17, 40-44. Minutes and shorthand, verbatim notes of meetings of the War Cabinet. Indispensable.

Class 24, volume 4. Memoranda of the Economic Offensive Committee.

Class 27, volumes 15, 16, 43, 44. Most important is volume 43 which contains verbatim, shorthand notes of the discussions of the Imperial War Cabinet Committee on Indemnity.

Class 28, volumes 4-7. Minutes of Inter-Allied Conferences, June 1918 to July 1919. Formal, usually unrevealing.

Class 29, volumes 1-4. The "P" series of memoranda on peace-making written from 1916 to 1919. The ideal origins of diplomacy.

Class 29, volume 28. Minutes of the British Empire Delegation to the Paris Peace Conference.

Class 32, volume 1. Minutes and resolutions of the Imperial War Conferences of March-April 1917 and of June-July 1918.

Class 37, volumes 139, 141-5, 147, 148, 150, 151, 158. Memoranda and other papers relating to the Paris Economic Conference of June 1916.

Records of the Foreign Office

Class 368, volume 1669. Commercial despatches relating to the Paris Economic Conference.

Class 373, box 7. Handbooks prepared by the Historical Section of the Foreign Office for the British Empire Delegation.

Class 374, volume 22. A bound set of the British Empire Delegation minutes, complete except for one set of minutes to be found in CAB 29/28.

Class 800, volumes 199, 201, 207, 212, 214-217. Correspondence and other papers of Foreign Secretary Balfour for 1917 to 1919. Mainly valuable for correspondence received by Balfour.

Class 800, volumes 222-225. Correspondence and telegrams to and from Lord Reading, Ambassador to the United States, 1918 and 1919.

Records of the Treasury

Class 172, volumes 100, 371, 639, 903, 905. Records of the Office of the Chancellor of the Exchequer. Very useful for the study of policy-making.

2 UNPUBLISHED PAPERS, LETTERS, AND DIARIES

Papers, Letters, and Diaries of Leopold S. Amery, in the possession of the Rt. Hon. Julian Amery. Valuable for the Conservative Party and the Cabinet Office during the War. Amery systematically kept copies of his own letters. His diaries are lively and informative.

Papers and Letters of Herbert Henry Asquith, Lord Oxford and Asquith, at the Bodleian Library, Oxford University. Valuable here for the Paris Economic Conference and Liberal politics during the War.

Papers and Letters of Arthur James Balfour, Lord Balfour, at the British Museum. Mainly important for Conservative politics.

Papers, Letters and Diaries of Lord Robert Cecil, Viscount Cecil of Chelwood, at the British Museum.

Papers and Letters of Sir Austen Chamberlain, at the Library of Birmingham University.

Papers and Letters of John C. C. Davidson, Lord Davidson, held by Lord and Lady Davidson.

Papers and Letters of David Lloyd George, in the Beaverbrook Library at the *Daily Express* building, London. An indispensable collection for this study, as for any study within the years 1916 to 1922.

Papers, Letters, and Diaries of Cecil Harmsworth, Lord Harmsworth, held by the present Lord Harmsworth.

Papers, Letters, and Diaries of W. A. S. Hewins, formerly held by Mr. Richard Hewins, now at the University of Sheffield Library. Important for the tariff reform movement, the Unionist Business Committee, and the economic policy-making of the war years. The reader must beware of Hewins' tendency to exaggerate his importance.

Papers and Letters of Andrew Bonar Law, in the Beaverbrook Library at the *Daily Express* building, London. A very full and informative collection, and a valuable complement to the Lloyd George Papers.

Papers and Letters of Philip Kerr, Lord Lothian, at the Scottish Record Office, Edinburgh. Valuable for letters and papers sent to Lloyd George, who employed Kerr as private secretary.

Papers, Letters, and Diaries of Alfred Milner, Lord Milner, at the Bodleian Library, Oxford University.

Papers and Letters of Sir William Wiseman, at Yale University.
Two collections I had hoped to use were unavailable during my research: The Papers of Sir Edward Carson, then incomplete and under a fifty-year rule at the Public Record Office of Northern Ireland; and the Papers of John Maynard Keynes, Lord Keynes,

then being used by the Royal Economic Society. The latter omission is partly redressed by the Society's 1971 edition of Keynes' writings.

3 Published Documents, Debates, and Statistics

Philip M. Burnett, *Reparation at the Paris Peace Conference From the Standpoint of the American Delegation.* 2 vols. New York: Columbia University Press, 1940.

Dod's Parliamentary Companion. Volumes for 1910, 1915, 1919, 1923, 1924 (second edition), and 1925. Checked against other sources.

Great Britain. Command Paper 8462. Dominions Royal Commission Report of March 1917.

Great Britain. *Census of England and Wales, 1921.* London: His Majesty's Stationery Office, 1921.

Great Britain. *Parliamentary Debates.* House of Commons. Fifth Series. Volumes 77 to 127.

Liberal Party Yearbook, 1919.

Royal Economic Society. *The Collected Writings of John Maynard Keynes.* Volume 16. *Activities, 1914-19: The Treasury and Versailles.* Edited by Elizabeth Johnson. London: St. Martin's, 1971. An excellent edition of Keynes' main economic and administrative writings during the War.

The Times Election Supplement, December 30, 1918.

United States Department of State. *The Treaty of Versailles and After: Annotations of the Text of the Treaty.* Washington: Government Printing Office, 1947. A valuable legal history of Versailles.

4 Newspapers and Periodicals

Major London and Provincial Publications

Birmingham Post
Daily Chronicle

Daily Express
Daily Mail
Daily News
Daily Telegraph
Economist
Evening Standard
Glasgow Herald
Gleanings and Memoranda by the National Union of Conservative Associations.
Herald (*Daily Herald* after March 30, 1919)
John Bull
Manchester Guardian
Monthly Proceedings of the Associated Chambers of Commerce
Morning Post
Nation
National Review
New Statesman
Observer
Round Table
Scotsman
Spectator
Sunday Times
Tariff Reformer
The Times
War Notes of the Tariff Reform League

Local Newspapers

Barrow Guardian
Cambridge Chronicle and University Journal
Cambridge Daily News
Daily Gazette (of Islington)
Halifax Daily Guardian
Halifax Evening Courier
Hertfordshire Express.
Kentish Gazette and Canterbury Press
Leicester Mail
Northwestern Daily Mail
Nottingham Journal and Express
Pioneer (of Leicester)

St. Andrews Citizen
Somerset Standard
Somerset and Wilts Journal
West London Press and Chelsea News

5 ARTICLES

Scholarly

Aronsfield, C.C. "Enemy Aliens, 1914-18: German-born Jews in England during the First World War," *Jewish Social Studies*, October, 1956.

Blewett, Neal. "Free Fooders, Balfourites, Whole Hoggers. Factionalism within the Unionist Party, 1906-10." *Historical Journal*. Volume 11. 1968.

David, Edward. "The Liberal Party Divided, 1916-1918." *Historical Journal*. Volume 13. 1970.

McEwen, John. "The Coupon Election of 1918 and Unionist Members of Parliament." *Journal of Modern History*. Volume 34. September 1962. A brilliant essay.

Rodman, Barbee-Sue. "Britain Debates Justice: An Analysis of the Reparations Issue of 1918." *Journal of British Studies*. Volume 8. November 1968. A strained argument that concepts of penal justice explain the issues of 1918. Neglects the economic cost of the War and related anxieties.

Wilson, Trevor G. "The Coupon and the British General Election of 1918." *Journal of Modern History*. Volume 36. March 1964. The first thorough explanation of the coupon, based on Wilson's Oxford D.Phil. dissertation.

Contemporary

Brailsford, H. N. "The Folly of Indemnities." *Herald*. December 7, 1918.

Chapman, John. "In East Fife." *National Review*. February 1919.

Cox, Harold. "Commerce and Empire." *Edinburgh Review*. October 1918.

———. *"The Case for an Indemnity."* Morning Post. December 2-4, 1918.

Gribble, Francis. "How Germany Can Pay." *Nineteenth Century And After.* Volume 79. May 1916.

Halévy, Elie. "Apres les Élections Anglaises." *Revue de Paris.* March 1, 1919.

Hobson, John A. "Rival Economic Systems in Europe." *Contemporary Review.* Volume 109. February 1916.

Law, Andrew Bonar. Interview with Edward Marshall. *Observer.* November 10, 1918.

Marriot, J. A. R. "Mitteleuropa and the Meaning of the Paris Pact." *War Notes* of the Tariff Reform League. January 1, 1917.

Masterman, C. F. G. "Rise and Fall of the Coalition." *Nineteenth Century.* June 1919.

Money, Sir Leo Chiozza. "Paying for the Cost of the War." *Daily Chronicle.* November 16, 1914.

———. "Can Germany Pay?" *Daily Express.* December 2, 1918.

Northcliffe, Alfred Harmsworth, Lord. "From War to Peace." *Daily Mail.* November 4, 1918.

6 Principal Works Consulted

Angell, Norman. *After All: The Autobiography of Norman Angell.* New York: Farrar, Straus and Young, 1951.

———. *The Great Illusion.* New York: G. P. Putnam's Sons, 1910.

Amery, Leopold S. *My Political Life.* 3 vols. London: Hutchinson, 1953. One of the best political autobiographies.

Birdsall, Paul. *Versailles, Twenty Years After.* New York: Reynall and Hitchcock, 1941. Reprinted by Archon Books, Hamden, Conn., 1962. Still one of the most sensible volumes on the Peace Conference.

Blake, Robert. *Unrepentant Tory: The Life and Times of Andrew Bonar Law.* New York, St. Martin's, 1956.

Fowler, W. B. *British-American Relations, 1917-1918: The Role*

of Sir William Wiseman. Princeton: Princeton University
Press, 1969. A model of historical research.
George, David Lloyd. *War Memoirs.* 2 vols. London: Odham's,
1938.
_____. *Memoirs of the Peace Conference.* 2 vols. New Haven:
Yale University Press, 1939. These and the preceding vol-
umes are still valuable, but must be checked against their
sources.
Gilbert, Martin. *Roots of Appeasement.* London: Weidenfeld
and Nicolson, 1966.
Gollin, A.M. *Proconsul in Politics: A Study of Lord Milner in
Opposition and in Power.* New York, Macmillan, 1964.
Hammond, J. L. *C. P. Scott.* London: G. Bell and Sons, 1934.
Hancock, Sir Keith. "Problems of Economic Policy, 1919-1939."
Survey of Commonwealth Affairs. Volume 2, part one.
Oxford University Press, 1940.
_____. *Smuts: The Sanguine Years.* Cambridge University
Press, 1962. A splendid biography.
Harrod, Roy F. *The Life of John Maynard Keynes.* New York:
Harcourt, Brace and Company, 1951. A rich portrait.
Hewins, W. A. S. *Apologia of an Imperialist.* 2 vols. London:
Constable, 1929.
Hirst, Francis W. *The Political Economy of War.* London:
E. P. Dutton, 1915.
Hobson, John A. *The New Protectionism.* London: T. Fisher
Unwin, 1916.
Hoffman, Ross J. S. *Great Britain and the Anglo-German Trade
Rivalry.* Philadelphia: University of Pennsylvania Press,
1933.
Johnson, Paul B. *Land Fit for Heroes: The Planning of British
Reconstruction, 1916-1919.* Chicago: University of Chicago
Press, 1968. A fine administrative history.
Jones, J. H. *The Economics of War and Conquest: An Examina-
tion of Mr. Norman Angell's Economic Doctrines.* London:
P. S. King and Son, 1915.
Jones, Tom. *Lloyd George.* Oxford University Press, 1951.
Judd, Denis. *Balfour and the British Empire: A Study in Impe-
rial Evolution, 1874-1932.* London: Macmillan, 1968.

Keynes, John Maynard. *The Economic Consequences of the Peace*. New York: Harcourt, Brace and Howe, 1920.

McCallum, R. B. *Public Opinion and the Last Peace*. Oxford University Press, 1944. Impressionistic, but lively and still useful.

McEwen, John M. *Unionist and Conservative Members of Parliament*. University of London Ph. D. dissertation, 1959. Exhaustive biographical study of the Conservative Party in the twentieth century.

Mackinder, Halford J. *Democratic Ideals and Reality*. New York: Henry Holt, 1919.

Martin, Laurence, *Peace without Victory: Woodrow Wilson and the British Liberals*. New Haven: Yale University Press, 1958.

Marwick, Arthur. *The Deluge: British Society and the First World War*. Boston: Little, Brown and Company, 1965. A fascinating, perceptive social history.

Mayer, Arno J. *Wilson versus Lenin: The Political Origins of the New Diplomacy*. New York: World Publishing Company, 1963.

———. *Politics and Diplomacy of Peacemaking: Containment and Counterrevolution at Versailles, 1918-1919*. New York: Alfred A. Knopf, 1967.

Nicolson, Harold. *Peacemaking, 1919*. New York: Harcourt, Brace, and Company, 1939.

O'Farrell, Horace Handley. *The Franco-German War Indemnity and Its Economic Results*. London: Harrison and Sons, 1913.

Pound, Reginald and Geoffrey Harmsworth. *Northcliffe*. New York: Praeger, 1960.

Rudin, Harry R. *Armistice, 1918*. New Haven: Yale University Press, 1944. Reprinted by Archon Books, Hamden, Conn., 1967.

Semmel, Bernard. *Imperialism and Social Reform: English Social-Imperial Thought, 1895-1914*. London: George Allen and Unwin, 1960. Excellent on the prewar philosophy and personalities of the tariff reform movement.

Taylor, A. J. P. *English History, 1914-1945*. Oxford University Press, 1965.

Tillman, Seth P. *Anglo-American Relations at the Paris Peace Conference of 1919.* Princeton: Princeton University Press, 1961. A superb monograph.

The Times. The History of The Times. 4 vols. New York: Macmillan, 1952.

Watt, D.C. *Personalities and Policies: Studies in the Formulation of British Foreign Policy in the Twentieth Century.* London: Longmans, 1965. Excellent on policy-makers and on biographical sources, public and private.

Wilson, Trevor G. *The Parliamentary Liberal Party in Britain, 1918-1924.* Oxford D.Phil. dissertation, 1959.

_____. *The Downfall of the Liberal Party, 1914-1935.* London: Collins, 1966.

_____. *The Political Diaries of C. P. Scott, 1911-1928.* Edited by Trevor G. Wilson. Ithaca: Cornell University Press, 1970.

Woodward, Sir Llewellyn. *Great Britain and the War of 1914-1918.* London: Methuen, 1967. Magisterial.

7 SUPPLEMENTARY SOURCES

Addison, Christopher. *Four and a Half Years, A Personal Diary From June 1914 to January 1919.* 2 vols. London: Hutchinson, 1934.

Angell, Norman. *The Peace Treaty and the Economic Chaos of Europe.* London: The Swarthmore Press, December 1919.

Bailey, Thomas A. *Woodrow Wilson and the Lost Peace.* Chicago: Quadrangle, 1963.

Barnes, George N. *From Workshop to War Cabinet.* London: Herbert Jenkins, 1923.

Beaverbrook, Max Aitken, Lord. *Politicians and the Press.* London: Hutchinson, 1926.

_____. *Politicians and the War.* 2 vols. London: T. Butterworth, 1928-32. Reprinted by Archon Books, Hamden, Conn., 1968.

_____. *Men and Power.* London: Hutchinson, 1956. Reprinted by Archon Books, Hamden, Conn., 1968.

Bentinck, Lord Henry Cavendish. *Tory Democracy.* London: Methuen, 1918.

Bergman, Carl. *The History of Reparations.* London: Ernest Benn, 1927.

Birkenhead, Second Earl of. *Frederick Edwin: Earl of Birkenhead, The Last Phase.* London: T. Butterworth, 1935.

_____. *Halifax.* London: Hamish Hamilton, 1965.

Butler, J. R. M. *Lord Lothian.* London: Macmillan, 1960.

Callwell, Sir C. E. *Field Marshall Sir Henry Wilson, His Life and Diaries.* 2 vols. London: Scribner's, 1927.

Cecil, Lord Hugh. *Conservatism.* London: Williams and Norgate, 1912.

_____. *Nationalism and Catholicism.* London: Macmillan, 1919.

Chelwood, Lord Robert Cecil of. *The New Outlook.* London: Allen and Unwin, 1919.

_____. *A Great Experiment.* London: Jonathan Cape, 1941.

Croft, Henry Page, Lord. *My Life of Strife.* London: Hutchinson, 1948.

Davis, R. O. *British Policy and Opinion on War Aims, 1914-1918.* Duke University Ph. D. dissertation, 1958. Good, but little on economic aims.

Dickinson, G. Lowes. *The Economic War after the War.* London: Union of Democratic Control, 1916.

Driberg, Tom. *Beaverbrook.* London: Weidenfeld and Nicolson, 1956.

Dugdale, Blanche E. C. *Arthur James Balfour.* 2 vols. London: Hutchinson, 1936.

Feiling, Keith. *The Life of Neville Chamberlain.* London: Macmillan, 1946. Reprinted with a new introduction by the author by Archon Books, Hamden, Conn., 1970.

Garvin, J. L. *The Economic Foundations of Peace.* London: Macmillan, 1919.

Garvin, Katherine. *J. L. Garvin: A Memoir.* London: Heinemann, 1948.

George, David Lloyd. *The Truth About Reparations and War Debts.* Garden City: Doubleday, Doran and Co., 1932.

Guinn, Paul. *British Strategy and Politics, 1914-18.* Oxford University Press, 1965.

Halifax, Edward F. L. Wood, Lord. *Fulness of Days.* New York: Dodd and Mead, 1957.

Hankey, Lord Maurice. *The Supreme Command, 1914-1918.* 2 vols. London: Allen and Unwin, 1961.

———. *The Supreme Control at the Paris Peace Conference, 1919*. London: Allen and Unwin, 1963.

Hirst, Francis W. *The Consequences of the War to Great Britain.* Oxford University Press, 1934.

Holborn, Hajo. *A History of Modern Germany.* 3 vols. New York: Alfred A. Knopf, 1959-1969.

Jones, Kennedy. *Fleet Street and Downing Street.* London: Hutchinson, 1920.

Labour Party. *Towards a New World, Being the Reconstruction Programme of the British Labour Party.* New York: W. R. Browne, 1919.

Lennox, Lady Algernon Gordon, ed. *The Diary of Lord Bertie of Thame.* London: Hodder and Stoughton, 1924.

Louis, William Roger. *Great Britain and Germany's Lost Colonies, 1914-1919.* Oxford University Press, 1967.

Millin, Sarah G. *General Smuts.* 2 vols. London: Faber and Faber, 1936.

Mowat, Charles L. *Britain Between the Wars, 1918-1940.* London: Methuen, 1955.

Murray, Arthur C. *Master and Brother.* London: John Murray, 1945.

Nicolson, Harold. *King George the Fifth.* London: Constable, 1952.

Oliver, F. S. *Ordeal by Fire.* London: Macmillan, 1915.

Owen, Frank. *Tempestuous Journey: Lloyd George, His Life and Times.* New York: McGraw-Hill, 1955.

Parrini, Carl P. *Heir to Empire: United States Economic Diplomacy, 1916-1923.* Pittsburgh: University of Pittsburgh Press, 1969.

Petrie, Sir Charles. *The Life and Letters of Sir Austen Chamberlain.* 2 vols. London: Cassell, 1940.

———. *The Life and Times of Walter Long.* London: Hutchinson, 1936.

Riddell, Lord. *Intimate Diary of the Peace Conference and After.* London: Gollancz, 1933.

Rodman, Barbee-Sue. *British Political Opinion and the German Question, 1918-1920.* Radcliffe Ph. D. dissertation, 1958.

Roskill, Stephen. *Hankey: Man of Secrets.* Volume 1, 1877-1918. London: Collins, 1970.

Salter, Sir James Arthur. *Recovery: The Second Effort.* London: G. Bell and Sons, 1932.

Steed, Henry Wickham. *Through Thirty Years.* 2 vols. London: Heinemann, 1924.

Tariff Commission. *The War and British Economic Policy.* London: The Tariff Commission, 1915.

Taylor, A. J. P. *Politics in Wartime.* London: Atheneum, 1964.

Taylor, H. A. *Jix-Viscount Brentford.* London: Stanley Paul, 1933.

Whyte, W. Farmer. *William Morris Hughes.* Sydney: Angus and Robertson, 1956.

Williams, Ernest R. *Made in Germany.* London: Heinemann, 1896.

Wrench, John Evelyn, *Geoffrey Dawson and Our Times.* London: Hutchinson, 1955.

Young, G. M. *Stanley Baldwin,* London: R. Hart-Davis, 1962.

Young, Kenneth. *Arthur James Balfour.* London: G. Bell, 1963.

Index